A Guide to Financial Regulation for Fintech Entrepreneurs

A Guide to
Financial Regulation
for
Fintech Entrepreneurs

STEFAN LOESCH

WILEY

This edition first published 2018
© 2018 John Wiley & Sons, Ltd

Registered office
John Wiley & Sons Ltd, The Atrium, Southern Gate, Chichester, West Sussex, PO19 8SQ,
United Kingdom

For details of our global editorial offices, for customer services and for information
about how to apply for permission to reuse the copyright material in this book please
see our website at www.wiley.com.

Wiley publishes in a variety of print and electronic formats and by print-on-demand.
Some material included with standard print versions of this book may not be included
in e-books or in print-on-demand. If this book refers to media such as a CD or DVD that
is not included in the version you purchased, you may download this material at http://
booksupport.wiley.com. For more information about Wiley products, visit www.wiley.com.

Library of Congress Cataloging-in-Publication Data is available:

ISBN 978-1-119-43670-6 (paperback) ISBN 978-1-119-43675-1 (ePub)
ISBN 978-1-119-43672-0 (ePDF)

Cover Design: Wiley
Cover Image: © chombosan/Shutterstock

Set in Garamond 10/12pts by SPi Global, Chennai, India

Printed and bound by CPI Group (UK) Ltd, Croydon, CR0 4YY

10 9 8 7 6 5 4 3 2 1

To Hartmann Karl Günter Loesch, 1937–2012

Contents

About the Book

Fintech companies are revolutionising the way financial services work. Their main strengths are superior agility, systems and customer focus, but established financial services have a strong advantage because they understand how to comply with regulations. This book teaches Fintech executives to attack incumbents in the regulatory arena, and at the same time to create moats against other Fintech companies.

When a company is starting up, regulatory requirements are small. However, they increase rapidly when a company starts growing and regulators start paying closer attention, or when regulators from other jurisdictions are getting involved. Regulators only have limited capacity, and if a company wants to be able to scale without being held back by the regulators, planning the regulatory strategy ahead of time is indispensable.

Going through regulatory texts is hard: even for the most basic financial services, the relevant regulations amount to thousands of pages of dry legalistic prose, describing the regulatory trees in detail but obfuscating the view on the regulatory forest. As a Fintech executive, this book gives you a map of the forest, allowing you quickly to identify the specific trees that matter for you. It clearly explains the purpose and the structure of the regulatory environment, and provides you with frameworks that enable you to develop an effective regulatory strategy.

The first part of the book explains why financial services regulation exists, what its goals are, and how Fintech executives can use regulation to gain a strategic advantage for their companies. The second part gives a more detailed map of the key regulations that Fintech companies have to follow, firstly identifying the most relevant ones, and then distilling the thousands of pages that still remain into about 100 pages in the book.

All EU regulations cited are (c) European Union 1995–2017 and used based on their reuse policy that can be found on https://ec.europa.eu/info/legal-notice_en which states that "Reuse is authorised, provided the source is acknowledged. The Commission's reuse policy is implemented by the Decision of 12 December 2011—reuse of Commission documents".

Acknowledgments

I am grateful for the help of Thomas Barker, Pascal Bouvier, Andy Condurache, Maxim Harper, Jonathan Howitt, Jerôme Legras, George Markides, Justin McCarthy, Oscar McCarthy, fiona Mullen, Sid Singh and Sean Tuffy at the various stages of this project. It goes without saying that all mistakes still left are mine and mine alone.

I want to thank my family—my wonderful wife Oksana and our two daughters Sophie Alexandra and Béatrice Hélène—for their support, and for putting up with me while I was researching and writing this book. I would also like to thank my parents, Christa Loesch-Goldschmidt and Wilfried Goldschmidt, just for being there for me and my family.

About the Author

S tefan is a theoretical physicist by training, holding a degree from the University of Bonn, and he spent some time at Ecole Polytechnique near Paris. He also holds an MBA degree from INSEAD.

Immediately after university he became a quant, developing pricing software for derivatives, where he lead Paribas' equity derivatives quant team worldwide. After the MBA he joined McKinsey & Co. as a consultant in the Corporate Finance practice, which is where he first got introduced to financial services regulation proper, in the form of the Basel 2 regulations. He then joined J.P. Morgan where he continued advising clients on Basel 2, helping them to position their balance sheets to optimise regulatory and economic capital and liquidity constraints.

After leaving J.P. Morgan he built an edtech platform for business schools to improve their online and classroom teaching. He was also invited to join the PRMIA Education Committee, and to co-edit and co-author the most recent revision of the PRMIA Handbook, the study guide for students taking the prestigious Professional Risk Manager™ exam. More recently he was serving as CTO of an early stage start-up in the non-traditional lending space. His current focus is on bridging the gap between crypto and traditional finance, setting up structures that allow both of those spaces to work together while being in compliance with the applicable regulations.

PART I

Fintech Regulation and Strategy

CHAPTER 1

Regulatory Strategy for Fintech Companies

The Fintech space—like the overall tech space a few years earlier—is evolving at breakneck speed, even though from a low base when compared to the incumbents currently present in the market. Financial services is a highly regulated industry—and for good reasons, as it is the lifeblood of a modern economy, and because it deals with people's live savings. Because of the lack of scale, Fintech has thus far mostly escaped regulation. However, this is coming to an end: as Fintech grows up and moves into the mainstream of finance, regulation on a par with that applied to other financial services is unavoidable.

Many people, especially in the tech world, see regulation as a nuisance, and something that at best needs to be reluctantly complied with. This is partially true—compliance with applicable regulations is tedious and a lot of work. However, from a strategic point of view this is not necessarily a bad thing: to the extent that a company is better able to navigate the regulatory environment than others, this can and will provide a competitive advantage.

This competitive advantage can be particularly important for tech companies because of way they slice up the underlying market: the current banking system is mostly designed on the assumption that customers want a one-stop-shop for all their banking needs, or even for all their financial needs, with most major banking groups now also sporting associated insurance and asset management divisions. Tech companies tend to have a very narrow focus in terms of the services they provide, and often even in terms of the segment of customers they target. They also understand the importance that scaling has for them: for many tech business models the first player who can reach significant scale in its segment can reach a position that is difficult to attack for followers, so being able to scale quickly and efficiently is a key part of a tech company's strategy.

There are very few national markets in the world—and especially in the Western world—that provide sufficient scale for a tech company that wants to play in the major league. This means that tech companies have to think about international expansion early on. For Fintech in particular this means that they will always have to deal with regulatory compliance in each and every market in which they operate. Compliance being costly is one thing, but from a scaling point of view more important is that regulatory compliance means delays: even before the first customer interaction takes place, a company has to ensure that it can comply with the applicable requirements, document this, and then seek authorisation or registration in the relevant jurisdiction. This process can be very time-consuming, especially if approached the wrong way, and more regulatorily nimble competitors can leapfrog Fintech companies that are seeing regulatory compliance as an afterthought rather than a core strategic skill.

The purpose of this book is to allow senior executives—especially those that come from a technical and single-product-focus background— to get to a point that allows them to understand the overall regulatory environment they are facing and to formulate a regulatory strategy, in particular during the scaling phase.

The financial markets are a highly connected system, and it is not possible to understand financial services regulation without a high-level understanding of the entire financial services space, and the range of products and services it offers. A big part of this book therefore is a description of the financial services space, intertwined with applicable regulation.

The first part of the book provides the main narrative. It is split into the following chapters:

1. a general introduction to regulations and their purpose, and how they impact a company's strategic planning (this chapter)
2. an overview of financial services regulations, looking at the types of regulations (ie, grouped by purpose), as well as their strands (ie, grouped by the way they are organised in reality)
3. a more detailed description of the regulations in place, looking at the sources from which they flow, then at various regulatory models, and finally a discussion of the areas most important for Fintech companies
4. an overview of the financial services industry split along the classic sectorial lines, interspersed with discussions about key applicable regulations
5. an overview of the key products offered by the financial services industry offered in the *retail* space, interspersed with discussions about key applicable regulations
6. an overview of the key products offered by the financial services industry offered in the *wholesale* space, interspersed with discussions about key applicable regulations.

The second part consists of tear sheets covering in more detail the most important regulations applicable to Fintech companies. A quick summary of each of those regulations is provided, and there is a discussion of the strategic importance of that particular regulation within the Fintech space. The tear sheets are cross-referenced against the regulatory text so that it is quick and easy to look at the exact regulatory requirements. All regulatory texts are linked on the companion site for easy access. In order to avoid duplication I had to choose a jurisdiction for which to provide those regulations, with the choice being between the US and the EU. I ultimately chose the EU because the regulatory structure is clearer. However, the large majority of rules and regulations will be very similar in the US, just with different references where to find the respective legislation.

1.1 Regulation

Whilst there is a general belief that markets work well in many instances, there is also an understanding that there are market failures, and that markets left to themselves can lead to suboptimal or bad outcomes. In many cases, market failures can be traced back to the fact that one party is better informed than the other one—not because they have failed to do their homework, but because structurally one party to the transaction finds it impossible or at least very expensive to acquire information that the other side has.

1.1.1 An Example for Beneficial Regulation: Taxis

Financial services are complex, so I want to start with an example where the market failure is very obvious: taxi services. First let's define the service, the classic street-hailed taxi service where a customer—possibly someone not living in that particular city—must go from point A to point B within that city, and where this is not a regular trip. Being at point A they'd therefore go to the closest busy street, or to the next taxi stand, and take a taxi to point B. What the customer wants is to get there (a) unharmed, (b) reasonably fast, and (c) at a reasonable and predictable cost. Unfortunately, if the customer just stands next to road waving his hand and a car stops, he will not have the information that would allow him to assess the points (a)–(c) above. For example, he'd like to know that the driver is sufficiently capable and not a psychopath, and that the car is safe in order to assert (a). To assert (b) he'd want to driver to be sufficiently skilled in navigating the city, and to assert (c) he'd either need to know that the driver is honest, or would need a benchmark to assess what the fair price should be.

It is interesting that technology changes how those constraints can be addressed. For example, since GPS units have become ubiquitous, being able to navigate the city is no longer a big issue, and even non-residents can assess the length of a trip, and whether or not the price demanded is fair. However, ignoring the fact that nowadays it is possible to quasi-street-hail taxis using a smartphone app, the issue of the honest and skilled driver with the sufficiently safe car remains: when a car pulls up at the kerb or waits at the taxi stand, the potential passenger has no means of getting all the information he needs. That is the fundamental market failure in taxi services, and in in absence of a mechanism to address this, potential customers might find it too dangerous to take a taxi, and therefore a mutually beneficial deal would not happen.

There are fundamentally two different ways in which this can be addressed: regulation and reputation. Let's start with reputation. In countries where taxis are not well regulated one tends to have large taxi companies that dominate the market. For example, when I was in Jakarta a while ago, I was strongly advised to only use cars of a specific company, and to always order a car by phone, lest rogue drivers manage to get hold of a car of that company. One impact of this was that it was rather difficult to get a cab when not in a location where some trusted friend or an honest concierge could order a car, and the company was able to charge premium prices because they had a quasi-monopoly on vetting reliable drivers.

In most cities, taxis are regulated. They are easily identifiable as taxis, and both the car and the driver must be in possession of a valid licence. Licensed taxis are equipped with an official meter that both the customer and the driver can see, and that is the sole basis for the fare that will be due at the end of the ride. The meter is regularly verified to ensure that it works correctly, and police makes spot checks on taxis in operation and fines offenders who do not comply with the aforementioned requirements. In this environment, customers do not have to worry whether or not a taxi they hail in the street conforms with the requirements (a)–(c) discussed above: provided the car is a licensed taxi, the customer can be assured that driver and car are vetted and that he therefore does not have to worry about taking this taxi—the market failure has been addressed.

1.1.2 Carry-over to Financial Regulation

In the previous section we have seen that information asymmetry can lead to a market failure in the market for street-hailed taxis, meaning that the market breaks down because potential customers are not comfortable with their potential providers and therefore do not engage in transactions. In financial services the situation is similar: for example, it is impossible for individuals to assess the strength of financial institutions, and therefore they might either not deposit money with those institutions, or withdraw it at the first sign of distress, both of which constitutes a market failure.

We have seen two mechanisms that can be employed to get around this market failure, notably:

* services are provided by companies whose size and market share are sufficient to allow them to develop a strong enough brand; those companies are able to charge premium prices
* services are provided by small companies or individuals, and there is a small number of private authorities who vet the providers and who have a brand strong enough to support this.

In the early days of banking, banks mostly employed the first solution, ie brand and reputation was the major means of addressing this issue. A testament to this are the splendid branches that banks built to credibly signal the solidity of their financial standing. As an example for this I'd recommend a visit to Société Générale's original branch next to Opéra in Paris, which is still open today and which was clearly and successfully built to impress. It turned out, however, that this strategy was not overly successful in financial services: even splendid headquarters could not prevent bank runs where everyone wanted their deposit back at once.

In modern banking there is also an element of the second solution, in that all major banks are rated by reputable rating agencies, and in the major developed economies most banks are rated AA, or at worst A. However, whilst rating agencies are an important data point in assessing the creditworthiness of a bank, in practice ultimately the only way to ensure that people leave their deposits with banks even in times of distress seems to be to make sure that (a) the banks are tightly regulated and risk is at an acceptable level, and (b) deposits are insured, and there are sufficient business continuity procedures in place to ensure that the distress does not spread through the financial system.

1.2 A Regulatory Strategy Framework

Whenever an industry is regulated this fundamentally alters its strategic landscape. The strategic impact of regulation cannot be understood generally, but must be analysed on a case-by-case basis. For example, in markets with natural monopolies—eg utilities or transport—regulation is often the only way that competition can be maintained. In other markets, the purpose of regulation is not competition, but, say, customer safety or systemic stability, in which case regulation is more often than not an additional barrier to competition. One universal truth, however, is that *in regulated environments, being able to play the regulatory game well is a key competitive advantage*, especially for new entrants trying to break into an existing market. This is doubly important for tech companies, where the focus is on being able to scale quickly and efficiently, and where regulatory moats can be both an opportunity for those who are on the right side of them, and a hurdle for those who are not.

Observation 1 (Regulation creates moats): All regulation—even when it is meant to increase competition—creates moats. Moats are good for companies, at least for those whose strategy means that they find themselves on the correct side of it. In an established business, the moats protect the incumbents. In a fast-changing yet highly regulated business segment, creating and taking advantage of regulatory moats can be key to becoming the new incumbent.

This is very important to understand: whilst regulation is a barrier to doing business, regulation is not necessarily bad for businesses, at least not for those businesses who find themselves on the right side of the moat. This is even the case when it is bad regulation: customers might pay more or receive a worse service than if the regulation was better or not present, and the market size might be reduced, but a specific company using that regulation to its advantage might still find itself in a very comfortable situation.

As an example I want to look at taxi companies in New York, especially before the arrival of Uber. This is a highly regulated market with a fixed service offering—the standard street-hailed yellow cab—at a fixed price, and with a very big moat: the number of medallions is fixed, so new players can only enter the market when the regulator auctions off new medallions, or when they buy them from incumbents who withdraw. In the years prior to the arrival of Uber, the price of medallions in the secondary market skyrocketed, suggesting that operating a taxi in New York was a very attractive business. The flip side of this was that customers were getting a worse deal than they'd have got in a more open market, as everyone trying to get a taxi in NYC during rush hour and/or rain can attest. So in this case, the regulation created a nice moat that restricted the overall size of the market, but that created a very comfortable environment for the cab owners that found themselves inside the moat.

Observation 2 (Eager regulators are assets): Regulators are naturally
of the reluctant type. Having an eager regulator is of great strategic
advantage for a business that wants to establish itself in a regulated
market.

By their very nature, regulators must be reluctant in embracing
innovation: they have a duty to protect markets, and those markets typically
require protection because they are important for the overall economy and/
or for a significant part of the population. Also, whilst those markets in their
regulated state might not be perfect, they tend to work sufficiently well. In
that environment, innovation poses an asymmetric risk: the downside is
destroying something that is essential in peoples' lives, whilst the upside is
an incremental improvement whose value, even if it works, is often uncer-
tain and not yet well understood. This means that regulators have a natural
bias towards being reluctant and not rocking the boat.

In addition, regulators are typically underfunded and stretched, and
their personal incentive structure is even more asymmetric as they'll get the
blame if things blow up, but not much of the credit for marginal improve-
ments. On top of this, in many cases the industries they are meant to regulate have a lot of resources to put into influencing regulation, both at the
political and at the regulatory level, and in many cases there is a strong
financial incentive for experienced regulators to move over to the other
side. All of this together means that regulators often have an even bigger bias towards reluctancy than they should naturally have. Plus there is
always the issue of regulatory capture, ie that regulators get too close to
those whom they regulate, and that they start defending the interests of the
companies they regulate against outsiders, especially against new entrants.

Having said this, there are two fundamentally different cultures within
the regulatory community, a *permissive* culture and a *pre-approval* culture.
Under the former, regulators are more comfortable with companies going
ahead and doing new things, to be regulated—or not—eventually, whilst
under the latter, regulators expect everything that might need regulation
to be pre-cleared from the beginning. Those cultures can also temporarily
shift, for instance when markets are perceived as not working as they
should. An example for this would be the period after the credit crisis.
In an environment like that one, regulators are often eager to help new
entrants to enter the market, for example by treating them more leniently
than proportionate regulation would imply, or by actively helping them, eg
in a regulatory sandbox environment. Those episodes where regulators are

eager are typically temporarily and geographically limited, and so being in the right place at the right time when this happens is an important strategic advantage.

Observation 3 (Regulatory scale): As long as the business scale is below the regulatory scale, incumbent businesses experience economies of scale when dealing with regulation, and therefore regulation creates a moat. Those scale effects disappear once the business scale becomes larger than the regulatory scale.

Active regulatory strategies can reduce or increase this moat. At the lower end, the moat is reduced if there is a proportionate regulatory regime in place; at the upper end, a certain moat is maintained if there are passporting or equivalence regimes in place, or at least some common regulatory rules that allow large players to reap economies of scale across multiple regulated markets.

The underlying reason here is that compliance costs do not scale much with the business volume, ie they have a significant fixed component. For example, bank regulators might require certain reports. The actual work of crunching the numbers for the report is done by a computer, and the cost of running a report pales against the cost of programming the computer. Not all regulatory cost is fixed, however: for example, any report will throw up a certain number of exceptions that will have to be followed up manually, and the cost of doing this will be proportional to the business volume. In any case, in the financial services segment regulatory compliance usually does impose a high fixed cost, and this does create moats.

Proportionate regulatory regimes are acknowledging not only that there is this high fixed cost component in compliance, but that it is often not necessary. For example, rules that are meant to keep the overall system safe if a bank defaults can be safely ignored when regulating a small bank whose default can easily be absorbed by the system. On the other hand, rules that are meant to protect the customers of this bank remain equally important, regardless of whether the bank is big or small. A proportionate regulatory regime would therefore allow small banks not to spend many resources on the first objective, but would not reduce the burden on the second one.

Things like common regulatory frameworks, equivalence regimes and passporting go the other way: they allow players present in multiple jurisdictions to reap some economies of scale, thereby benefitting from regulatory moats. To explain what those terms mean, *common regulatory frameworks* indicates that the requirements are similar—for example, a company might still have to submit reports to all their regulators, but all the reports can be the same or at least very similar.

Under an *equivalence* or *passporting* regime, the host (local) regulator assumes that the home regulator (where the company is based) does a good job and leaves the main regulatory burden with the home regulator. The difference between equivalence and passporting is one of degree—the latter term is in particular used in the EU where it refers to the unconditional right of businesses resident and regulated in one market to operate across the entire EU Single Market, whilst equivalence is an agreement between two regulatory jurisdictions that the two systems are currently equivalent, but that can be withdrawn at short notice.

Observation 4 (Trailblazers and close followers): It is hard to be a regulatory trailblazer, in terms of cost, effort, and time to market. The best position from a regulatory strategy point of view is that of a close follower, with the exception of where the trailblazer's business model has some hard-to-replicate features that they manage to slip into the regulation. Distant followers will find regulatory compliance the easiest as rules are already set, but their lack of scale and market share might hinder them.

Being a trailblazer is hard, in every business. Trailblazers spend a lot of time working on dead ends before finally coming up with the right solution. However, when solving business problems, intellectual property law, copyright law, or simply institutional knowledge often mean that trailblazers create a moat that protects them. This is not the case in regulatory interactions: here a lot of time and effort is spent convincing the regulators that allowing that particular new-and-untested business model is a good idea in the first place. After that, coming to an agreement as to what kind of documents, analysis, and reports the regulators need to see, and more generally what the regulatory framework should look like requires a lot of effort. Regulators will often lean on companies to do the leg work on that as they themselves lack the resources and incentives to do so.

Once all those issues are resolved, however, regulators no longer need convincing, and the document requirement and regulatory frameworks are in place. All a competitor has to do is to contact the regulators, and they'll guide them through the authorisation process. There is a slight twist if the trailblazer can shape the regulation in a manner that plays to their own strengths and to their competitor's weaknesses, but this is rare with a good regulator.

Observation 5 (Power of the precedent): When regulation has not settled yet, precedents are very powerful. In descending order of power, key precedents are:

1. Someone else doing the same thing in the same jurisdiction, regulated by the regulator in question.
2. Doing the same thing, in a different jurisdiction, regulated by the regulator of that jurisdiction.
3. Similar regulation with a clear carry-over being in place in that particular jurisdiction, or in another one with sufficient reputation.
4. The possible regulatory concerns are understood and agreed, and there is a written regulatory draft framework that addresses them.
5. The business is up and running at a not-insignificant scale, and is well-liked by the public, and/or is in line with the current public opinion (eg 'the financial system has failed us and needs to be renewed').

In a new area with no established best practices—and with a significant downside risk and much less upside—nothing can calm regulatory minds as much as giving the confidence that what is being done is not actually new, and that the risk is limited. That, in a nutshell, is the power of the precedent: theoretical arguments are good, but real-life experience is better.

The last solution—operate now, regulate later—is the odd one out. It can work, especially in lightly regulated industries, or where the regulator is not particularly powerful vis-à-vis the company in question. For example, where the company is global and operating in numerous locations whilst the regulators are local, losing the right to operate in a given location might not be catastrophic for the company, but the regulator might face a public backlash if the service is popular elsewhere. This strategy in particular allows to bootstrap the regulation cases where no regulator wants to go first: once one regulator has agreed on a certain regulatory scheme the company moves up from precedent (5) to precedent (2). It is, however, a rather risky undertaking, and in the financial services space it is not necessarily recommended, even though some segments—notably the crypto space—are sometimes seen as operating in that way.

> **Observation 6 (Skilful regulatory interaction)**: Regulatory inter-action is a skill that can make a big difference in terms of cost, effort, and time to market.

Every junior consultant learns very quickly there is a very narrow point when one should go to see the senior partner in charge to discuss the new deck of slides. Going to see them when you think you have everything tied down and finished is dangerous: maybe you misunderstood something, or you were not given a key piece of information when receiving your brief, or the partner simply feels out of the loop and needs to put his or her own imprint on the deck. In any case, you'll have done a lot of superfluous work, and will have to redo a number of things. Going to see the partner too early is dangerous as well. First, it is bad for your reputation, because then you are seen as someone who is not particularly skilled and needs a lot of help. Also, the partner will see this as a brainstorming session rather than as an opportunity to tie down loose ends, and he or she might come up with many different ideas that you'll have to pursue, the majority of which end up being wrong, redundant, or simply not important enough to be pursued within the limited timeframe of the project.

Exactly the same points apply to regulatory interactions: if you pre-sume too much, the regulator might simply disagree with you, and/or get annoyed that they have not been involved at an earlier stage. If you come too early, on the other hand, with no clear idea of what kind of regula-tion you consider appropriate, then the regulator will initially assume that you are not particularly competent in this area, and that you need extra supervision. Moreover, they will treat this meeting as a brainstorming ses-sion and you risk end coming out of it with not much to show other than a big shopping list for more analysis and reports that the regulator would like to see for the next meeting. So here as well, hitting the sweet spot is extremely important in order to reduce the workload, and to keep the pro-cess on track.

> **Observation 7 (Local regulation matters)**: Even in a passporting regime, the local regulations still matter, if not de jure then de facto, so all local regulators should be kept informed and on-board.

In passporting regimes—and in the weaker equivalence regimes of course—the local regulator will always be able to throw a spanner in the wheels if they feel that a company is not following local rules that they consider important, even if passporting means that they do not have to follow the rules. If the local regulator is unreasonable, ultimately the regulated company will be able to rectify this when going through the appeals process, but this is a costly and lengthy endeavour, and possibly not a good strategy for start-ups with limited resources. The best strategy is usually to address such conflicts early on, and to comply with local regulatory demands where this is economically justifiable.

Observation 8 (Regime choice matters): Jurisdictions within a passporting environment might offer two choices to start-up companies that are subject to regulation: compliance with a lightweight local framework, or with a more complex cross-jurisdictional framework that can be passported.

To give a concrete example, let's consider an alternative lender who does not take deposits and does not lend to individuals. In the UK this lender can choose to follow either a lightly regulated local model, or to get a banking licence. In Germany, every lender needs a banking licence, so alternative lenders either have one, or work with a bank. If the UK company wants to do business in Germany and has a banking licence, it can simply passport it. If it only has a local licence, it might not be able to passport it at all, and even if it manages to do so, it will need a local banking partner, which means probably that it will need to redesign a lot of its processes and systems.

This choice is ultimately down to individual circumstances, and should be given serious thought by the start-up's executives, ideally together with competent advisors. The local regime probably allows for a quicker and less-costly time-to-market, and an easier pivot if need be. The passportable regime, on the other hand, might save time scaling and, importantly, avoids the risk of getting stuck in a business model that does not scale.

The last observation is not really an observation but it is a meta-observation about the interaction of all that we have previously discussed (see also Figure 1.1).

FIGURE 1.1 A Regulatory Strategy Framework

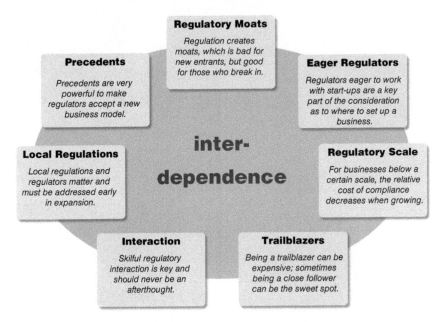

Regulatory Moats

Regulation creates moats, which is bad for new entrants, but good for those who break in.

Precedents

Precedents are very powerful to make regulators accept a new business model.

Eager Regulators

Regulators eager to work with start-ups are a key part of the consideration as to where to set up a business.

inter-dependence

Local Regulations

Local regulations and regulators matter and must be addressed early in expansion.

Regulatory Scale

For businesses below a certain scale, the relative cost of compliance decreases when growing.

Interaction

Skilful regulatory interaction is key and should never be an afterthought.

Trailblazers

Being a trailblazer can be expensive; sometimes being a close follower can be the sweet spot.

Final Observation (Interdependence): All the previously mentioned observations depend on each other, and it is important to look at them jointly rather than in isolation.

CHAPTER 2

Overview of Financial Services Regulation

2.1 Types of Regulation

Regulations are about addressing market failures. There are a number of market failures in the financial services space, and it is useful to classify the different strands of regulation according to the market failure that they are meant to address (see Figure 2.1).

- **Prudential regulation.** Micro-prudential regulation addresses the issue that single institutions have incentives to take excessive risks, and macro-prudential regulation addresses the same issue for markets as a whole; many of them have a tendency to operate in destructive boom and bust cycles.
- **Market structure regulation.** Market structure regulation addresses the issue that markets are not operating optimally, eg because of asymmetric information.
- **Conduct regulation.** Conduct regulation addresses the issue that customers are not able to properly assess the respective risks and rewards of financial products, and that they can't see ahead of time who'll treat them fairly once they are tied in.
- **Public interest regulation.** Public interest regulation addresses the issue that the financial system can be used for illicit purposes, for example money laundering or terrorist financing.

2.1.1 Prudential Regulation

Banks, and more generally the financial system, are critical for the functioning of an economy, so ultimately authorities will always step in once a critical solution develops. The knowledge of this fact feeds back into the behaviour

FIGURE 2.1 Types of Regulation

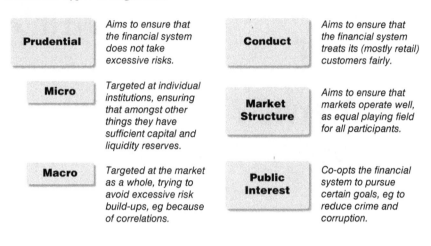

of all actors involved. For example, shareholders of banks know that they'll get the upside of any risky investments the bank makes, but don't have to bear the downside below a certain level. They therefore have an incentive to invest the depositors' money as riskily as possible to benefit from this free option. If depositors are confident they will be bailed out by the state if things go wrong, they might not particularly mind. So as soon as there is a reasonable belief that the state will bail out failing banks and/or their investors and/or their deposit holders, there must be regulatory oversight to ensure that risks are kept at bay. The regulation that is meant to ensure the safety of financial institutions and financial infrastructure is commonly known as **prudential regulation**.

Within this prudential regulation, there are two strands, **micro-prudential regulation** and **macro-prudential regulation**. The former deals with the stability of individual institutions without considering their context, and this was the main focus of prudential regulation before the crisis. Up to that point it was widely believed that if all banks are considered safe, then the system can be considered safe as well. Since then, regulators have realised that this is not necessarily the case. To give an example, banks might choose to hold a portfolio of reasonably liquid assets in case they run into liquidity problems, and regulators might consider this sufficient, given the liquidity they see in the market. However, if many banks hold similar assets, and if there is a general liquidity stress, all companies might all try to sell those securities at the same time, and they might find that markets seize up. Macro-prudential regulation is meant to discover and address those risks.

Micro-prudential regulation

On the micro-prudential side, regulators want to ensure that individual institutions are safe and well run. For banks, for example, the major prudential requirements are that:

- they hold sufficient capital to be reasonably certain that depositors and other senior liability holders don't suffer any losses in case of distress
- they hold sufficient liquid assets to be reasonably certain they will be able to repay obligations when they come due
- they competently assess, manage and mitigate all risks they face, including operational risks.

The last point includes business continuity planning. It is important that a bank failure does not interrupt the business for their customers. So even if a bank is in the process of winding down it must be possible for their customers to participate in the payment system, up to the point where their accounts can be transferred to a viable entity.

For players other than banks, the prudential requirements are very similar when their particular circumstances are taken into account. For example, for insurance companies all of those points apply. For funds, the main prudential requirements are that they have adequate risk management processes in place, that assets are properly segregated and are in particular not commingled with the management company's own assets, and generally that the fund's operations are safe. Finally, for payment systems and other infrastructure items, operational risk and in particular business continuity tend to be the most important requirements.

A key purpose of micro-prudential regulation is to protect the customers of the business. This means that there is a priori no lower size limit below which it becomes less important: whether a bank is established in a single small town and serves a few hundred customers out of a single branch or whether it is a large national bank serving tens of millions of customers does not matter in this respect, as every single customer should be protected to the same level by micro-prudential regulation. Regulation is meant to be proportionate; however, in many cases, the small banks have simpler products and processes, so the regulatory burden can be lighter.

There is an important carry-over of this into the Fintech space: even if a start-up has only a few thousand customers, to the extent that the start-up offers products or services that are only offered by regulated entities, and unless it has been clearly agreed otherwise both with the customers and the regulators, those customers can expect the same level of protection as if they were a customer of one of the regulated businesses. It is therefore crucial for a Fintech start-up to understand the regulations that apply to their regulated competitors. Also, for early-stage Fintech companies there is a real risk that companies cease operations, so regulators expect contingency plans in place that allow for an appropriate level of business continuity.

Macro-prudential regulation

Macro-prudential regulation is about protecting the interconnected system as a whole, not individual players. Size matters here: macro-prudential regulators will usually ignore an institution that has only a few thousand customers—or even a few ten-thousands of customers for that matter—and similarly they are likely to ignore individual start-ups if their business volume is insignificant in the overall scheme of things.

There are, however, a number of exceptions to this general rule. For example, in some cases there are many small players that are similar to each other or share resources, eg small credit unions serving local communities. Regulators will look for systemic risk among those, as well as single points of failure like centralised data or payments infrastructure. A similar example from the start-up world would be bitcoin mining: even if miners were not as concentrated as they are now, systematic regulators would look at what could make the system fail, eg a reliance on mining pools, or central servers used to update the mining software, or coordinated attacks.

Also, growth and growth potential matters: in the old world of bricks and mortar finance, things changed slowly. This is different in the modern environment where markets can grow from insignificant to systemically important within a few years—see for example the development of CDS and securitisation markets in the early 2000s. We have not seen that in Fintech yet, but it has the same potential of massive growth when their service offerings become popular. Whenever there is massive growth, macro-prudential regulators are worried, often with good reason.

For banks, the most important considerations are size and interconnectedness.

After the crisis, the Financial Stability Board has decided to identify Globally Systemically Important Banks (G-SIBS), later renamed to Globally Systemically Important Financial Institutions (G-SIFIs) that would be subject to enhanced supervision and increased capital requirements. It is usually not the core lending businesses that cause the regulators to worry about the systemic importance of the banks, but it is more their securities and derivatives trading businesses and how they connect to their peers.

Whilst banks are on top of the list when it comes to systemic risk considerations, they are by no means the only ones on it. Systemic regulators oversee all important parts of the financial infrastructure, for example the clearing houses, the major payment systems, and stock and derivatives exchanges. If systemic regulators pay attention to specific Fintech players in the next couple of years, then this is probably in that area rather than in areas like lending. For example, if start-ups are directly or indirectly connected to a major interbank payment system then the regulators will want to be comfortable that the start-up's systems are either secure enough or well enough insulated from the system not to be able to wreak havoc under any circumstances.

The toolkit of macro-prudential regulators is mostly analytic—they collect and analyse data, and if they have specific concerns they ask for specific reports, or for stress tests under scenarios they are worried about. In their active toolkit they can ask institutions that they are systemically important to hold larger amounts of capital, and in severe cases they can also request that positions that they consider excessive are reduced in an orderly manner. Another important tool is living wills and resolution plans: for companies that are considered systemically important there must be a detailed plan as to how they can be wound down without risk to the overall financial system. It is similar to a business continuity plan but much more detailed, and it is created in close interaction with the regulators.

2.1.2 Market Structure Regulation

Market structure regulation is about making sure that markets are as close to being efficient as is reasonably possible. The main issue to address here is usually information asymmetry in its various guises. The argument is slightly subtle, however: in the real world, information is not free, but it costs resources to acquire, and those who spend those resources acquiring it should make an adequate return on their investment—after all, they contribute to price discovery. To the extent this price discovery works, the price in the market then is fair, and everyone buying or selling does so at this fair price. On the other hand, a market with too much private information—especially when this private information is concentrated with a small number of players—becomes unattractive to everyone who is not in possession of private information and liquidity dries up, to the point that the market possibly collapses.

So market structure regulation tries to address the situations where some participants are in a structurally superior position. For example, it outlaws insider dealing, ie, it makes it in many cases a criminal offence to trade a security when in possession of material non-public information. Other regulations ensure that players do not have different access to key market information—for example that some players are not allowed to see orders significantly earlier than others, or also that companies must release information such as annual reports or ad hoc messages to all investors at the same time.

It also addresses natural oligopoly issues that often arise in financial services, in part because of regulatory moats. So in order to ensure competition, regulators can require access to key infrastructure on fair and non-discriminatory terms, thereby allowing the smaller players to compete with the larger ones. An important example for such regulations is PSD 2, which requires banks—and other payment institutions, including larger Fintech companies—to provide their account query and payment API to other players, effectively allowing customers to substitute the large banks' electronic banking system with that of a third-party provider or aggregator.

2.1.3 Conduct Regulation

Financial markets are at the same time important, and complex for many people to understand, with an added difficulty that many developments play out over a long horizon, which gives people less opportunity to learn from experience.

As an example let's have a look at savings deposits: there are a number of investments out there that look very similar to but more attractive than term savings deposits, for example bonds issued by those banks. Whilst the bonds might look similar, they can be quite different, especially when Tier 1 or Tier 2 capital bonds are involved—and many retail investors do not understand that difference. First, bonds are not usually covered by the deposit protection schemes, so if a bank defaults those bonds will suffer a loss. Moreover, this loss can be dramatically higher on capital-type bonds, something that was not necessarily clear to the customer when they bought them. Those customers might simply have seen bonds offered by the same bank with attractive yields. Unless there has been a crisis recently, looking backwards does not help to assess the risks on those bonds, but, as many bond holders discovered in the crisis, this does not mean that those risks won't materialise in the future.

Conduct regulation is in place to ensure that customers are treated fairly. What this means depends on the exact regulatory regime in place—some are more protective than others—but the principle is that customers should be put in a position to make informed decisions with respect to their finances. For example, some jurisdictions might simply require customers to be provided with sufficient information, others might require the financial services company to ensure that their customers understand the information they have been given, others might prevent certain customers from acquiring in certain instruments entirely, and others finally might give companies the fiduciary duty to act in their customers' best interest.

A typical regulatory system divides the customer base into three tiers:

- private clients
- professional clients
- market counterparties.

The first tier are all those clients who do not operate in the financial markets in a professional capacity. This includes most retails clients, but also small and medium-sized companies and public bodies etc. The second tier are clients who operate in the financial markets professionally and on a regular basis. For example, this would be the treasury operations of large and some mid-sized companies, investment managers, insurance companies, etc. Note that this distinction is to be made on a by-product-class basis: for example, if a treasury operation is regularly engaging in forex hedging but rarely does interest rate swaps, then it might be considered a professional client when trading forex products, but a private client when trading interest rate swaps. The third tier are other financial institutions that are considered equal trading partners to the institution in question, not clients.

The difference between the tiers is the amount of consideration financial institutions have to give to their needs. In many cases, when dealing with private customers, financial institutions have to make an effort to understand the needs and circumstances of their clients, and must make sure that the products are suitable for them. They are also subject to very specific transparency requirements, for example they might have to produce *key facts* sheets that in easily understandable terms contain all major considerations important for the client to assess the product. For professional clients there will usually be no requirement to assess suitability, and the transparency requirements are more lightweight—for example, they might be expected to understand deals based on the term sheet and the deal documentation. Market counterparties finally do not profit from any specific protection, other than the usual commercial rules with respect to acting in good faith.

The classification is done jointly by the financial institution and its counterparty. Sophisticated clients have an interest to be treated as professional clients because it will allow them to deal on more favourable terms, and it will allow them to access a wider range of products and services. Financial institutions, however, cannot just take a client's declaration at face value and must make a reasonable effort to determine whether clients do indeed qualify for being in the professional clients tier in the areas in which they want to transact.

Direct conduct regulation also includes data protection and privacy rules that regulate what level of protection customers can expect by regulated institutions and their partners in this area. This is important as customers are not in a position to audit their provider's systems and processes in this respect, and might not even be able to ascertain whether or not the protections provided in a company's terms and conditions are adequate.

2.1.4 Public Interest Regulation

Financial institutions' conduct is also regulated *for the common good*, for example for crime prevention and similar public policy purposes. The key areas covered with those regulations are the anti money laundering (AML) area, the combat terrorist finance (CTF) area, and the Anti-Bribery Corruption (ABC) area, which includes the politically exposed persons (PEP) processes. More widely there is a cyber security and cyber crime angle, which means that there is also some overlap with data protection regulation that otherwise sits mostly in the conduct space.

For AML the issue is that criminals can use the regular financial system to launder the proceeds of crime, ie to make it appear that those proceeds come from legitimate ventures, which then allows them to benefit from this money wherever they please. In the ABC and PEP area the purpose is similar, except that instead of targeting crime the main purpose is to combat corruption, whether or it is criminal in the country in question, and also to support with politically motivated embargoes. The thrust of CTF goes in the opposite direction: terrorists might use the regular financial system to move around the resources that they need to prepare their activities.

All those regulations enlist the financial system as a deputy in the fight against crime, corruption, and terrorism, and also to support politically motivated actions, in particular embargoes. It puts a liability on each and any participant to be vigilant in this respect, including checking customer data against the numerous watch lists, and to profile the transactional behaviour where appropriate. The central element in all those processes are the Know Your Customer (KYC) rules: financial institutions must know their customers—and where necessary the ultimate beneficiaries behind their customers—to assert whether or not flows of funds they observe correspond to legitimate activities, and that the persons involved do not appear on any of the relevant lists.

The cyber security and cyber crime angles are independent from those discussed above, but the common denominator is that companies must perform some duties out of public interest over and beyond what they'd be doing out of self-interest. For example, some companies might consider being hacked in some more unusual scenarios an acceptable risk when assessing how much to spend on systems security, whilst regulators—having the financial system and its customers in mind—might want companies to harden more against cyber attacks.

2.2 Strands of Regulation

Most financial services nowadays are regulated. This regulation has developed over time, and for practical reasons it has developed along the lines of the regulated sectors. So bank regulators would be in charge of applying bank regulation to banks, insurance regulators would be in charge to apply insurance regulation to insurance companies and so on. Even in the past this did not work entirely without hiccups, especially when industries restructured. For example, there was a trend towards *universal banks* or *financial conglomerates*, and the same company (or group of companies) might provide, say, banking services, insurance services, fund management, and brokerage. By and large that was not an issue as the different activities would be run out of different entities within the group, so the bank subsidiary would be regulated by the bank regulator, the insurance subsidiary by the insurance regulator etc. There are, however, group-level effects: for example, banking and insurance subsidiaries might have common treasury operations, and/or rely on intra-group funding which has to be taken care of at a group-level. Also, one of the key reasons why companies would join into financial conglomerates would be the ability for cross-selling, which means that ideally salesforces and IT systems would be joined up.

With Fintech we now have a slightly different dynamic in that companies tend to be ultra-focused, at least to begin with. This focus could be a product focus, in which case the operations might fit neatly into one of the traditional areas of regulation. For example, a robo-advisor would be regulated similar to an investment advisor, and for an app that allows friends to share bills some bank-like regulation might apply (unless there is specific regulation in the payments space that recognises non-bank payment services providers, as is the case for example in the EU). There are products that are more difficult to fit into existing categories, especially if they fit into some kind of market-place category. For example, peer-to-peer lending or crowdfunding do not slot neatly into pre-Fintech categories that did not really foresee individuals providing finance to each other on a large scale. Also, applicable regulations would be partly from the banking space (eg money laundering, consumer protection) whilst some would be from the market infrastructure space (eg the requirement to treat all customers equally).

The company focus could also be a customer focus. For example, a company could focus on providing a complete set of financial services to a very narrow set of customers. This company might focus on distribution, meaning that it would not create the products itself, but rely on partners— eg banks, insurance companies, asset managers—whose products it would white-label and sell on to its own customers. Regulating this company like a financial conglomerate would certainly not be the way to go. On the other hand, solely relying on the fact that the backend product providers are regulated would probably not work either, as at least some of the applicable regulations (eg money laundering, data protection, conduct) are relevant for the front-end provider as well.

Before we go on I want to illustrate this issue with a comparison of one product (a standard bank account) to two products that can be functionally very similar, but that belong to different regulatory universes (a money market fund and a gift card).

2.2.1 Regulating Products Versus Regulating Institutions

One fundamental issue when regulating a market is to decide what exactly should be within the regulatory scope and what should be out. To show that this is harder than it looks I want to give an example, looking at the *savings account* product.

Example: Current accounts versus money market funds

A current account is an account whose main purpose is to allow the owner to participate in the country's payment system—cards, cheques, transfers, ATMs—and to hold the funds necessary to do so. Many money market accounts allow for exactly the same benefits, albeit with a number of important differences:

- bank deposits are protected by deposit guarantee schemes; money market funds are not
- deposits are general liabilities of a bank that uses the funds for their overall balance sheet; money market funds are invested in specific high-quality and highly liquid assets
- deposit accounts usually benefit from an overdraft facility, avoiding payments to bounce; money market funds don't.

Many of the securities that money market funds invest in are either banks' short-term debt, or asset-backed securities that in turn serve to finance loans. Therefore, overall the picture is very similar: customer deposits serve to finance loans to other customers, either via a bank balance sheet, or via asset-backed securities. Also, if money market fund investors expect to be bailed out by the government—as they have been in the financial crisis—they might not care about the lack of deposit protection.

From a regulatory point of view banks and funds are very different, as they are subject to very different regulations. For example, banks have very strict guidelines on how much capital they have to hold against their lending, whilst there is no such requirement for funds. Also banks will be expected to contribute to some deposit protection fund, either ex-ante, or ex-post when an event has actually happened. This constitutes a regulatory arbitrage, as what is economically essentially the same product is provided with a very different level of regulatory requirements.

Example: Savings accounts versus gift cards

Now let's look at another common product, the gift card. Here a customer has purchased a card that can be used to purchase specific products, and/or in specific stores. In some cases the restriction might be significant, eg it might allow one only to purchase, say, music, or smartphone apps. However, there are less restrictive cards, eg those issued by department stores, that might give access to a large range of goods, including food and other everyday items. Those cards are almost as useful as cash, or as a pre-paid debit card.

Now regulators have a dilemma: on the one hand they do not want to regulate retail stores that issue gift cards if they are genuinely used as such and the amounts involved are not too high. However, to the extent that the gift cards become more like cash—and possibly represent significant value—regulation can become more important, for example in the AML/CTF space.

Regulating products

To conclude this section, it is often difficult to design product-based regulation. In the example above we have seen that *some* funds and *some* gift cards can look very similar to deposit accounts; however, not *all* funds do, and neither do *all* gift cards. It would be good to be able to apply the equivalent of *duck typing*—it walks like a duck, and it quacks like a duck, so it must be a duck—but whilst regulators often try to do so, it is not always possible:

First, the nature of law makes it difficult to write regulation on a functional or product level because there is the tension between making the law unambiguous and predictable, and making it flexible enough to allow for variations around a theme when the market offers products that are similar in nature, but different in important details, in particular also in the legal form.

The question is often where to put the boundary, as can be seen in the gift card example: there is a spectrum of design choices, and on one side of it—say not transferrable, can only be used for very restricted purposes, possibly a time limit—it is almost certainly not electronic money, whilst on the other side of it—say card-based, and accepted in a wide variety of stores—it almost certainly is, as the difference to a regular pre-paid card is very small.

Legislating this is hard, especially ex-ante: it is usually possible to look at existing products and services and then write legislation that sorts them correctly into those where it should apply and where not. However, once the legislation is written, new products can be designed that end up on the wrong side of the boundary, either deliberately—a process often referred as regulatory arbitrage—or by chance, in which case existing legacy regulation can and does impede the development of innovative products and services.

An attempt to solve this dilemma is to go down the route of principles-based regulation which—as opposed to classic rules-based regulation—is meant to allow for more regulatory flexibility. In practice this is not a dichotomy but rather two opposite ends of a continuous spectrum, as principle-based regulations also have some hard rules, just fewer of them, and vice versa. Principles-based regulation can solve some of the issues, but it comes at a cost: for example, there is less regulatory certainty, and regulators become more powerful so regulatory capture and even corruption can become more of an issue.

Second, apart from the nature of law there is a more mundane issue, that of organising regulation (in this context, see also Figure 2.2 for a graphic presentation of the financial services segment on the products/institutions grid, and Figure 2.3 for an illustration of how regulators are traditionally organised). When regulating a firm, it is both important to understand the nature of the firm as a whole and what is happening at the detailed product level. Therefore the regulatory team has to pull in both product specialists and people who have a high-level view. This is easy if the organisational structure of the regulator mirrors the organisational structure of the industry it regulates: for example, traditionally there will be a banks team, an asset management team, and an insurance team. Within the banks team there will be specialists for lending, payments, and deposits and they'll work together to get an overall view. However, more recently we have seen both fund-based checking accounts and dedicated payment institutions, so suddenly the payment specialists also have to work on the fund side, and might even need their own department.

This might not seem overly complicated at first sight, but the issue is that the nature of Fintech means the business models are deconstructed and reconstructed in a different manner at scale, and the emerging companies do not fit any longer into mutually exclusive boxes. Regulating this

FIGURE 2.2 Company Classification: Product vs Institutions Grid

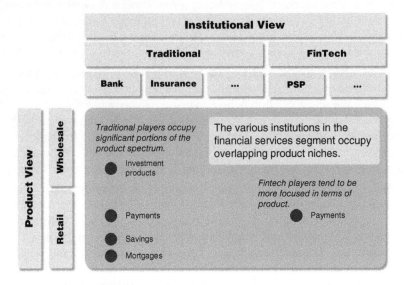

FIGURE 2.3 Typical Regulatory Alignment

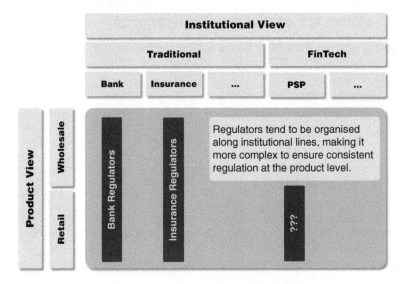

is a challenge, because the regulatory organisation has to follow what is happening in the markets. To some extent regulators will be able to operate with multidisciplinary teams. However, it is well known that matrix reporting structures (two reporting lines) are difficult to operate, and cube or hypercube reporting structures (three or more lines) are even worse.

Eventually regulators will be able to find a new organisational structure that is both manageable internally and that fits their external environment—we already see the transformation happening, and initiatives like regulatory sandboxes and sharing of best practices are evidence for this. However, this will take time, and the regulatory structure will always lag behind the structure of the market. As long as the market is permanently playing with and transforming business models, the regulators forcibly will remain a few steps behind.

What this means in practice is, for example, that deposit takers will be regulated as banks, money market funds will be regulated as funds, and many gift cards will probably not be regulated at all. There will be some regulatory distortions, and regulators will monitor how important those distortions are. If they become too big—in a business-volume-weighted sense—regulators will try to address those distortions. However, this takes time, and in the meantime all those companies are operating and competing under the existing regulations.

2.2.2 Strands of Financial Services Regulation

Financial services regulation is usually organised along the classic industry sectors which are

- banking and payments
- insurance and asset management
- market infrastructure.

Within those sectors, there are a number of lines along which regulation can be split, for example:

- prudential (robustness of institutions and the system) vs conduct (eg fair treatment of customer) vs market structure (eg product innovation and availability)
- by subsector (eg banking, payments; or insurance, mutual funds, pension providers etc; or exchanges, clearing houses).

There are also a number of regulations which cut across all sectors, the most important ones being:

* money laundering
* terrorist finance
* financial crime
* data protection and privacy.

2.2.3 Global Strands of Regulation

The financial system is exceedingly global, and therefore regulation is becoming global as well. One reason is that this makes it easier for companies to expand into other national markets, thereby increasing competition and improving customer choice. Also, globally uniform regulation avoids regulatory arbitrage, so business will be located and regulated where it makes sense from a business point of view rather than where the regulatory barriers are lowest.

Banking

One area where global harmonisation is very advanced is the banking sector, where the Basel Committee for Banking Supervision (BCBS; a committee made of international regulators) defines the so-called 'Basel Accords'. We are now into the third revision of those regulations, with the fourth one being work in progress.

Securities, markets and asset management

In other areas there is also some international harmonisation, but it is less strong. For example, in the securities, markets, and asset management space there is the International Organization of Securities Commissions (IOSCO). They provide technical guidance and advice in a number of areas related to the securities space. Some of the advice is more formal, the most important piece in this respect being the *38 Principles of Securities Regulation* from 2010, which contains high-level guidance on regulators and their interaction, auditors, rating agencies, issuers, investment funds, and intermediaries, and which has been endorsed by the G20 and the FSB. They also publish less authoritative staff working papers on topics of interest, for example the 2014 paper on the crowdfunding sector.

Insurance

In the insurance space, there is the International Association of Insurance Supervisors (IAIS). According to their own words, the IAIS is:

> *the international standard setting body responsible for developing principles, standards and other supporting material for the supervision of the insurance sector and assisting in their implementation. The IAIS also provides a forum for members to share their experiences and understanding of insurance supervision and insurance markets.*

They are the author of the *Insurance Core Principles* document that sets out the 26 core principles of how an insurance company should be run, and that, at almost 400 pages in size, is closer to the Basel framework than the terse 10-odd pages of the IOSCO *38 Principles* document.

2.2.4 Strands of Regulation in the EU

Within the EU there are a number of regulations that apply to all sectors, notably in the areas of data protection and privacy, which is covered by the General Data Protection Regulation (GDPR), which is as of 2016 in its second revision, and in the area of money laundering, terrorist finance, and financial crime, where the Anti Money Laundering Directive (AMLD) is as of 2015 in its fourth revision.

There are also general rules covering all consumer contracts, including financial services contracts, in the 1993 Consumer Contracts Directive.

Banking and payments

On the banking side, there is the EU's implementation of the Basel Accords.

The currently active implementation is loosely referred to as Capital Requirements Directive 4 (CRD4), which consists of the Capital Requirements Regulation (CRR) and the Credit Institutions Directive (CID), both published in 2013. They in turn are based on the 2010/2011 Basel 3 Accord. Basel 4 is work in progress, but whilst there have been some publications at the Basel level there is little visibility regarding if and when this will impact EU legislation.

On the prudential side, another key regulation is the Banking Recovery and Resolution Directive (BRRD) of 2014, which deals with failing banks, and there are a number of conduct regulations on the consumer side, notably the Consumer Credit Directive from 2008 and the Mortgage Credit Directive from 2014. Also, the Deposit Protection Scheme Directive, which is in its second revision as of 2014, is important in this space.

On the payments side, there is the Payments Services Directive (PSD), which as of 2015 is in its second revision. There is also the Electronic Money Directive from 2009 that is covering things like pre-paid payment cards. There is also the Cross-Border Payments Regulation from 2009, which deals with the fees for Euro-denominated cross-border payments.

Insurance, pension, and fund management

On the insurance prudential side, the equivalent of the banks' Basel/CRD regulations is Solvency 2, ie the second revision of the Solvency Directive, published in 2009. On the pension side there is the Institutions for Occupational Retirement Provision Directive (IORPD) from 2003.

In the asset management space there is the Undertakings for Collective Investment in Transferable Securities Directive (UCITSD), which is in its fifth revision as of 2014 and covers retail-focused mutual funds. There is also the Alternative Investment Fund Manager Directive (AIFMD), which covers alternative investments like hedge funds, private equity, and venture capital, and there is the Packaged Retail and Insurance-based Investment Products Regulation (PRIIPR) from 2014.

Markets

The big directive in the markets space, covering market places, intermediaries, advisors, etc. is the Markets in Financial Instruments Directive (MiFID), which as of 2014 is its second revision, and which consists of the MiFIR regulation and the MiFID2 directive. The central entity under this regulation is the investment firm, which, like the banks and insurers, is one of the types of regulated entities with whom most end-customers are most likely to interact.

There is also the European Market Infrastructure Regulation (EMIR) from 2012, which deals with clearing houses (aka central counterparties aka CCPs) as well as with trade repositories collecting trade data. Finally, there is the Market Abuse Regulation (MAR), which is as of 2014 in its second revision, and which replaces the previous MAD directive, and there is the Rating Agencies Regulation (RAR) from 2009 which deals with rating agencies.

CHAPTER 3

Regulation in Practice

U ltimately, regulations are simply laws that have been decided upon by a legislative body, that is, implemented by an executive body, and whose implementation is overseen by a judicial body.

As legislation, it is implemented in the way all legislation is implemented: the legislative body—typically the parliament—enacts primary legislation. This primary legislation gives explicit power to some other agencies—typically part of the executive—to enact secondary legislation that acts within the framework of the primary legislation and that deals with minutiae and details that would overload the primary legislation process. The process itself, in particular at the primary legislation level, is not particularly interesting in the context of this discussion. What is interesting, however, is how legislation across different jurisdictions is harmonised, and I will discuss this, and the bodies that are responsible for secondary legislation, in the section that follows.

Financial regulation is very important for the functioning of the economy, and every jurisdiction has multiple executive bodies that oversee its implementation. EU legislation refers to them as 'competent authorities', and in common language they are mostly referred to as 'regulators'. I will stick mostly to that second term, but we must keep in mind that it can refer both to dedicated regulatory authorities and to other authorities that have been given executive functions in this context, such as departments within a country's finance department or inside a central bank. I will discuss those regulators and how they interact for a number of jurisdictions in the section thereafter.

Discussing the judicial bodies responsible is not particularly interesting, as the arrangement here is very straightforward: ultimately, all dispute resolution is backstopped by the national court system, and in the case of the EU the Court of Justice of the European Union (CJEU), often also referred to under the acronym ECJ and distinct from the ECHR, which is a completely different court. Many specific areas of regulation also create

35

a number of dispute resolution mechanisms below the court system, eg specific ombudsman-type services for customer complaints, and appeal mechanisms to, for example, the European Agencies (EBA, EIOPA, ESMA) in the case of disagreements between regulators and regulated entities, or among regulators. I will discuss some of those mechanisms in the section on executive bodies, as it is often those who host the dispute resolution mechanism, and I will usually mention it in the description of the specific regulation when this is the case.

Finally, in the last section of this chapter I will discuss a number of specifics around the regulation of Fintech companies.

3.1 Sources of Regulation

Regulation is anchored around primary legislation that has been implemented at the appropriate level. By default this is the national level, but there are important exceptions. For example in the United States, insurance regulation is based at the state level, and bank regulation can either be at the state or the federal level, depending on whether the bank has a state charter or a federal charter. In the European Union, on the other hand, a lot of regulation is legislated at the supra-national level, in a slightly complex process involving national-level legislators as well, which I will discuss below.

Regulatory legislation is complex and technical, and the broad-brush principles have to be interpreted to ensure coherent application on the ground. Therefore, primary regulatory legislation generally leaves a lot of the technical details to secondary legislation. Wherever there is a legislator enacting regulation there tends to be one or multiple agencies tasked with implementing this legislation, loosely referred to as 'regulators', and those regulators are usually also in charge of enacting the secondary legislation. The balance between the frontline regulatory task, and the duty to create secondary legislation can vary. For example in the EU, the EU agencies EBA, EIOPA, and ESMA are mostly in charge of proposing secondary EU-level legislation that is then enacted by the European Commission, and do very little on-the-ground supervision, whilst local regulators do more of the latter, and spend comparatively little time on secondary legislation for their own jurisdiction.

The financial system is highly interconnected at all levels, and it is therefore important that regulation is coordinated and harmonised at all levels as well. I have already mentioned two examples where two levels of legislation are involved, namely the US, where it is the states and the federation, and the EU, where there is legislation at the EU and the national level. Those examples are extraordinary, however, in the sense that in both those jurisdictions real legislative power is held at both levels, and that there is a well-established system in place that coordinates those two levels, not only for regulations. In the international arena there is no such coordination system, and therefore it had to be built from scratch, typically involving coordinating committees where a number of the interested parties are represented.

In what follows, I will first discuss coordination and harmonisation at the international level, and then harmonisation and coordination within the United States and within the EU. Finally, I will finish this chapter on sources of regulation with a discussion of harmonisation that spans the legislative and the executive angle, notably passporting and equivalence. Those are both frameworks by which companies that have been authorised in one jurisdiction can operate in another jurisdiction without having to go through a full-scale local authorisation process. This topic is very important for Fintech companies wanting to scale and I will go into more detail on this further below.

3.1.1 International Harmonisation

Harmonisation of rules

The international harmonisation of regulation happens in a number of supranational forums where national regulators and legislators, plus typically the EU as an independent party, convene and discuss to what extent regulations should be harmonised. At a political level, the highest-level group addressing this is the G20 forum of heads of state or finance ministers who—supported by their senior regulators—decide upon a high-level roadmap of where they want international regulation to go. The main focus tends to be the avoidance of crisis. The G20 only meet occasionally, and they are supported by the Financial Stability Board (FSB), which is a permanent institution that drives the G20 agenda between the meetings.

On a more technical level, there are three organisations that deal with the global harmonisation of rules in their respective sector: the Basel Committee for Banking Supervision (BCBS) for banks, the International Association of Insurance Supervisors (IAIS) for insurance companies, and the International Organisation of Securities Commissions (IOSCO) for market places. To the extent that they have to cooperate, eg for the supervision of financial conglomerates, they have their Joint Forum. All those committees are regularly producing policy documents that can be found on their respective websites. Some documents are more impactful than others, but for example the Basel bank regulations that have been produced by the BCBS now form the basis of the bank regulatory framework in all major countries.

Another important international organisation is the Financial Action Task Force (FATF), which coordinates the global fight against money laundering, terrorist finance, and more generally financial crime. It is a forum to create harmonised rules in this area, and the FATF regularly reviews and comments as to whether national practices are in line with those rules.

Harmonisation at firm level and regulatory colleges

Harmonisation of rules at the abstract level is important, but for firms operating cross-border it is arguably even more important to understand what the rules are that apply to them. By default every subsidiary is subject to the rules of the jurisdiction where it is incorporated. This, however, cannot be seen in isolation, and there is also the group-level view to consider. In order to deal with this, regulators establish for every major financial group a so-called 'regulatory college' where all national regulators for whom the group in question is important participate, and that is led by the group's home regulator, ie the lead regulator in the jurisdiction where the group holding company is regulated.

There are a number of conventions and international agreements about how those colleges operate, but essentially they must agree on respective responsibilities, in particular with respect to control, inspection, and information sharing, and on how to deal with sanctions and emergency situations should the need arise. This process can become quite challenging to manage due to the diverging interests of the participants, which is one of the reasons why EU regulation is always very specific on the respective rights and responsibilities of home and host regulators.

3.1.2 Harmonisation Within the EU

The international organisations mentioned above only have advisory powers, and it is up to the respective legislators to implement those rules, or not, as the case may be. The European Union on the other hand has real rule-making power (see Figure 3.1 for an overview of the process of how regulation is created both nationally and in the EU). To the extent that it falls into the EU's area of competence, the EU has can make laws that the Member States—and to a varying degree some associated countries like those in the EEA—and their courts have to follow. Note that for the interest of brevity I will no longer make this distinction. When I refer to Member States this might will in many cases include the associated countries, but should be checked on a case-by-base basis.

FIGURE 3.1 How Regulation is Created

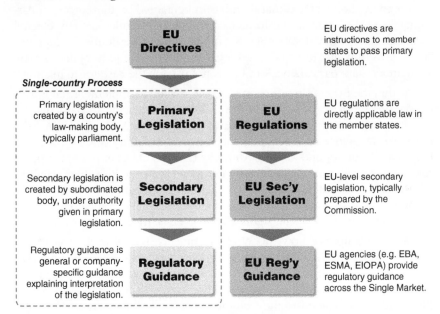

The EU possesses two major legal instruments, *Regulations* and *Directives*:

- **EU Regulations.** EU Regulations are EU-level laws that are automatically considered local law of any Member State as soon as they become active; they can be directly relied upon in all local courts, with the CJEU being the ultimate arbiter in case of dispute.
- **EU Directives.** EU Directives are EU-level laws that must to be transposed into local legislation by the Member States within a given time period, filling in the gaps where needed; the role of the CJEU on those is more limited as permissible difference in implementation must be taken into account.

Whether the EU uses Regulations or Directives to pursue a legislative goal depends on a number of factors, for example to what extent local law is already harmonised, so that that one common regulation across all Member States is possible. Other important considerations are local differences: using Directives allows the EU to leave some gaps in the legislation to be filled at the Member State level. For large legislative projects—eg the implementation of the Basel framework for bank regulation—it is often necessary to use both Directives and Regulations to achieve the legislative goal.

The legislative process in the EU is driven by the European Commission, who prepare the legal text that then has to be agreed by the European Parliament and the Council, the former consisting of deputies directly elected by the citizens of the Member States, and the latter representing the Member States' governments. In some cases legal instruments require ratification by all Member State parliaments, but this is not usually the case for regulations.

Within the EU the Commission is usually tasked to implement secondary legislation, and it is supported in this task by EU agencies, in particular by the three regulatory agencies, the European Banking Authority (EBA), the European Insurance and Occupational Pensions Authority (EIOPA), and the European Securities and Markets Authority (ESMA). Other important support roles in this respect are played by the European Systemic Risk Board (ESRB), whose task is to look at systemic risks across the system, and the European Central Bank (ECB), which also has some responsibilities—including supervisory ones—in the financial stability area, even outside the Eurozone.

As an example of how this works in practice I want to look at PSD 2 and in particular the *Regulatory technical standards on authentication and communication* that define certain security standards in the payment systems. After a consultation process those standards are drawn up by the EBA, and are submitted to the Commission, who will then transform them into secondary legislation. The language for this can be found in Directive 2015/2366/EU (PSD 2) (Art 98):

> *(1) EBA shall, in close cooperation with the ECB and after consulting all relevant stakeholders, including those in the payment services market, reflecting all interests involved, develop draft regulatory technical standards addressed to payment service providers [...]*

> *(4) EBA shall submit the draft regulatory technical standards referred to in paragraph 1 to the Commission by 13 January 2017. Power is delegated to the Commission to adopt those regulatory technical standards in accordance with Articles 10 to 14 of Regulation (EU) No 1093/2010.*

In some cases the agencies can decide themselves about implementation guidelines, without the need of approval by the Commission. An example for this, again from PSD 2, is how regulators should design a complaints procedure (Art 100):

> *(6) EBA shall, after consulting the ECB, issue guidelines, addressed to the competent authorities, in accordance with Article 16 of Regulation (EU) No 1093/2010 on the complaints procedures to be taken into consideration to ensure compliance with paragraph 1 of this Article. Those guidelines shall be issued by 13 January 2018 and shall be updated on a regular basis, as appropriate.*

3.1.3 Harmonisation Within the US

The United States is a federation, and this can be felt very strongly in the regulation of financial services, which in most areas is still ultimately done at the state level. There is also a strong separation at the product/segment level, ie between banks, insurance companies, and markets, where for the latter there is also a distinction between securities markets and commodity markets.

The general rule is that there are different state-level laws for all those segments, and there is a drive to harmonisation from the federal level. In some areas there is a federal charter allowing companies to operate across all states, but in most the main drive is to ensure that local regulations do not drift too far apart. Often this happens on a voluntary basis, like in the case of the Uniform Commercial Code (UCC), which despite being voluntary is widely implemented. Each of the segments also have their own body where state-level regulators come together and agree on model laws and regulations for their respective sectors.

There are also federal agencies that contribute to the harmonisation of regulations across state lines. Most are confined to a particular segment and discussed below, but there is also the Consumer Financial Protection Bureau (CFPB), which cuts across and is in charge of consumer and small-business protection.

Insurance

Insurance regulation is still grounded at the state level, and—ignoring subtleties around admitted and non-admitted insurers—companies that want to operate across multiple states must essentially be chartered in every state in which they operate. There is some coordination at the federal level through the National Association of Insurance Commissioners (NAIC), which, as the name implies, is a forum for all local regulators to get together and discuss regulation, among other things. The NAIC develops what it refers to as *Model Laws, Regulations, and Guidelines*, which are templates for laws, regulations, and guidelines to be implemented at the state level. In this sense they are similar to EU regulations—with the important exception that the adoption of model laws is entirely voluntary: states might choose to adopt them as they are, or with any modifications they wish to make, or not at all.

There has been an ongoing discussion about an optional federal charter for insurance companies for a while now, but it has not happened, and it does not look like it will happen anytime soon. A couple of the recent major financial reform acts, however, have had an impact on the insurance industry. In particular, the Gramm–Leach–Bliley Act established some mandatory minimum standards that local insurance laws have to fulfil, and the Dodd–Frank Act established the Federal Insurance Office (FIO). The

FIO does not have regulatory power as of yet, except in cases where it involves international agreements. Its main task is currently studying the US regulatory system, with a view to proposing how it could be reformed and harmonised.

Banks

The bad news is that, if anything, banking regulation is more complex than insurance regulation as there are different types of banks that offer the same—or essentially the same—products and services, but that roll up into slightly different regulatory frameworks. The good news is that there is a national charter for banks, and ultimately institutions that want to operate across state lines can cut through a lot of complexity by operating under a national charter.

All nationally chartered banks must be members of the Federal Reserve System, and are therefore placed under its regulation, as well as under the regulation of the OCC, which is enforcing a certain degree of harmonisation in regulation. For state-chartered banks, the Conference of State Bank Supervisors (CSBS) plays a similar role to that of the NAIC in the insurance space, as a forum for harmonising regulation, and to develop model solutions that states can adopt or adapt.

The Federal Deposit Insurance Corporation (FDIC) is in charge of insuring deposits in both nationally and state-chartered banks and thrifts. In this function it has also an oversight role and is able to impose certain regulations—especially prudential regulation—on the insured institutions.

In parallel to the banking system there is the credit union system, where companies can either operate under a national charter—overseen by the National Credit Union Administration (NCUA)—or under a state charter. For the latter, the NCUA has a certain coordination role between local regulators. The NCUA also has an equivalent role to the FDIC in the credit union space.

Markets

Markets is a wide field with many different operators. The first important consideration is what is actually traded on the market. Key markets are those for securities, where the oversight at the federal level lies with the Securities and Exchange Commission (SEC). For commodity futures and other derivatives, the federal oversight lies with the Commodity Futures Trading Commission (CFTC). Both of those regulators are able to drive a certain harmonisation at the federal level. However, it is important to understand that even for the large market operators state-level regulation is still important, and for example the New York regulator is an important player in markets regulation simply because of the important market players operating within that state.

Market regulation is not only about regulating the market places themselves, but also about regulating those who provide market access and advice, in particular for retail customers, as well as fund managers. Again there is usually the possibility of going for a state charter or for a federal charter, depending on the type of the organisation. Federal charters are typically overseen by the SEC.

The equivalent role of NAIC and CSBS in the markets is played by the Financial Industry Regulatory Authority (FINRA), which despite its officially sounding name is a private corporation and was created by the merger of the National Association of Securities Dealers (NASD of NASDAQ fame) and its equivalent organisation on the NYSE, which again plays a role in harmonising regulations across the US.

3.1.4 Passporting and Equivalence

One of the key reasons behind the harmonisation of regulations is to enable companies to engage in cross-border business without having to go through a full regulatory approval process in every jurisdiction in which they operate. In current regulatory practice there are two different levels of authorisation:

- **Equivalence.** Regulatory equivalence means that rules are similar enough that the regulators are confident that the firms covered by them can operate in each other's markets—or portions of each other's market, eg only covering sophisticated investors—with a reduced level of local oversight.
- **Passporting.** Regulatory passporting means that the rules in the two jurisdictions are so close that only very limited local oversight is needed, and that therefore the regulator of the company's home jurisdiction is responsible for looking after the company's entire business, including in passported jurisdictions.

The EU is a good example for demonstrating the similarities and differences of the two concepts as it implements both: most financial services that are provided by companies resident and authorised in any EU Member State are passported across the entire Single Market. The EU also operates an equivalence regime under which companies resident in third countries can operate in the Single Market, but in a much more restricted manner, for example:

- Equivalence is available for a much smaller set of services than passporting—equivalence must first be established on a jurisdiction level, and can often be withdrawn at short notice; passporting is enshrined in EU law and cannot be withdrawn.
- Under passporting, most decisions are up to the home regulator, ie there is (mostly) a single regulator that a company has to deal with; under equivalence the role of the host regulator is more important.

A very important point to make here is that *established in the EU* does not mean that the group headquarters must be in the EU: it simply means that the group must establish a subsidiary within the EU into which all the passported business must roll up. This subsidiary will then be regulated on a stand-alone basis by the EU regulators, which usually means that compliance becomes more cumbersome, and there might be a need for higher overall capital and liquidity requirements.

Equivalence

When regulators declare their rules within a certain area to be equivalent, this indicates that either set of rules is as good as the other. In this case the regulators might grant each other's regulated companies access to their own markets, subject to a number of operational guidelines with regard to the respective rights and responsibilities of *home regulators* and *host regulators*, and how they'll interact—in particular, how they'll share data. Typically, market access via equivalence is within a very narrow range of product, services, and customers, with the latter almost always being professional or sophisticated counterparties that are believed to be able to look after themselves if need be.

I want to go through an example of how equivalence works in one specific area in the EU; whilst this is not a universal process and it depends on both area and jurisdiction, it gives a sufficiently good idea of the regulatory blueprint used to establish equivalence. The specific example we look at is the EMIR regulation (Regulation EU 648/2012) dealing with central counterparties:

In the first instance, the Commission must declare that the third-country regime in which a company that seeks equivalence is established is indeed equivalent (Art 13):

> *(2) The Commission may adopt implementing acts declaring that the legal, supervisory and enforcement arrangements of a third country [are equivalent and effectively applied and enforced].*

This is generally outside the remit of the company—the equivalence decision is as much a political one as an economic one, and the timeframe under which equivalence can be established is unpredictable.

Equivalence can be withdrawn at short notice. In fact, if the Commission finds that the regime is no longer equivalent it must withdraw equivalence within 30 days, and there is no transition period or grandfathering (Art 13):

> *(4) Where the [Commission determines] an insufficient or inconsistent application of the equivalent requirements by third-country authorities, the*

Commission shall, within 30 calendar days of the presentation of the report, withdraw the recognition as equivalent of the third-country legal framework in question.

Once equivalence has been established, ESMA—which in this case is the relevant regulator within the EU, in other cases it might be EBA or EIOPA— must establish cooperation agreements with the relevant regulator (Art 25):

(7) ESMA shall establish cooperation arrangements with the relevant [regulator]. Such arrangements shall specify at least:

(a) the mechanism for the exchange of information between ESMA and the [third-country regulator], including access to all information requested by ESMA regarding CCPs authorised in third countries;

(b) the mechanism for prompt notification to ESMA where a third-country [regulator] deems a CCP it is supervising to be in breach of the conditions of its authorisation or of other law to which it is subject;

(c) the mechanism for prompt notification to ESMA by a third-country [regulator] where a CCP it is supervising has been granted the right to provide clearing services to clearing members or clients established in the Union;

(d) the procedures concerning the coordination of supervisory activities including, where appropriate, on-site inspections.

Establishing equivalence at the regulatory regime level does not automatically give the right to provide services—it is a necessary precondition, but not a sufficient one. In the case of this particular equivalence framework, companies have to go through a recognition process with ESMA (Art 25):

(1) A CCP established in a third country may provide clearing services to clearing members or trading venues established in the Union only where that CCP is recognised by ESMA.

In this process, companies send their applications to ESMA, which in its sole discretion decides whether or not the application is granted. ESMA has 210 working days—ie about a year—to make this decision, or longer if the initial application is deemed incomplete (Art 25.4):

The CCP [...] shall submit its application to ESMA. [...] Within 30 working days of receipt, ESMA shall assess whether the application is complete. [...] Within 180 working days of the submission of a complete application, ESMA shall inform the applicant CCP in writing, with a fully reasoned explanation, whether the recognition has been granted or refused.

At this point—and only at this point—the company can take up its business with counterparties established in the EU, provided the application has been successful.

Passporting

Companies that are established within the European Union's Single Market do not have to rely on equivalence to provide their services on a cross-border basis. As the rules are already the same—within the parameters established by the relevant directives and regulations, ie taking into account permissible variations across jurisdictions—the different regimes are known to be equivalent. In fact, they are super-equivalent in the sense that the variation in rules is much smaller than would be the case under the typical equivalence regime. In this case, companies can provide services under a regime that is known as 'regulatory passporting'.

Companies that are authorised in an equivalent regime have the right to apply for authorisation under equivalence provision, meaning *being authorised in their home country is a necessary condition for authorisation under equivalence.* On the other hand, companies that are authorised in their home country have under a passporting regime the right to operate under this passport, meaning *being authorised in their home country is a sufficient condition for authorisation under passporting.* There are a number of administrative hurdles to overcome, but overall, gaining access to a market via passporting is much preferable to gaining access via equivalence.

Companies must be established in the business they want to passport in their home Member State—they can't just go *forum shopping* and establish themselves in a particular jurisdiction for regulatory reasons without doing substantive business there.

To go through the mechanics of passporting I use the example of the PSD2 (Directive EU 2015/2366), which is one of the key regulations for start-ups active in the payments area who want to provide their services cross-border within the EU.

Importantly, contrary to the equivalence example we have seen above, the company that wants to passport their authorisation into another Member State applies to their home regulators, ie the regulator who regulates them in their home country. In practice this greatly simplifies things—companies can use their own language, communicating with a regulator whom they know and who knows them, and who has previously authorised them, so who is a priori thinking positively about them (Art 28):

(1) Any authorised payment institution wishing to provide payment services for the first time in a Member State other than its home Member State, in the exercise of the right of establishment or the freedom to provide services, shall communicate the following information to [its home regulator...].

The home regulator is required to forward the information to the relevant host regulator within one month; the host regulator has one month to assess the information and—if need be—voice concerns to the home regulator (Art 28):

(2) Within 1 month of receipt of all of the information [... the home regulator] shall send it to the [relevant host regulator]. Within 1 month of receipt of the information [...], the [host regulator] shall assess that information and provide the [home regulator] with relevant information [...] in particular of any reasonable grounds for concern in connection with the intended engagement.

Whilst the home regulator has to take the concerns of the host regulator into account, it is ultimately up to the home regulator to take the decision on the application (Art 28):

(2) Where the [home regulator does] not agree with the assessment of the [host regulator], they shall provide the latter with the reasons for their decision. If the assessment of the [home regulator] in particular in light of the information received from the [host regulator], is not favourable, the [home regulator] shall refuse to register the agent or branch [...].

The overall deadline for going through the process from the point where the information has initially been provided is three months, and the company should be ready to go. Note that it must give notification of when it will actually start its operations to its home regulator (Art 28)

(3) Within 3 months of receipt of the information [the home regulator] shall communicate their decision to the [host regulator] and to the payment institution. Upon entry in the register [...] the agent or branch may commence its activities in the relevant host Member State. The payment institution shall notify to the [home regulator] the date from which it commences its activities. The [home regulator] shall inform the [host regulator] accordingly.

Home and host regulator are meant to cooperate in the supervision. However, the home regulator is in the lead. Non-compliance is to be dealt with by the home regulator (Art 30):

(1) [Where] the [host regulator] ascertains that a payment institution [...] does not comply [...] it shall inform the [home regulator] without delay. The [home regulator ...] shall, without undue delay, take all appropriate measures to ensure that the payment institution concerned puts an end to its irregular situation. The [home regulator] shall communicate those measures without delay to the [host regulator] and to [any other regulator concerned].

Whilst most interaction is via the home regulator, the host regulator of the jurisdictions where a company is established, there are some responsibilities that companies have vis-à-vis the host regulators in the countries where they are operating. For example, host regulators can ask for regular reporting according to their own templates, eg for statistical purposes, and they can expect to have a central point of contact in their territory (Art 29):

> *(2) The [host regulator] may require that payment institutions [...] shall report to them periodically on the activities carried out in their territories. Such reports shall be required for information or statistical purposes.*
>
> *(4) Member States may require payment institutions operating on their territory [...] to appoint a central contact point in their territory to ensure adequate communication and information reporting [...].*

To the extent that home and host regulators don't agree, the relevant European agency, here EBA, is in the first instance the judge and mediator (Art 27):

> *(1) Where a competent authority of a Member State considers that, in a particular matter, cross-border cooperation [...] does not comply with the relevant conditions set out in those provisions, it may refer the matter to EBA [...].*

So overall, passporting is a much more streamlined process than equivalence, and whilst it has still a number of practical hiccups—partially caused by host regulators who are not always content to leave key decisions on their territory to other regulators—it in many cases works sufficiently well to be able to grow a cross-border business.

3.2 Regulatory Models

There are probably as many regulatory models as there are jurisdictions, and I will discuss a number of them in turn. Those models mostly follow a number of common themes:

First, the more complex a market, the more complex its regulatory system. So it is no surprise that the US, which has the most advanced and complex financial markets system in the world, also has a very complex regulatory system consisting of a significant number of institutions—public, private, and in-between—with varying responsibilities. Countries with less complex financial markets tend to have a simpler regulatory system, which also manifests itself in the number of regulators it has.

Second, a country's central bank is almost always involved in regulation, especially in bank regulation. The reason for this is that central banks control a country's money, often run or at least support their country's payment systems, and they are lenders of last resort to the local banks, so they have a strong interest that those banks are well run.

Third, regulation is usually split along the three major sectors: banking and payments, insurance and asset management, and markets and market infrastructure. This split might manifest itself as departments within a unified regulator, or there might be independent—but usually cooperating—regulators for the different sectors.

An interesting distinction is whether regulators are *government bodies* or whether they are *self-regulatory organisations* (SROs), or whether they are something in-between. The US Federal Reserve System, for example, is a body that is neither entirely private nor entirely public. In practice this distinction is, however, not as important as it might seem, as all regulatory institutions ultimately operate under the supervision of the government, and in accordance with internationally agreed rules and principles where applicable. Having said this, SROs will generally be part regulator, part industry association, and depending on the specific association the balance might swing one way or the other.

3.2.1 The US Regulatory Model

The first thing to mention with respect to the US financial markets is that they are not fully integrated. Integration in the insurance segment is particularly bad, with insurance businesses being regulated at the state level. The banking segment has numerous financial institutions that are chartered and operate at a federal level, but there are numerous others—especially by number, less so by aggregate business volume—that restrict their business to a single state, and that are chartered and regulated at the state level. For those players the local state regulators are usually the most important and often the only ones, with a notable exception being the FDIC, which has a regulatory role for all banks whose deposits it insures. Even for federally chartered institutions, the state regulator has some say for the business conducted in their state, making New York's regulator, the NYDFS, one of the most powerful regulators in the country.

Let's start our journey through the US regulatory landscape with the Federal Reserve System, or Fed for short. The Fed is the central bank(ing system) of the United States, and therefore in charge of the dollar and the US monetary policy. It also runs a number of payment systems. The banks in the system are private or semi-private institutions, and every federally chartered commercial bank must be a stockholder of one of the banks in the system. Every Fed is responsible for regulating the commercial banks who hold its stock.

The other big banking regulator is the historically named Office of the Comptroller of the Currency (OCC). Its role is to charter, regulate, and supervise all national banks and thrift organisations, as well as the federal branches and agencies of foreign banks. The OCC covers both prudential and conduct regulation of the banks it supervises, meaning that it is in charge of the safety and soundness of the system and it must ensure that banks treat customers fairly. The OCC's responsibilities also include the anti money laundering, terrorist finance, and related regulations and the inclusiveness agenda, aiming to ensure that the financial system is open for all.

Within the banking sector there are two other important institutions, the first being the Federal Deposit Insurance Corporation (FDIC), which administers the deposit insurance for federally chartered banks in the US, ie it indemnifies depositors of failed member banks from the dues it collects from its members. In order to reduce the risk of a pay-out the FDIC also has prudential regulatory powers, and it also had a conduct regulation role for its member banks. It does not, however, cover credit unions, which—if on a national charter—are chartered and regulated by National Credit Union Administration (NCUA), which also runs the deposit protection scheme for their members.

An indicator of the complexity of the US financial system is who represents them at the Basel Committee for Banking Supervision (BCBS): the Board of Governors of Fed and the OCC as the two main regulators for nationally chartered banks, the New York Fed as the local regulator of the main banking location, and the FDIC as regulator of many of the smaller banks.

The Financial Crimes Enforcement Network (FinCEN) is the US Financial Intelligence Unit (FIU), ie the agency that is responsible for the complex around money laundering, terrorist financing, and financial crime in general. It is part of the Treasury Department, and its role is both to collect and to analyse data, and to follow up on leads and pursue them together with the law enforcement agencies and other relevant actors.

In the securities and markets sector, the most important player on a federal level is the Securities and Exchange Commission (SEC). It is an independent agency of the US government whose primary task is to enforce the federal security laws. It is heavily involved in the rule-making process itself, assisting the government in producing primary legislation and being responsible for some secondary legislation in this space, and it is representing the US at IOSCO. The SEC oversees securities exchanges, securities brokers and dealers, investment advisors, and mutual funds, with a focus on disclosure, fair dealing, and securities fraud. It also runs EDGAR, which is the electronic public repository for company filings like the Form 10-K, the annual report listed companies have to file.

The Financial Industry Regulatory Authority (FINRA) is a private organisation, chartered by Congress to oversee the broker-dealer industry, covering the 4,000-odd broker-dealer firms that mostly operate in the retail markets. Its role is to develop standards and best practices in the conduct space, ie covering areas like investor protections, disclosure and suitability, and also broker qualifications and advertising standards. FINRA also oversees broker-dealers' compliance with those rules, and more generally works on market transparency and investor education. SEC's and the FINRA's work are complementary, in that they focus on the same market segment, where the SEC looks at the issuer end, and FINRA's responsibility lies mostly with retail distribution.

The Municipal Securities Rulemaking Board (MSRB) is a self-regulatory organisation with a federal charter that is tasked to oversee the US municipal bonds market. This market is a very important market in the US, both for municipalities to raise money, and for investors seeking an alternative to bank savings accounts. The MSRB oversees the entire vertical, making rules for and overseeing all entities operating in this sector, with the goal of protecting both issuers and investors, as municipalities—contrary to other issuers—are often not sophisticated market participants. The MSRB works closely with the SEC to the extent that their areas of responsibility overlap.

The CFTC is an independent agency of the federal government, overseeing the commodity futures and derivatives markets. After the 2008 financial crisis, the previously unregulated swaps markets have been added to its portfolio, and also forex operations covering the retail market. This was a step change in terms of responsibilities, with the new markets added being more than 10 times bigger than those it had previously overseen. The CFTC is not only overseeing the dealers and exchanges in this space, but importantly also the clearing houses (CCPs) and data repositories that have become mandatory after the crisis. The National Futures Association (NFA) is a self-regulatory organisation for the markets the CFTC oversees whose membership is mandatory for a large majority of the companies operating in those markets. It is tasked with screening and registering companies operating in this market, overseeing compliance with applicable rules and regulations and taking enforcement actions if need be. It is also running an extra-judicial dispute resolution procedure between member companies and their customers.

In the insurance sector the National Association of Insurance Commissioners (NAIC) does not have any meaningful supervision role; as previously discussed, it is mostly involved in rule making.

The Consumer Financial Protection Bureau (CFPB) is a federal agency—located within the Federal Reserve, and affiliated with the Treasury—that regulates consumer financial products and services across all sectors of the

US financial markets. It was established in 2011, consolidating responsibilities that were prior to that spread over a number of different agencies. Its core mandate is *to provide a single point of accountability for enforcing federal consumer financial laws and protecting consumers in the financial market place*, and for this it has taken on a number of supervisory and law enforcement responsibilities, it is operating an ombudsman service, it is analysing the market place, and it provides financial education.

It should be noted that the US market is much more markets-driven, meaning that there are fewer institutions that hold financial assets, and more that originate them and distribute them to the market. This is particularly important in the banking market, where securitisation is a very significant source of credit. To the extent that originators are non-banks they will not be overseen by the banking regulators but rather by the markets regulators, notably the SEC. The US Treasury which directly or indirectly oversees a number of those regulators plays an important role here to avoid overly large differences in regulation. Also, the CFPB tends to be involved regardless of the legal form of the relationship.

3.2.2 The EU Regulatory Model

EU-wide regulatory institutions

As already discussed in the discussion on secondary legislation in the EU, there are the three European agencies, ie EBA for banks and payment institutions, EIOPA for insurance companies and other asset gatherers, and the ESMA for markets and market infrastructure who play an important rule in refining the regulations that come out of EU, providing secondary legislation and technical guidance. Those agencies also have some supervisory role, in particular in areas of where there is a third-country equivalence regime in place that is covering the entire Single Market, and where the respective agency is often the designated lead regulator as far as the EU business is concerned. Those agencies also run an extra-judicial appeal process, especially in respect of cross-border and passporting issues.

In addition to those three agencies there is also the European Systemic Risk Board (ESRB), which has an analytical and advisory role, and the European Central Bank (ECB), which both works on the analytic side and has some supervisory powers. Those five agencies share the responsibility for Europe-wide macro-prudential supervision, meaning that they are in charge of identifying and addressing systemic risks that build up across the system. For most regulated companies, the most relevant visible impact those agencies have on their day-to-day business are probably the stress tests that they design on a regular basis, and where the respective regulated companies must assess the impact of a number of regulator-defined stress scenarios on their portfolio and on their operations. Otherwise they'll mostly be interacting with their home regulator and—to a much more limited extent— with their host regulators if they operate in more than one country within the Single Market.

Local regulatory systems

Locally the countries in the EU run a number of different models. For example, in some jurisdictions the central bank is also responsible for the regulation of the entire financial sector, an example for this being the Czech Republic, where the Czech National Bank (CNB) also is in charge of financial services regulation. In other jurisdictions there is a single regulator, but this regulator is distinct from the central bank. However, even in those countries the central bank usually still has a small role in regulation, in particular macro-prudential regulation. Examples for this are Germany, where the Bundesanstalt für Finanzdienstleistungsaufsicht (BaFin) is the main regulator; Austria, where it is the Finanzmarktaufsichtsbehörde (FMA); Sweden, where it is Finansinspektionen (FI); and the Netherlands, where it is the Autoriteit Financiële Markten (AFM).

In yet other jurisdictions the regulators are split according to the major financial services sectors. In those cases the central bank often is responsible for bank regulation. Examples for this are Italy, where the Istituto per la Vigilanza sulle Assicurazioni (ISVAP) is in charge of insurance regulation, the Commissione Nazionale per le Società e la Borsa (CONSOB) is in charge of markets, and the Banca d'Italia (BdI) is in charge of banks. Another example is Spain, where the respective regulators are the Direccion General de Seguros (DGS) for insurance companies, the Comisión Nacional del Mercado de Valores (CNMV) for markets, and the Spanish central bank Banco de España (BdE) for banks.

Finally there can be a functional split between the different agencies. For example in the UK, the Financial Conduct Authority (FCA) is in charge of conduct supervision and micro-prudential supervision across all sectors. This includes the payment system whose supervision has been broken off in the Payment Systems Regulator (PSR), which is a semi-independent part of the FCA. Macro-prudential supervision in the UK is mostly the remit of the Prudential Regulation Authority (PRA), which has joint supervisory authority with the FCA for firms that are considered of systemic importance. Also operating in this area is the Financial Policy Committee (FPC), which provides high-level financial policy guidance, and the Special Resolution Unit (SRU), that is in charge of winding up failing banks without threatening the integrity of the system. All three—PRA, FPC, and SRU—are part of the UK central bank, the Bank of England (BoE).

3.3 Fintech Regulation

All financial services regulations are applicable to Fintech companies, with two important caveats. First, there is a principle of *proportionality*: as discussed previously, regulation is not an end in itself, but a means to achieve a certain end, typically to address a market failure. The smaller a company is, the less damage it can do, and the less it is subject to regulatory oversight. There is one important distinction to make: proportionality mostly applies in the area of macro-prudential regulation and market structure, because in those areas size matters. However, any company can do damage to its customers, so even small companies must comply with conduct rules, micro-prudential rules ensuring appropriate levels of safety for customer assets, and public interest regulations, eg in the money laundering and terrorist finance space.

The second caveat is that regulation does not always catch up immediately with what is happening in the market. Especially when business models are new, and/or do not map properly onto the classic regulated businesses, it is often not clear which exact regulation applies, how it is to be interpreted, and who the regulator in question is. That is a chance, but it is also a risk that suddenly a regulator steps out of the woodwork and imposes restrictions or even fines. Ultimately a start-up company with limited resources must weigh the risk of getting bogged down in regulatory discussion with a number of regulators, most of which might not have clear idea what to do in this respect either, with the risk of being told off at a later stage.

Start-ups, however, should have a good view on the regulations in place in the product areas in which they are operating. In particular, if start-ups are competing head-on with regulated businesses, they should know the regulations that those businesses have to comply with, and they should spend some senior management time and effort to adapt their own strategy accordingly.

Key senior management considerations

A number of questions that senior management should ask themselves are the following (see also Figure 3.2):

1. Are there regulations that apply to our business?
2. Are there regulations that make sense if they applied to our business, and is the only reason they don't apply because our business model is not yet on the regulatory radar?
3. Are there regulations—or regulatory principles—that apply in the product space that we are covering?
4. Are there regulations that apply to traditional competitors but not to us, and do they really not make sense either in their case or in ours?

5. What are the implications of the answers to the above points with respect to product design? Are there product features that would make it better suited to the regulatory environment?
6. What are the technology implications of the above points? In particular, would it be better to take certain design decisions now, or leave them to later? What data should we collect?

If there are regulations where the answer to question (1) is 'yes' or 'probably yes' then it is highly advisable to talk to the relevant regulator. Any regulations where the answer to question (2) or (3) is 'yes' should be high on the priority list, as they'll almost certainly become a requirement in the future. Those under (4) are more ambiguous: there is a risk that they'll be extended for level-playing-field reasons, or maybe they might be entirely scrapped, so they should be on the radar but need not necessarily be acted upon. The points (5) and (6) are key strategic question in terms of product and system development that companies should consider. A company should in this respect also keep the regulatory strategy framework that we've developed in Chapter 1 in mind: when expanding into new markets, regulators might have different views, and the better the compliance situation is, the easier a roll-out will be.

FIGURE 3.2 Regulatory Assessment Worksheet

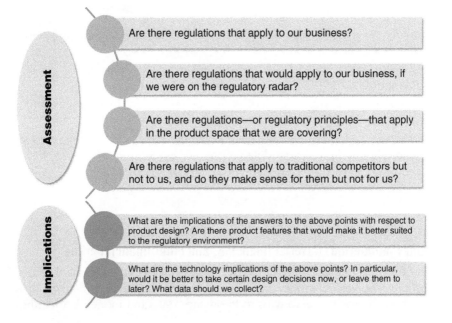

One instrument often used with early-stage start-ups is a *non-action-letter*: after some initial discussions, the start-up formally approaches the regulator with a description of its business activities, processes, and volumes, especially in the areas that relate to regulated parts of the financial system. If the regulator has been persuaded that those are adequate it might issue a non-action-letter, ie expressing its opinion that the start-up's business activities processes are adequate given the environment described. This letter is limited in time, and conditional on the environment not substantially changing from that which had previously been described, in particular also in terms of business volume.

A no-action-letter does not provide 100% legal certainty that everything is correct, especially if things go wrong. Also, it only covers the regulator who has prepared the letter, so it should not be taken as an indication that all applicable regulations have been complied with, or that all relevant regulators are on board. Having said this, in most cases having a non-action-letter is better than not having one, and it is worthwhile spending some senior management time on it.

3.3.1 Regulation Applicable to Most Fintech Businesses

Most of the regulations applicable to a Fintech business depend on the sector in which it is operating, and/or which products it is offering. However, there are a number of regulations that apply to most Fintech businesses, notably:

1. taking reasonable steps to avoid money laundering, terrorist financing, and other financial crime
2. keeping customer data safe, and ensuring that customers' privacy is respected
3. ensuring an adequate level of customer protection, including ensuring that a product is suitable where this is required
4. ensuring that there are adequate continuity and wind-down plans in place should the business default
5. ensuring that the company does not endanger critical financial infrastructure.

I'll go through these one by one.

Money laundering, terrorist financing, and other financial crime

Most financial services businesses have to take into account the risk that they become involved in money laundering, terrorist financing, or other illicit financial activity. The acronyms to know are AML (anti money laundering) in the criminal space, ABC (Anti Bribery Corruption) and politically exposed persons (PEP) in the political space, and combat terrorist finance (CTF) in the terrorism space.

Money laundering and ABC is mostly being looked for at the boundaries of the financial system. For example, if a business accepts cash or other bearer assets—arguably including digital assets like bitcoin—it must make a reasonable effort to assert where those assets are coming from, and possibly report the transaction to the central bank, or whoever the designated authority is. There is a proportionality aspect to this investigation: small amounts and occasional transactions are less relevant than large amounts and frequent transactions. Details differ by jurisdiction, but the materiality threshold usually is lies in the region of $1,000–5,000 or equivalent.

Terrorist finance—and more generally financial crime as well as politically motivated embargoes—is about money being used to support illicit goals. Unlike money laundering, this is an issue that needs to be considered throughout the system, not only at the boundaries. One key element here is the PEP process—or equivalent watch lists in the terrorism and crime area—that contain individuals or companies that are suspected of illicit activities or subject to an embargo for other reasons and whose participation in financial services is restricted.

The central process in all those areas is what is usually referred to as Know Your Customer (KYC): a financial services company is under an obligation to know the real identity of its customers—and the beneficial owners behind them if relevant—and to make a reasonable effort to ensure that it is not being misled. This means that before it can provide services it needs to verify official ID documents—which can be difficult if the sign-up is over the Internet—and often it often needs an address history and to make adequate enquiries on those using available public databases. Also, it needs to get an idea of the size of funds involved and, if sufficiently large, will seek assurances that they come from and are being used for legitimate purposes.

Data protection and privacy

Data protection and privacy rules are among the most important rules that all Fintech companies have to comply with, and they are also some of the most difficult ones because they are currently in flux as regulators try to catch up with what happens in the industry. Also, they are very different among the different jurisdictions, partially because of the regulatory lag referred to above, and partially because views differ on how regulation in this particular area should look like. Therefore any Fintech company should seek advice as to which rules apply in the jurisdictions they cover and how those rules are expected to change, and make sure that their product and systems strategy is compatible with that.

One of the strictest data protection regimes in place is that of the EU, so I'll describe that as a current maximum requirement that other jurisdictions might or might not follow. Note that 'data' in this context refers to *personal data* of *identifiable natural persons*, so company data is not protected under this legislation. The scope is nevertheless very wide: for example, a picture of the face—or even a tattoo—can be considered *identifiable* if there is a good chance that it allows someone to identify this person with a database search, even if this search has not yet been made.

The key requirements that everyone involved in data processing has to follow—and that are ultimately the responsibility of the owner of the data, ie the data controller, even if they employ data processors—are the following:

- Data must be collected and processed lawfully, fairly and in a transparent manner in relation to the data subject (*data lawfulness, fairness and transparency*).
- Data must be collected and processed for specified, explicit and legitimate purposes, and not further processed in a manner that is incompatible with those purposes (*purpose limitation*).
- Data must be adequate, relevant and limited to what is necessary in relation to the purposes for which it is processed (*data minimisation*).
- Data must be accurate and, where necessary, kept up to date (*data accuracy*).
- Data must be kept in a form which permits identification of data subjects for no longer than is necessary for the purposes for which the personal data are processed (*storage limitation*).
- Data must be processed in a manner that ensures appropriate security of the personal data, including protection against unauthorised or unlawful processing, and against accidental loss, destruction or damage (*data integrity and confidentiality*).

Those rules are very general, so here it is worth looking at specific technical requirements that are and will be enacted as secondary legislation. For example, the point on data integrity and confidentiality can be interpreted widely, and companies should check whether, for example, operating in a cloud server, virtual server, or container environment is appropriate for the data processing in question, or whether, say, a bare metal environment is required, and/or there are certain data centre certification requirements.

It is important to understand that, contrary to what many people in the tech scene often seem to believe, under this regulation people *own* their personal data, and the company only holds it for them, looks after it, and processes it to the extent allowed by the owners. People have the right to obtain their data in machine-readable format, allowing them to hand it over to another company if they choose to do so. They also have the *right to be forgotten*, and unless the EU has declared a jurisdiction adequate with respect to data processing rules, data transfer is subject to restrictions.

Breaches can attract substantial fines—up to €20m, or 4% of global turnover, whichever is higher—and the more cavalier a company behaves with respect to following the rules, the higher the expected fine in case of a breach. Fines of this order of magnitude can put a start-up out of business, so it is worth paying close attention to those rules.

Customer protection and suitability

Depending on the product or service offered and the nature of the customer, a provider of financial services might have the duty to ensure that the product is suitable for either the individual customer, or at least the group of customers the product is marketed to. Not taking this into account exposes the company to a risk, in particular if things go bad, as the PPI misselling case in the UK showed. This duty is mostly relevant in areas where customers have to take decisions now that can have a significant impact in the future, for example in areas related to investments and insurance.

It also depends on the customers. A widely used model relies on the following customer classification:

1. retail and other inexperienced customers
2. professional and expert customers
3. market counterparties.

The general principle is that the first group needs special protection, and the company has a duty to ensure that products offered are suitable, with exceptions only in cases where it is very clear from the context that this is not the case (eg, some execution-only brokerage services). This duty spans across the whole production chain, meaning that when designing a product, due consideration must be given to suitability concerns, and the marketing and sales strategy must take this into account. This process should be well documented, and it must include parties further down the line that are involved in the distribution process.

For the second group there are generally some fair dealing requirements, and for the third group it is mostly *caveat emptor*, ie only the regular safeguards against fraud and non-good-faith dealing apply.

Firms should keep in mind that the risk profile is asymmetric: if customers have been sold unsuitable investments and those investments go up in value, they won't complain. In the opposite case, however, they might seek restitution on the basis that the investment was unsuitable. In many cases, there is a fine line separating an acceptable suitability assessment from an unacceptable one. For example, it is often acceptable to rely on a customer's self-reported net worth to assess affordability. On the other hand, there can be no encouragement to lie, and red flags must not be ignored.

There is also a micro-prudential aspect to customer protection: their funds must be safe from risks other than those inherent in the product offered. If funds are commingled with the firm's own assets, this usually means the firm must be regulated as a bank, and be part of the deposit guarantee scheme. If the firm is not a bank, it must hold the funds in separate accounts from its own with a bank, and it might need to be part of an investor compensation scheme, depending on the services offered.

Customer protection in this respect, however, is wider, and it is not restricted only to customer funds. For example, a payment services provider on which the customer relies for important payments must ensure that their service level is adequate so as to ensure that those payments are sufficiently reliable, or must at least ensure that the customers retain their normal banking relationship to fall back on when things go wrong.

Continuity and wind-down plans

All financial services have to work with their regulators to have a specific plan in place that ensures that even in the case of default, critical services are not interrupted. Under those plans, both continuity (*How can we continue running key portions of this business?*) and wind-down (*How can we wind down this business with minimal damage?*) should be considered. This planning has a systemic angle, ie default should not endanger the system, and it has a customer angle, ie default should not interrupt services that customers critically rely upon, like being able to pay their rent on time.

For start-ups, the systemic angle is probably secondary due to their limited size. However, contrary to established financial services firms, start-ups have a significant risk of default, so regulators do commonly require an adequate plan in place that ensures that customers do not face interruptions in critical services should the company default. To provide an example, a payment firm that relies on pre-paid funds might have to ensure that their customers maintain a regular banking relationship, and keep this data up to date to ensure that in the case of default funds can be returned without delay.

Systemic protection and critical infrastructure

Because of the limited size of start-up Fintech companies, systemic risk is not usually the most important of regulatory concerns. Having said this, there is also a growth angle: regulation always takes a while to implement, and even longer to be confident that is has been implemented correctly, so fast-growing companies might be treated as if they were systemically important before they are. Also, fast growth puts a company's processes and governance model under strain, so not only there is a risk that a fast-growing company becomes systemically important soon, there is also a risk that by the time it has become important, its processes will have suffered, and hence regulatory attention might come earlier than expected.

Also, modern technology allows even small companies to technically disrupt a major system—for example, a malfunctioning client application connected to a major exchange or to a major payment system could bring the system down. This is, of course, mostly the responsibility of the operator of the major system to ensure that this does not happen, but regulators will generally not be very lenient with start-ups whose badly designed system risks causing a major disruption, and might be sympathetic to the major operator simply disconnecting them.

3.3.2 Regulation Specific to Fintech Businesses

The actual rules for Fintech businesses currently differ from country to country, even in supposedly homogenous environments like the EU. One reason for this is that the EU Directives still allow an important variation in regimes across the Member States; for example, in Germany, any company lending money *or* taking deposits must have a banking licence, whilst in other countries a banking licence might only be required if a company is taking deposits. This in turn means that market-place lenders must organise themselves differently, as either they need a banking licence, or they need to cooperate with a bank who legally is the lender, and who then backs the risk into the market-place lender, eg via derivatives.

United States of America

Depending on the regulatory environment, for a Fintech company it can be difficult even to find out who one's regulator should be. Especially in the US, there are a large number of regulators that every financial institution has to deal with, and it looks as if very few of them are willing to step back and to rely on other regulators' work in this respect. Every state has their banking, their insurance, and their securities regulator, and they might consider any company whose products or services fall into their regulatory remit, and that is either based in that state or has customers based in that state, to be subject to their regulation.

In addition, there are federation-level regulators to consider for any company that wants to operate across state lines, ie pretty much every single Fintech company. One regulator that has taken a keen interest in all things Fintech is the OCC, and it almost certainly will be involved. To the extent that the products or services involve consumers, the CFPB will also want to be involved, and for businesses at risk of being involved in money laundering or terrorist finance there is also the FinCEN to consider. Otherwise, it depends on the business in which a Fintech company is operating. If it is banking and payments, the local Fed might want to be involved, if it is securities- or derivatives-related, it will be the SEC or the CFTC, and possibly relevant SROs like FINRA, MSRB, or FTA.

European union

Most jurisdictions within the EU operate a two-tier system: there are the regulatory entities that operate under the framework defined by the EU rules, and there are entities that operate under local rules. Companies in the first group might be regulated as, for example, a *credit institution* in the case of a lender, or an *investment firm* in the case of an exchange, a broker, or a financial advisor. EU regulation applies to those firms, and to the extent that there are passporting rights, they can use those rights to establish their business across the Single Market.

Then there is often a second layer of regulatory business models that allow firms to provide similar services to those offered by firms in the first group, under similar but typically less cumbersome rules which have been created using opt-outs or optionality in the EU rules, or are restricted to areas that are not covered by EU regulation. This second layer is often there to account for smaller, second-tier players that have been historically present in the market and/or are serving a particular customer niche. This second level of regulations allows firms to provide services locally, but it does not grant them any of the passporting or equivalence privileges that the EU-conform business model has.

For start-up companies, that can be a hard choice to make: on the one hand, the local regulatory model is almost certainly easier to comply with, which is good to bootstrap the business. On the other hand, scaling the business cross-border will first require a re-authorisation under one of the EU-standard regulatory models, which might lead to additional costs and delays. At the very least, any company that intends at some point to scale cross-border should have an understanding of what this involves in terms of business requirements and authorisations, and should make sure that there is a pathway to compliance which is in line with the scaling ambitions in that company's business plan.

The regulatory set-up in Europe is generally less complex than in the US. As described in the section above, European countries usually have either one financial regulator, or one for each of the three sectors. An exception is the UK, where large firms can be regulated by the FCA and PRA, but for small firms it is only the FCA. Also, the reporting obligations under the money laundering rules are often to the central bank, even in jurisdictions where the central bank is not the regulator. When relying on regulatory passports, the passporting procedure is described in detail in the relevant regulation, usually along the lines that I have discussed in the example above: the main regulatory interactions are with the home regulator—and they importantly also deal with the initial introduction to the host regulator—so in the host countries only minimal regulatory interaction should be necessary.

Some jurisdictions operate what they call a 'sandbox' for innovative start-ups. This means two things: first, businesses are given a helping hand when navigating the regulatory framework relevant to them, and their requests for approval are often given priority and expedited so that those companies can scale more quickly. Second, companies might obtain certain waivers which—similar to no-action letters—will be limited in time, and tied to the business not exceeding a certain scale. This allows companies to take a much more gradual and proportionate approach to regulations, and requirements grow in line with the complexity of the business.

Functionally it is not that different from the no-action letters, except that the approach here is more formalised. Some other jurisdictions, however, are not particularly keen on the sandbox approach, with arguments along the line that regulation is proportionate anyway, and there is no need for a special regime for early-stage start-ups. Also, to the extent that sandbox capacity is limited, it has an element of the regulator actively supporting start-ups they consider winners. For a regulator, this is an awkward position to be in, especially if in the future there are problems.

Summary

Regulated Fintech companies are first and foremost regulated financial service companies, so the regulatory considerations here are not too different from what they are in the traditional case, with a number of exceptions due to where those businesses are in their lifecycle, and what kind of products and services they offer.

Macro-prudential considerations are not usually a concern, unless the company is already relatively big and it is growing quickly. Market structure concerns sometimes do matter, but they are often on the side of the new entrant and its ability to shake up things a bit. Micro-prudential considerations might be a concern if customer money is at risk, however, and where there is a reasonable expectation on the side of the customer that this is not the case. To give an example: if a company provides payment services and holds customer funds commingled with its own funds, then micro-prudential considerations are of concern, and in fact the regulator is likely to expect the company to apply for a banking licence. Alternatively, the company could choose to not commingle the funds but hold them in a third-party account with a bank, in which case the regulator might be more relaxed about micro-prudential considerations.

The flip-side of not being overly concerned on the prudential side is that regulators will want the company to plan for its own failure. This might not quite amount to the living wills required under the BRRD, but there should be some continuity planning in place that ensures that customers do not overly suffer from a default of the company. For example, a peer-to-peer lender or a crowdfunding company should have certain back-up agreements and arrangements in place that ensure that the loans or crowdfunding investments are still being serviced, ie that payments are being passed through, or that the companies funded have a way to directly communicate with their customers.

For money laundering and related regulations, again proportionality applies. There tends to be a materiality threshold somewhere between $1,000 and $5,000, and companies where a typical customer relationship involves sums significantly below that might not have to be too bothered about KYC and associated duties. If, however, materiality thresholds are reached, then the regulations are likely to apply in full. This is particularly important for companies that enable cash transactions, or that enable transfers into countries with weaker AML or CTF standards, or that sit at the boundary of financial and digital assets, eg exchanges that allow the buying and selling of crypto currencies.

The one concern that regulators will have regardless of whether a company is a Fintech start-up company or an established financial services player is conduct: customers must be treated fairly, must have all the necessary information to take a decision, and must have the necessary competence and knowledge to do so, etc. However, sometimes the specific requirements around conduct, eg in terms of assessing the customer's degree of financial sophistication and documenting this process, are less stringent. In other cases—eg crowd-funded equity for start-ups in the UK—the regulator either restricts this product to investors either *certified as sophisticated or high net worth* or *who confirm that they will not invest more than 10% of their net investible assets in these products* to strike a balance between making this product accessible and protecting customers from taking excessive risks.

CHAPTER 4

The Financial Services Industry

Financial services is a catch-all term for all those institutions that provide services in the realm of finance to their customers, whether those customers are individuals or companies, and whether the latter are a small SME or a large multinational corporation, or some other entity like, for example, an investment fund. Within financial services there exist a number of segments (see also Figure 4.1):

- Classic and Corporate Banking
- Specialised Lending
- Investment Banking and Advisory
- Payments
- Asset Management
- Brokerage and Transaction Services
- Insurance
- Others.

I'll go through these different sectors in turn. It is important to understand, though, that this is a somewhat artificial split. There are numerous business models in financial services, and many of them are either ultra-specialised within one of the segments above, or they straddle multiple segments at once.

4.1 Classic and Corporate Banking

Classic and corporate banking is about the core banking business of gathering deposits, making loans, and moving money around, both for

FIGURE 4.1   Classifying Financial Services by Institution

individuals and for companies. Often those institutions offer ancillary products, eg brokerage and custody, asset management, or even insurance. There are a large number of business models in this space, which differ in size, and product and customer specialisation.

Banks also have a number of ownership models: the large majority (by aggregate size) issue equity to shareholders, and are listed on a stock exchange. There is also a large mutual sector (eg building societies, Volksbanken) where the banks are owned by their customers, and finally there is a large state-owned/state-sponsored sector (eg savings banks, Sparkassen, cajas). Many of the institutions in the mutual and state-sponsored sectors are small, sometimes tiny. In this case they often form associations that operate under the same branding, and that join forces on central services such as IT to save cost. Institutions within the same association often do not compete with each other, eg by restricting themselves to a single geographic area.

The most common business model in this space (by aggregate size) is the **universal bank** that covers all customer segments (retail, mid-market, corporate) and that offers a wide range of products, including corporate banking and investment banking. If it also provides insurance services that are sometimes referred to as **bancassurer**.

As the companies in the **mutual bank** and state-sponsored **savings banks** sectors are smaller, they typically only serve the lower-sized end of the market, ie they serve retail customers and small to medium-sized businesses. In some instances they can also serve larger corporates, typically through specialised institutions that are part of a larger associative group and that do not serve the group's core markets of retail and small business customers. There are also institutions that focus on a single customer segment, eg medical professionals, or shipping companies.

Sometimes banks are associated to large industrial companies. For example in the Korean *chaebol* model, each of those chaebol industrial groups has an associated bank that serves it, and that is also open for external business. In the West, many large manufacturers—auto manufacturers in particular—have associated banks or finance companies that provide financing to their customers, and that I'll briefly discuss in the section on specialised finance providers.

Regulatory Angle. The main framework for banks are the Basel-related and other prudential regulations (CRD, BRRD, DGSD in the EU). There are also conduct regulations in place. Those are mostly local, but there exist some at the EU level as well (CCOD covering all consumer contracts, CCRD covering consumer credit, and MCD covering consumer mortgages).

Banks must also comply with the money laundering and related rules (AMLD in the EU). Also, payments systems regulations apply (PSD in the EU) as well as potentially e-money regulations (EMONEYD in the EU). To the extent that banks manufacture and/or distribute investment products, the relevant rules for those apply (MiFID and PRIIPR in the EU). See also the rules that apply to the asset managers (UCITS, AIFMD in the EU) in this respect.

4.2 Specialised Lending

Whilst a lot of lending is done via banks, there is a segment of financial service providers who lend money or provide credit protection, but who are not banks. The most important distinction in this respect is that they do not take customer deposits.

The first big sub-segment here is that of **leasing companies (captive** or not) or **vendor finance providers**. They all lend against capital assets—typically moveable assets that can be repossessed if need be—starting from office equipment (phones, computers, even furniture), via cars, heavy machinery, turbines, and all the way up to aircraft and comparably priced assets. *Captive* companies are associated to specific manufacturer, and they only provide financing for purchases of the assets produced by the manufacturer. An important representative of this particular segment are **auto banks**, who are often proper banks—they take deposits—and who are associated with the large car manufacturers. *Non-captive* finance companies tend to focus on one or a few verticals, eg office equipment, or furniture, or certain types of cars.

The second big sub-segment here is **factoring** and more generally **working capital finance**. Factoring businesses—also known as invoice financing businesses—lend only against *accounts receivable*, ie unpaid invoices. Working capital lenders are also lending against other portions of a company's *working capital*, most often inventories of raw materials or finished goods.

Another important segment is **trade finance**. Banks often operate in this area, as do government-sponsored entities. Trade finance can have a working capital finance aspect—financing goods whilst they are in transit for example—but often it is a mere *credit guarantee* where the trade finance provider indemnifies the seller against a default of the purchaser. In this sense this is similar to regular **credit insurance**, where an insurer indemnifies a creditor if there is a default, again something often provided by banks. In the trade finance area, however, the credit aspect is less important than the fact that the trade finance provider has the capability to pursue a claim in a foreign jurisdiction, something which is very difficult and costly for smaller businesses to do.

A specialised form of credit insurance which is unrelated to trade are the **monoline insurers**. They provide credit guarantees for securities, notably US municipalities, and structured finance instruments. However, their importance has decreased markedly since the financial crisis.

Regulatory Angle. To the extent that the specialised lending relates to consumer credit, the same consumer protections as for banks apply. For corporate lending it depends: in some jurisdictions, lending to corporates is very lightly regulated and might not even require a licence; in others, for any kind of lending a banking licence is required, with all the implications this has. Monoline insurers are regulated under the local insurance regulations.

Last but not least, I want to mention **mortgage originators** and **mortgage servicers**. The former are originating loans—mostly mortgage loans because those are the easiest to underwrite—and they either sell those loans to interested investors like insurance companies, or they have a warehousing agreement with an investment bank who eventually securitises them. The buyers can typically not service them, meaning they are not in a position to communicate with the borrowers, receive and reconcile payments, and foreclose on the mortgage if need be, which is where the servicers come in. This so-called 'originate-to-distribute' model was particularly popular with subprime mortgages, and after the crisis it has lost much of its volume.

Regulatory Angle. Stand-alone mortgage originators—to the extent that they exist—are locally regulated. Depending on the jurisdiction, they have a certain duty of care to ensure that the products are suitable for the customers in question. Also, to the extent that it relates to consumer credit—and it mostly does—the same rules as for banks apply in this respect. Servicers—to the extent that they operate on a stand-alone basis and not as, for example, part of a bank—are mostly covered by the general customer protection and fair dealing rules that apply across all businesses.

4.3 Investment Banking and Advisory

The term '**investment banks**' describes companies engaging in a wide range of loosely related business activities that are connected to the financial markets. The two major business lines are the **advisory** business, which is mostly advisory on **mergers and acquisitions**, and the **markets** business.

Within the markets business there is the **capital markets** segment, which is usually separated into **equity capital markets**, which deals with primary issuance of equity securities; **debt capital markets**, which does the same for debt securities; and **securitisation**, which securitises assets, ie packages them into stand-alone special-purpose companies that are financed by issuing a range of securities, both debt- and equity-like. Another important area here is the **syndicated loans** business, which deals with tradeable loans to large companies, the latter often owned by private equity companies, and of sub-investment-grade credit quality.

Also within markets is the **sales and trading business**, which covers secondary trading of securities—ie the trading of securities that are owned by someone else than the issuer—as well as derivatives trading. The securities business is often referred to as **broker/dealer** business because the institution sometimes serves as broker, where they are intermediating between clients without taking a position, and sometimes as dealer where they are buying and selling securities on their own account to facilitate customer business (see the section on brokers for more details). Derivatives trading in this context is always a dealer-style business, ie the institution acts as a counterparty for the trade (eg a swap or option trade) for the whole lifetime of the trade.

Regulatory Angle. Large investment banks nowadays are mostly regulated as banks, therefore bank prudential regulations in particular apply. Smaller firms, both in the trading and the advisory space, can be regulated as investment firms (MiFID in the EU; CRD also applies to investment firms). To the extent that they are actively trading, they must take into account of the various market and market infrastructure regulations (EMIR, MAR in the EU).

4.4 Payments

In the payments space there are a large number of specialised service providers that are competing with the banks, as well as a number of **IT infrastructure providers** that are dealing with the backend of the payment systems.

To use the terminology of the Payment Services Directive, there are the following, not mutually exclusive, distinctions:

• payment institutions
• payment service providers
• single payment service providers
• payment initiation services and account information services
• three- and four-party card schemes.

Payment institutions (PIs) is a catch-all term for institutions that fulfil services in the payments space, and that are not banks; for example, they can run payment accounts, operate payment networks, access the standard payment systems, provide fx services, etc. Because they only operate in the payments space they are more lightly regulated than banks, making their establishment easier.

Payment service providers or **PSPs** are companies that serve as a payment gateway for their customers, especially for online merchants. They allow those customers to accept payments from different sources (eg different cards, direct debit, possibly payment vouchers) via a single API, so the merchants don't have to worry about connecting to all the different payment sources. They can also run payment accounts for customers, in which case they are also referred to as **account servicing PSPs**.

PSPs should not be confused with **single payment service providers** (**SPSPs**), which are fully integrated payment providers running their own payment infrastructure, eg **remittance** and **money transfer** businesses, or **bill payment services** allowing one to pay bills from, say, supermarkets or corner shops.

Card schemes are the well-known credit- and debit card networks; **three-party schemes** are vertically integrated, ie the whole operation is run by one institution, whilst **four-party schemes** include a bank, and the credit card company acts as a partner and service provider to the issuing bank.

Payment initiation service providers (**PISPs**) are providers that allow customers to initiate payments that are then either executed via PIs or banks; their purpose is to provide a better and possibly more specialised user experience in the payments space. **Account information service providers** (**AISPs**) are similarly single-purpose institutions. The service they provide is to retrieve account data from one or several of a customer's payment accounts, and analyse it or present it in a better way. Typically AISPs could also offer PISP services, but not necessarily vice versa.

Regulatory Angle. The payment systems regulatory framework applies here (PSD in the EU), and possible also the e-money framework (EMONEYD in the EU).

4.5 Asset Management

This segment groups all financial service providers who are dealing with investing other people's money. To look at the big picture first, there are **discretionary managers**, where people—or algorithms—decide where assets are invested, and there are **index managers**, where investment is determined by an index (eg, S&P 500) and all the manager does is implement this strategy as efficiently as possible. Funds can come in an **open-ended** fund structure where the funds continuously accept new money and offer redemptions—possibly through an exchange-traded **ETF** structure, where investments and redemptions are dealt with through a clever structure on an exchange—or they can come in a **closed-ended** structure, where units can be traded on the market, but additional funds cannot be accepted nor can units be redeemed during the lifetime of the fund. Related is the **certificate business**, where certain investment strategies, typically derivative-based, are repackaged into tradeable securities.

Coming back to the *discretionary managers*, there are a number of different types. The most common one is the **mutual fund**, which purchases securities, typically equities or bonds, depending on the mandate. There are also **hedge funds**, who are given more freedom in what kind of strategies to engage in; in particular, they can short securities, meaning they profit when securities fall; they can employ leverage, meaning they can borrow additional money to invest in a larger securities portfolio then their invested funds would allow; and they can engage in derivative trading strategies.

There are also the **private equity** (PE) and **venture capital** (VC) areas, which mostly invest into the equity of unlisted companies. The difference between them is that private equity invests in large mature businesses that might have been publicly listed at one point, and that benefit from the high leverage and investor focus that private equity can provide. Venture capital funds, on the other hand, invest in start-up companies, and there are funds that focus on the different stages of the company development. Part of that space are also **angel investors,** who invest at a very early stage, even ahead of the VC funds.

Lastly, one should mention **private banking** and **family offices** here. The former is *banking for rich people*, and whilst it is a full banking relationship, the focus tends to be on managing the clients' significant assets. A family office is similar, except that in this case a client—or a group of connected clients—employs a dedicated personal asset manager.

Regulatory Angle. Asset management usually has important rules at the local level in terms of requirements, legal form, and authorisation. In the EU there are also higher levels of rules for retail investments (UCITS) and for alternative managers (AIFMD). When selling or designing investment products, especially in the retail market, some of the provisions for investment firms apply (MiFID), and also the general consumer protection rules apply.

4.6 Brokerage and Transaction Services

This segment groups all financial service providers that are dealing with buying, selling, and holding securities and other financial instruments.

4.6.1 Broker and Investment Research

Brokers are generally intermediaries between buyers and sellers, and they sometimes also provide ancillary services, such as *custody* and *financing*. The most widely known brokerages are **retail brokerages**, who allow retail customers to purchase exchange-traded securities—mostly equities, but sometimes also bonds. Retail brokers usually provide an end-to-end service, ie they execute the transaction, and then work with a custodian—often, but not necessarily, an associate company—for custody and reporting.

There are also brokers operating in the professional markets, for example **interdealer-brokers**, who match buyers and sellers for derivative transactions, eg in the market of foreign exchange options. Brokers never enter into a transaction as a principal—all they do is to identify two dealers who want to do a specific trade, typically at the service of the one side who contacted them with a specific deal request that they then shop around for in the market. Another important group of entities here are the **broker/dealers**, who I already mentioned above, and who typically are part of investment banks. They run a securities inventory, so if clients want to sell securities they can either find them a suitable counterparty, or buy those securities on their own account with a view to finding a buyer later. They also enter into derivative transactions as principals. Broker/dealers often also run what is referred to as a **prime brokerage** business, which is targeted at hedge funds and provides ancillary services such as custody, financing, and reporting.

Traditionally, brokers and dealers also provide **investment research** to their clients, ie they have analysts who specialise in certain classes of securities (say, telecom stocks) and who provide information and views to potential buyers and sellers of those securities. In the European Union this business is currently under threat because of newly introduced guidelines that forbid providing this service as an ancillary service without charging for it. As a consequence there is a shift towards independent investment research that is being sold as a stand-alone product from independent research firms.

4.6.2 Transaction Services, Clearing, and Reporting

Transaction services providers are all those firms who support the trading activities of others. In this group we have **custodians**, who hold the securities on behalf of the beneficial owner. In the past this amounted to physically holding paper-based securities certificates in a safe, and tracking their ownership; more recently it is mostly an entirely electronic bookkeeping system, provided the securities exist in dematerialised format. A related function is that of a **registrar**, who knows where all the securities are held, and who arranges things like dividend and coupon payments, as well as communication, for example in respect of the annual shareholder meeting.

Securities clearing houses ensure that money and securities are exchanged without one side defaulting on the deal, meaning that they ensure that securities only change ownership when payment is received. There are also **derivatives clearing houses** (aka **central counterparties**), who fulfil a similar function, but for derivatives trades—we'll come to that in more detail in the chapter on products below. Finally, we have **exchanges** and other **trading venues** which provide a market-place where they can be traded, and that might provide additional services such as providing company- and price-specific information, and supervising that the securities comply with their listing requirements.

There are also a number of business models in that space that deal with collecting information, and making it accessible to either the public or to regulators, either in a raw or an aggregated forward. One of those models is **trade repositories**, which collect details of trades executed, be it on public or semi-public markets or OTC, and who make this data available to the regulators and, in an aggregated format, to their clients. Under the EU MiFID2 regulations there are also a number of very specific information services roles that deal with reporting trades from venues, eg **consolidated tape providers** (**CTPs**), that consolidate trade information from different venues into a single stream, and **approved publication arrangements** (**APAs**) and **approved reporting mechanisms** (**ARMs**), whose responsibility is to support investment firms in their reporting duties vis-à-vis the public and the regulators respectively.

Regulatory Angle. Custodians and registrars are generally regulated locally, with a view to ensuring the safety of the assets and the reliability of services. There are some mentions of them in related regulations, eg AIFMD, UCITSD, and MiFID. Clearing houses are regulated in the EU under EMIR, as are trade repositories. CTPs, APAs, and ARMs are defined in and regulated under MiFID.

4.7 Insurance

Insurance companies are pooling and distributing risk among their customers. For example, in the **property & casualty** insurance segment, clients who face a specific risk—eg that their home is broken into, or destroyed by fire—pay an insurance premium. Those customers where the risk materialises are then made whole by the insurance company.

Some insurance companies provide ancillary services, most importantly those in the **health insurance** market, where insurers not only provide indemnification but often are in a position to provide services more cheaply, for example because they are in a position to provide those services themselves, or because they have significant purchasing power in that market.

Another important insurance segment is that of **life insurance**, which deals with the risk of either dying prematurely, and therefore leaving dependents without the necessary means, or living too long, and therefore using up all one's assets. Especially the latter insurance is usually paired with an asset management business, so that people pay into insurance plans throughout their lives to reap the benefits during retirement.

Finally there are **reinsurance** providers, who insure insurance companies against excessive losses, eg because of a large natural event like a hurricane that affects a lot of the primary insurance's customers at the same time.

Regulatory Angle. The regulation in this space has a very strong local bias—partially because life and health insurance products in particular are crucial to individuals' lives, and any issues can take a very long time to play themselves out. In the EU, from a prudential point of view the Solvency Directive (SOLVD) applies.

4.8 Others

There are a number of financial services providers that don't fit into the categories above. For example, there are **rating agencies**, who assess the credit quality of borrowers. They are similar to the **research** functions mentioned above, except that they provide letter ratings for the creditworthiness of securities ('AAA', 'AA', etc.). Those ratings are in practice very important, eg for regulatory purposes, or to define fund management mandates for bond investors.

Regulatory Angle. Rating agencies are now usually subject to direct regulation (RAR in the EU). Also, ratings are a cornerstone of most prudential regulatory frameworks, eg Basel (CRD in the EU).

CHAPTER 5

Retail Financial Services Products

A lready today the variety of the business models in financial services means that economically very similar products are offered by a wide range of players, and the emergence of Fintech players with new and often ultra-focused business models will further exacerbate that issue. Traditionally, regulation has been defined on the basis of the business model— *you are a bank, hence we apply bank regulation.* This gets more and more difficult, and whilst legislation often is a bit slow to adapt, regulators in practice already often employ duck typing methods on a product level— *your product looks like a duck, and it sounds like a duck, therefore we regulate it like a duck.* So after having discussed the structure of the financial services segment in the previous chapter, I now focus on the products and services offered, and give some indication of how they are regulated.

Because of its sheer length I have broken down this topic into two chapters: one for products typically offered to retail and small business customers, and another one for products typically offered for wholesale customers. This is not entirely clean, as there are a number of products that are offered to the entire customer base—say, payment accounts. Those are either discussed in the chapter where it makes more sense, or in both if the product has significant different features in those segments. The product segments we'll be looking at in this chapter are (see also Figure 5.1):

1. payments and deposits
2. retail and SME/mid-market lending and credit
3. retail investments
4. insurance
5. financial advisory.

FIGURE 5.1 Classifying Financial Services by Product (Retail)

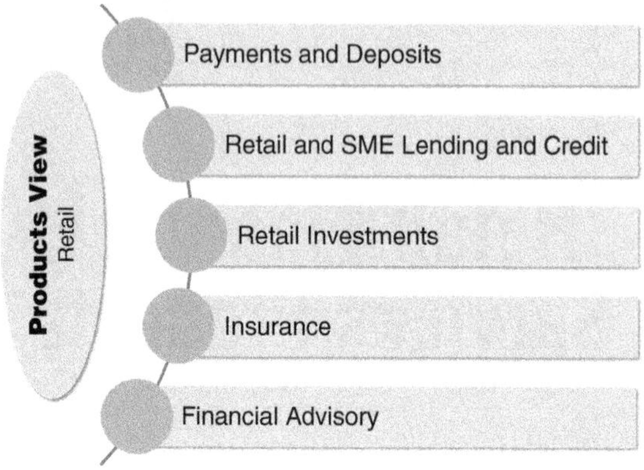

In the next chapter we will then cover:

1. wholesale credit
2. wholesale and specialist asset management
3. primary markets and origination
4. sales, trading, brokerage, and exchanges
5. settlement, custody, and ancillary services
6. advisory and research.

5.1 Payments and Deposits

5.1.1 Payments and Transaction Accounts

One of the fundamental products banks offer are **payment services**, ie the ability to send money to/receive money from others, both domestically and cross-border. A closely related service is that of **transaction accounts**. Whilst not strictly necessary for making payments—for example cash-in cash-out transfers (aka **remittances**) do not require them—in most cases a transaction account is needed to participate in a payment system, both as a sender and as a recipient of funds. Transaction accounts typically earn little or no interest and there might be periodic fees for holding the account itself, as well as fees for additional services like payments and obtaining hard copy statements.

The very large majority of payments in number terms—albeit not necessarily in terms of value—are **domestic payments** in domestic currency. However, **cross-border payments** and **cross-currency payments** have always been important for businesses and, with more and more cross-border commerce being facilitated by the Internet, are now becoming more important in the retail space as well. Customers who have a regular need for cross-currency transactions sometimes have **multi-currency transaction accounts** that allow them to manage their foreign exchange more efficiently.

There are three major products in the payment area, all of them typically offered by banks: **bank transfer**, **cheque**, and **card payment**, the latter being separated into **cardholder present** payments that are done using a card reader and the physical card, and **cardholder not present** payments that are done via the Internet or telephone. Whilst not strictly a payments distinction, there are three types of cards on the market: **debit**, **monthly debit**, and **credit**. The first two require payment in full—either immediately, or at the end of the month—and the latter is effectively a credit line, allowing to delay payment in return for an interest charge. There are also specialist payment providers, typically for cross-border payments, for example **remittances services** that allow cash-in cash-out transactions.

Regulatory Angle. To the extent that payment services are often provided by banks, bank regulations (CRD in the EU) apply. This is in particular the case when the payment service is attached to a payment account, and the funds in this account are commingled with the company's assets. Otherwise, the applicable regulations in this space might be those for a payment institution (PSD in the EU), or for an e-money institution (EMONEYD in the EU). To the extent that funds come from outside the regulated system—eg via cash deposits, or from a country with a weak supervisory system—AML regulations are extremely important. For outgoing payments, CTF rules must be taken into account, so KYC procedures in this sector are very important.

It is important to mention **money market funds** here, who in many cases appear like regular transactions accounts. For example, they can send and receive transfers, and it is possible to have cheques and a payment card.

The key difference is that they do not benefit from a deposit guarantee, but they rely on asset separation for protection against default of the bank.

> **Regulatory Angle.** Money market funds are an important product to demonstrate how regulatory arbitrage can be used to create an interesting value proposition: for customers this product is identical in terms of day-to-day usage to current accounts, and many customers apparently ignore or don't care about the fine print with respect to deposit guarantees. Because of lighter regulations—and because it does not trigger contributions to deposit protection schemes—this product is cheaper to 'manufacture', hence interest rates paid can be higher. Regulators are aware of this regulatory arbitrage, but it is not easy to address and not necessarily a priority.

5.1.2 Deposit Accounts

The term '**savings accounts**' covers a wide range of products. They are differentiated from transaction accounts in that the funds there are not usually immediately accessible—or at least only at a penalty—and earn interest in return. With **term deposits** the funds are locked up for a certain period, and it is impossible getting them returned earlier, unless they are **breakable deposits** which can be redeemed early at a cost. There are also **structured deposits**, where the interest depends on, say, the performance of an equity index, but the principal is still guaranteed, and there are all kind of deposits with more complex rules, for example the annual interest might increase in later years, or bonus interest might be added after a few years. A related product is the **certificate of deposit**, which is a term deposit in the form of a security, meaning that they can be sold if need be, and if a buyer can be found.

There is a crossover asset management product—money market funds—that in most practical aspects behaves like a bank account, that does not benefit from a deposit guarantee and that is discussed in the funds section.

Deposit guarantee schemes are typically state-sponsored schemes which guarantee the principal amount of a deposit for a range of eligible customers, usually retail customers. The amount is typically limited per-customer and per-bank, and there might be other deductibles.

Regulatory Angle. Institutions that hold customer deposits commingled with their own funds must in most jurisdictions be regulated as banks (CRD in the EU; also DGSD for the deposit protection). However, there are companies, especially in the Fintech space, that provide a convenient front-end for banking-like or investment services, with the funds being held in a third-party bank or at another appropriate regulated depositary. In this case the company in question might be regulated as a payment institution (PSD in the EU) or as an investment firm (MiFID in the EU), or under some local regulation.

5.2 Retail and SME/Mid-market Lending and Credit

Lending and credit is one of the most important product segments in the financial services space. Here I discuss the following market segments:

1. retail credit
2. SME/mid-market lending and credit
3. specialised lending
4. trade finance
5. credit guarantees and credit insurance.

The segments below are discussed in the corresponding section within the wholesale credit chapter:

1. large corporate credit
2. real estate, project, and other asset finance.

A number of different players exist in the space, notably banks who refinance themselves in part via customer deposits, specialised lenders who refinance themselves in the wholesale markets, and originator/investor structures where, in contrast to the first two groups, the originators do not lend from their own balance sheet. In this case loan servicing is often outsourced to specialist providers.

The originator group has two distinct models, a broker model and a securitisation model. In the broker model, the originator matches borrowers and lenders. Traditionally, lenders could, for example, be insurance companies. More recently, investors could be private individuals and specialist funds investing via a P2P lending platform. In the securitisation model, originators slice loan portfolios into low-risk and high-risk tranches, and sell them to investors separately, typically via investment banks.

Regulatory Angle. How the activity of lending is regulated is highly dependent on the jurisdiction. In some, everyone engaging in lending requires a banking licence, therefore bank prudential regulations in particular apply (CRD in the EU; also BRRD). In others, only lenders who are also taking deposits are subject to banking regulations, and other lenders can be authorised under a local regime. The reasons to impose prudential requirements are two-fold: first, to protect depositors and/or the state-sponsored deposit protection schemes, and second to ensure systemic stability. Therefore, small lenders not taking deposits will typically be less of a regulator's concern than those where either of those conditions is not fulfilled. AML rules are not relevant for lending, but CTF rules are, so KYC rules and establishing the use of proceeds is usually required (AMLD in the EU).

To the extent that regulated entities invest in loans, or securitisations, their own prudential regulations apply. For insurance companies, that will entail a capital requirement as well, albeit a different one than for banks (SOLVD in the EU). For funds it is more about the assets being eligible under the investment mandate, both from a legal and possibly ratings point of view (UCITS, MiFID, AIFMD in the EU). Originators might or might not be subject to specific regulation, in most cases probably as investment firms (MiFID in the EU), which gives them some duties vis-à-vis their investors, especially if those are not professional investors.

Key prudential rules are capital and liquidity requirements: banks and insurance companies must hold a certain amount of equity against every loan, the amount of which depends on its riskiness. For example, for an average risky loan regulators might require $10 in own funds for every $100 lent. Similarly they might require that a certain proportion of the remaining $90 is refinanced via longer-dated debt, for example term deposits longer than a year, or 3- to 5-year bonds issued by the lender.

5.2.1 Retail Lending and Credit

The **retail** segment consists of private individuals. Often this segment also includes very small businesses, especially when the credit given to the business is cross-secured on the owners' personal assets.

Regulatory Angle. An important additional consideration when dealing with retail customers is that consumer protection rules (CCOD, CCRD, MCD in the EU) and data protection rules (GDPR in the EU) apply. This can become a thorny issue when the originator or servicer—often thinly capitalised entities against whom recourse is difficult—have breached the rules and the customer seeks restitution, which might eventually come out of the investors' pockets.

By size, the most important product in the segment is the **mortgage loan**, ie lending against the value of a personal property. Usually this will be the borrower's primary residence, but it might also be a **buy-to-let** property, or it might be business premises in the case of a very small SME. The mortgage can be **recourse**, meaning in default there is a claim against the other assets of the borrower, or **non-recourse** meaning there is no such claim. This is not a customer choice, but it depends on the applicable law in a given jurisdiction.

In the US, there is a large **conforming** mortgage market, this term referring to the fact that the mortgages *conform* with the terms of the mortgage agencies who'll guarantee their performance, against a fee, thereby removing most of the risk. The **non-conforming** market is the rest, including for example the **jumbo** market of very large mortgages. Historically, it also contained **Alt-A** and so-called **subprime** mortgages of lower credit quality, but those markets have lost importance after the crisis.

The key part of mortgage lending is the actual *mortgage*, ie a registered claim over the property. Most jurisdictions run a mortgage register where it is possible to register a claim over every property in that particular jurisdiction and to see if there are prior claims, ensuring that it is not possible to obtain more than one mortgage loan against any given property. The register is either run by the state, or a state-chartered private company. It is also possible to place a nominee claim owner in the official register, and then keep track of the actual claim at the nominee level, allowing for mortgage claims to change hands without having to go back to the local register, which is often still paper-based.

It is sometimes possible to also register second-lien (aka subordinated) claims that are only paid once the first-lien claim is paid in full. In the US, the corresponding loans are referred to as **Home Equity Loans** or **HELs**. Depending on the quality of the information in the register, some jurisdictions may offer **title insurance** if a prior claim surfaces after a deal has been closed.

Regulatory Angle. Prime mortgage loans—ie loans to good credit quality owner-occupiers where the borrower has sufficient equity in the property—attract very low capital requirements under the bank prudential regulations (CRD in the EU) because of their low risk—it could be as low as $1 per $100 loaned, or even less. However, if a bank's lending portfolio is predominantly high-quality mortgage loans, then the non-risk weighted leverage ratio could become the binding constraint, in which case capital requirements would be a multiple of that. Lower-quality loans—buy-to-let, Alt-A, subprime, HEL—attract higher capital requirements, some of them substantially so. Title insurance is locally regulated, and highly dependent on the jurisdiction because it depends on the laws governing mortgage claims.

Secondary mortgage registers relying on nominee reference in the primary register are an interesting structure from a legal point of view. They can be considered infringing on consumer rights, and their legality should be checked in every jurisdiction based on the applicable mortgage law.

Another important product in the retail space is the **credit card loan**, ie revolving credit that is associated to a payment card. The way it works is that there is a credit limit on the card, and customers can make purchases up to that credit limit. Customers obtain a credit card statement once per month, and if they pay the bill in full, no interest is due. Otherwise they have to make at least the minimum payment of typically 5% of the outstanding balance, and whatever is not repaid is being rolled over indefinitely, accruing interest at a significant rate.

Regulatory Angle. Like mortgages, credit card loans have a special segment in the Basel regulations (CRD in the EU). They represent a higher default risk, and therefore their capital requirements are higher. They are also often subject to specific consumer protection rules.

The last major product in this space is the **overdraft facility** which allows a customer's payment account to go into overdraft up to a certain overdraft limit, either against a fixed overdraft fee, or against an interest rate, or both. Sometimes there is a requirement to clear an overdraft within a certain time frame, as its purpose is not that of a permanent loan facility, but to ensure that payments from that account don't bounce, potentially causing significant cost and distress.

Two more products in the retail space are the **unsecured personal loan** and the **auto loan**, the former being a general-purpose loan—often to consolidate credit card debt at a lower rate—the latter being a loan to purchase, and being secured on, a vehicle. Both of those loans are often extended by specialised consumer lending companies instead of banks, and in the case of auto loans also by the so-called 'auto-banks', ie banks associated to the major automotive producers, providing financing for their product. An auto loan is economically similar but legally different from a leasing contract: in the former the car is owned by the borrower, whilst in the latter the car is owned by the leasing company.

For small businesses there are a number of additional products, and I will discuss most of them with other business products below. One product I want to mention here, however, is the **cross-collateralised business loan** where private assets (property, possibly a car) are additional collateral for a small business loan or overdraft line. They also might make use of the products discussed under the specialised lending heading below.

Regulatory Angle. Other lending requires capital in line with its riskiness. For overdraft facilities—like for the very similar credit lines that are discussed in the section on corporate lending—some consideration must be given that they might be drawn before a default, so capital requirements are based not only on the drawn amount but also the authorised amount.

Last but not least, there are loans extended by **pawnbrokers** and by **payday lenders**. The former take possession of valuable assets—eg jewellery—and lend against them at a steep discount. If the owner defaults on the loan, the pawnbroker takes possession of the asset and sells it to recover their losses. Payday lenders lend to customers who need a bridge until the next payday, typically small amounts at a very high rate, and amounts can spiral out of control quickly if the original due date is missed.

Regulatory Angle. Pawnbrokers and payday lenders are often regulated as local law specialised lenders. Consumer protection rules (CCOD, CCRD in the EU) apply to the extent that customers are consumers.

5.2.2 SME/Mid-market Lending and Credit

The **mid-market** (US terminology) or **SME** (European terminology) segment is that of companies larger than those in the previous segment, but smaller than those in the large corporate segment discussed in the wholesale chapter. Boundaries are not clear, but typically mid-market companies have tens to hundreds of employees, do not usually have a significant presence abroad, and are privately held.

The major credit product for mid-market companies is the **loan** product, in a number of shapes depending on the specific purpose. For example, **equipment loans** are loans secured against equipment purchased, possibly with **instalment payments** in line with the economic depreciation of the assets. Especially long-term assets might be financed with **balloon** loans, meaning they are partially paid down during the lifetime of the loan, but there is a large *balloon* payment at the end; or with **bullet loans**, meaning there is no paydown of principal at all during the lifetime of the loan. Finally there are **zero-coupon** loans, meaning there is no payment whatsoever during the lifetime of the loan and even interest is rolled up until the end.

Another important product in this space are **credit lines**. Some are just **general-purpose lines** that allow businesses to deal with unforeseen fluctuations in finances, similar to account overdrafts. For those lines, companies pay both a *commitment fee* for having the line, and *interest* on the drawn amount. Credit lines can be **revolving**, meaning that they must be periodically repaid, eg for seasonable businesses financing inventory build-up. Derivatives lines are credit lines needed for the derivatives business, and are discussed in the wholesale chapter as they are of higher importance there.

Regulatory Angle. Customers in this space are not protected under the consumer protection rules, so for lenders who do not take deposits the regulatory load in this segment can be very low. However, AML/KYC rules might become more complex, especially with shell-type companies, as beneficial ownership might have to be established (AMLD in the EU). If prudential regulations apply, then the rules around capital and liquidity requirements are the same as for retail loans (CRD in the EU). In practice it might, however, become more difficult as the products become more complex, for example when the borrower has flexibility in the repayment schedule, or can redraw funds, in which case some expected exposures must be considered.

5.2.3 Specialised Lending and Leasing

The specialised lending segment is about lending against specific assets, with the loans being structured to account for the characteristics of those assets.

One big class of products in this segment is that of **asset finance** or **leasing**, where the former term tends to refer to big-ticket assets, whilst the latter is more neutral. This segment starts from the very small—eg photocopiers, computers, even office furniture—to the very big, eg aircraft or shipping vessels. An important asset in the leasing sector is *cars*, both for personal and professional use. As a general rule, most moveable assets can be obtained under a leasing contract. Leases can be **operating leases** and **capital leases**, the difference being that in the former the customer is expected to return the asset, whilst in the latter they are expected to keep it. Closely related to leasing is **vendor financing**, where the vendor arranges a loan to purchase the asset. Economically, vendor financing is equivalent to a capital lease.

Similar to leasing is *working capital* finance, where the lending is done not against fixed assets but against working capital, ie *accounts receivable* (aka unpaid invoices or inventories). **Invoice financing**, also referred to as **factoring**, can be structured in a number of different ways, depending on who takes the risk that the customer defaults, who takes care of assessing the credit risk of the customer, and who deals with collections. With **inventory financing**, a company can raise funding either against its *raw materials inventory* or its *finished goods inventory*. It is important in this case that the lender has good visibility on current inventory levels. For finished products the lender also must take the value of the items when the company defaults into account—consider for example IoT widgets that rely on a company-run server to operate.

Regulatory Angle. Specialised lending and asset finance is often done by lightly regulated companies relying on wholesale financing, at least in jurisdictions where corporate lending does not require a banking licence. Especially on the shorter end of the business—ie the working capital side—supervision is not particularly important, as customers who receive a bad service can switch providers without too much of a risk to themselves. On the longer end it depends on the asset in question: for example when leasing a turbine from the manufacturer, the product risk is significantly bigger than the financial risk, so, again, tight regulation is not necessarily useful. To the extent that this business is done by banks, the usual bank regulations apply. If there are capital requirements, a key consideration is to what extent the claim over the collateral asset increases recovery rates, and whether it makes a difference within the regulatory capital framework that is applicable.

5.2.4 Trade Finance

The trade finance segment is about supporting international trade, and most governments play a very active role in that market, as it allows them to support their own export industry. The main product here is the **letter of credit** (LoC), which is a credit guarantee rather than a loan, ie a promise to indemnify the vendor if the buyer fails to pay. An LoC allows companies to export their goods without having to assess the credit quality of the buyer and—importantly—without having to take the risk of having to pursue claims in a foreign jurisdiction. Conversely, it allows importers to withhold payment until goods have arrived and have been checked for conformity with the specifications.

Trade credit often involves two institutions, one in the country of the exporter, and one in the country of the importer. The reason for this is that banks in the country of the exporter will usually not have the skill to assess the credit quality of the importer, so they can't issue a guarantee. On the other hand, the exporter will find it difficult to work with a bank in the other country, so they rely on someone from a local bank, who provides a front.

> **Regulatory Angle.** The market itself is very lightly regulated. However, trust is important, so as far as private sector players are involved they tend to be regulated businesses for that reason. If entities are regulated as banks, the bank regulations apply.

5.2.5 Credit Guarantees and Credit Insurance

A **credit guarantee** is a third-party guarantee to a lender that guarantees that if the borrower defaults, the third party will step in and make them whole. **Credit insurance** is similar, except that in the case of a guarantee the third party might have a claim on the borrower, whilst in the case of insurance that is not usually the case. Everyone can guarantee credits, but a commercial credit guarantee is usually provided by a bank, whilst credit insurance is usually provided by insurance companies. This is mostly an SME product, enabling business that might otherwise not take place because of credit reasons.

An important application of credit insurance is also in the US municipal loan market, where municipalities issue bonds that are guaranteed by a *monoline insurance company*. Before the crisis, monolines also guaranteed structured finance assets (ie, securitisation tranches, often related to subprime mortgages), which lead to substantial losses.

> **Regulatory Angle.** To the extent that those products are provided by entities subject to prudential regulations, those regulations apply (in the EU, CRD for banks and SOLVD for insurance companies).

5.3 Retail Investments

The key legal difference between deposits and investments is that the former are commingled with the company's assets, and in some cases benefit from deposit guarantee schemes, whilst the latter are held in a separate account which is bankruptcy-remote in the event of a default of the asset manager. There is a crossover asset management product, **money market funds**, that in most practical aspects behaves like a bank account and that I have discussed in that section.

A key distinction in the asset management space is between **active management**, where discretionary investment decisions are taken by human fund managers, and **passive management**, where the investment strategy is fixed in advance. There is also **algorithmic management**, which is in-between the two, but in practice closer to active management when taking into account the people who develop and supervise the algorithms.

Another important distinction is between open-ended and closed-ended funds. In **open-ended funds**, net new money contributed is invested into new assets, and net money withdrawn is met from assets being sold. To avoid withdrawals beyond the liquidity of the underlying assets, there is often a notice period, and in times of distress funds can become **gated**, ie they can refuse withdrawals until liquidity improves.

Closed-ended funds have a maximum amount that can be invested, and withdrawals are not possible. Instead, the fund has a certain expected lifetime, and the proceeds are distributed when the investments are realised. Often closed-ended funds are *listed*, meaning their ownership interest is in form of shares that can be traded on an exchange, so whilst investors can't withdraw money, they can sell their shares, provided they find a buyer.

> **Regulatory Angle.** The investments themselves will be covered by the regulations for asset management and/or asset managers (UCITS or AIFMD in the EU, but there are significant local differences between jurisdictions). To the extent that the funds are quoted on an exchange, the regular securities laws also apply (MiFID in the EU).

5.3.1 Active Segment

The main distinction in the *active* segment is between **mutual funds** and **alternative investments**. The latter are often referred to as **hedge funds**, and are not usually open to retail investors, which is why they are discussed in the wholesale chapter. Mutual funds are real money investors, ie they are only allowed to invest in actual securities, and the amount they invest in securities is limited to the funds they receive. This means they can neither borrow additional funds to lever their investments, nor can they employ derivatives. Typically their investment mandate further restricts the eligible securities, for example to *S&P 500 equities*, or *EUR-denominated corporate investment grade bonds*.

There are also funds that invest in specialist asset classes. For example, real estate funds that invest in commercial real estate objects such as office or commercial space, or multi-tenant residential property, and there are aircraft and shipping funds and a few others investing in specialist asset classes. In many circumstances those funds are structured so that retail investors can invest, and sometimes there are tax advantages associated with this. Depending on the mandate, the funds can either invest in the underlying assets, or in loans backed by those assets, or in both.

Regulatory Angle. Mutual funds—at least those marketed to retail investors—are highly regulated (UCITS in the EU). The most important part is conduct regulations, that are meant to ensure that customers can make informed decisions and are treated fairly, which often includes a duty to have processes in place to avoid financially unsophisticated investors engaging in investments not suitable for them. There are also prudential rules, for example with respect to safekeeping of client assets, and to ensure that clients are financially and operationally protected in the event of the default of a manager, custodian, or any other actor in the service chain.

5.3.2 Passive Segment

Within the **passive** segment, there are a number of very different models, notably **index funds**, **exchange-traded funds (ETFs)**, and **investment certificates**.

Index funds are replicating the performance of an investible index, for example the S&P 500. By definition, an investible index represents a portfolio of securities whose composition is determined by a set of rules, eg *the 500 largest US companies.* Indices are rebalanced periodically, but not too often, to avoid spurious portfolio changes due to market volatility. In some cases, the rules fully determine the composition of the index, and in others there is a certain discretion that the rebalancing committee can apply when choosing which securities to include.

The number of **investible indices** has multiplied recently, to allow for passive investment strategies that still express some view, eg with respect to industry sectors or geographies. **Index provision** is a business in itself, and index providers receive a fee which is non-negligible when compared to the overall fee some passive managers receive. Therefore some ETF providers are vertically integrating into creating investible indices themselves in order to capture this part of the value chain.

Many index funds are organised as open-ended mutual funds, others as ETFs. From a customer point of view, the key difference is that ETFs are open-ended funds that can be purchased and sold on an exchange, and a clever mechanism ensures that—contrary to what happens with exchange-listed closed-ended funds—the prices are never too far away from the funds' net asset values.

ETFs can be either **cash ETFs** or **synthetic ETFs**. With the former, a purchase of ETF shares results in a commensurate purchase of index assets for the fund, and a sale results in a commensurate sale. With synthetic ETFs, the underlying portfolio is mostly meant to ensure that a certain amount of assets is available in the fund as collateral, but the actual fund performance is ensured via derivatives. This means that there is some external party—which may or may not be related to the company offering the ETF—undertakes to replace the collateral assets that *are* in the funds with the index assets that *should be* in the funds if need be. That does not make a difference when everything is going well, but if the derivatives counterparty defaults and the portfolio assets are illiquid—which they often are—this can lead to substantial losses by the time the collateral assets have been sold.

Investment certificates, finally, are exchange-listed securities whose payoff structure is linked to the performance of one or more financial indicators. Technically, it is a package of a bond and a derivative. Usually, no meaningful arm's-length secondary market exists, but issuers are prepared to purchase their certificate back at current fair value, minus a discount. A popular structure in the certificate space is a call option payoff with capped upside based on a major index like the S&P 500. In this case the certificate returns increase in line with the index returns, but there is a minimum repayment amount, and often a maximum also. A related product is **structured deposits**, which have a similar risk profile, but where the investment is not in form of a security, but in form of a deposit, and where the principal amount—but not interest—is covered by deposit insurance.

Regulatory Angle. The funds themselves will typically be covered by UCITS in the EU. To the extent that they are listed, MiFID also applies. Often those products are sold on an execution-only basis, in which case rules on providing investment advice to retail investors might not apply; however, rules regarding appropriateness of marketing still apply, especially for certificates that often provide a more complex risk than ETFs. Also, there are specific rules with respect to marketing in MiFID for firms who manufacture investment products in MiFID, which oblige them to ensure that the product is suitable for the target market, and that the marketing strategy is compatible with this. For structured deposits in the EU the DGSD applies. PRIIPR also applies, to the extent it is related to package retail products.

5.4 Other Products

There are a few other products in the asset management space that do not neatly fit into the above categories. The first one is **private banking**, which is a full-service banking relationship to wealthy customers, with a strong focus on managing their assets efficiently. In many cases the private banker even has a mandate to trade and invest on behalf of the customer, along the lines of the individual mandate established but without having to get every single trade confirmed, so it is a bona fide asset management relationship. Taking this relationship one step further is the **family office**, where a wealthy individual or group of individuals employ their own asset manager, who in this case often also deals with other aspects of the client's finances, eg settling their bills or managing a large asset transaction like the purchase of a property.

Regulatory Angle. Private banking is regulated like a regular banking relationship, with the exception that the clients are usually considered eligible for investments that are reserved for sophisticated investors. If the private banker has a discretionary mandate to invest the clients' assets the rules for fund managers also apply. Family offices are often unregulated as the asset managers are employees of the asset owner.

Also in this space is **life insurance**, because whilst fundamentally it is a risk-sharing insurance product, it has a strong savings and asset management character, as the individuals pay into the insurance contract throughout their life, with the intent of reaping the benefits in retirement. It is discussed in more detail in the section below.

5.5 Insurance

The **insurance** segment deals with the mutualisation of risk, meaning that a large number of individuals or companies who face similar risks agree to pool them.

Insurance relies on risks being not too highly correlated and not being subject to excessive amounts of private information on the side of the customers, therefore some risks are *insurable risks* and others are *uninsurable risks*.

Regulatory Angle. Insurance regulations tend to be highly local, to the extent that in the US insurance regulation is done on a state level, with only moderate coordination on the federal level. In the EU, prudential regulation of insurance companies is unified under the Solvency Directive. Insurance operations benefit from a regulatory passport across the EU, meaning they have both a right to establish subsidiaries and branches, and to serve customers directly. Whilst not strictly necessary, insurance to consumers is more likely to be provided through local entities; companies tend to be more comfortable doing cross-border business.

5.5.1 Property and Casualty Insurance

Property and casualty insurance deals with specific event risks. To give a few examples, in the retail market there is **home insurance**, which insures home owners or tenants against break-in and things like water damage etc, and there is **car insurance**, which deals with at least damage done to others as a consequence of the insured person driving a car, and possibly with damages to the insured person's car. In the professional space there are all kinds of indemnities, eg against malpractice, and in the company space those can insure themselves against a number of risks, eg fire on their premises. Smaller companies will usually only have access to off-the-shelf insurance contracts, but larger ones, as well as very wealthy individuals, might be able to negotiate highly personalised insurance contracts with the underwriters of specialist insurance syndicates.

> **Regulatory Angle.** Property & casualty insurance is the least critical insurance from a regulatory point of view as the quality of service is reasonably well observable based on actual settlement history. However, the regular consumer protection rules apply.

5.5.2 Health Insurance

The underlying aim of **health insurance** is to insure individuals against the cost associated with major illness. Most health insurance contracts also deal with more regular occurrences, eg annual check-ups, or recurrent doctor visits due to minor illnesses like colds, and therefore health insurance has a strong health management component. It also lowers the cost of treatment because insurance companies have a large purchasing power in the health market, and are therefore able to obtain substantially better prices than individuals seeking treatment.

> **Regulatory Angle.** Health insurance regulation differs widely by country, and it also depends strongly on what is provided by the state out of general taxation. Regulation tends to focus more on the social angle than on the market structure angle, as it is often desirable from an overall societal point of view that people with elevated risk and preconditions are being offered insurance rates that are subsidised by those with a lower risk. In a private or semi-private healthcare market this requires regulation that balances the risks between insurers, to avoid someone attracting all the good risks by offering very low rates.

5.5.3 Life Insurance

Life insurance products broadly cover two risks: first, the risk of dying too early, leaving one's dependents without sufficient funds to support themselves, and second, the risk of dying too late, and therefore outliving one's resources in retirement.

The first one is a straightforward insurance product: especially at the age where it matters most—beginning of career, family with young children—mortality is low, so the risk can be insured on an annual basis against a reasonably modest premium, with current premiums being in line with current pool pay-outs.

The second risk is more complex. Premiums received today relate to an insurable event many decades out, so there is an investment risk, and also there is very limited feedback early on if underwriting standards are inadequate. Also, the sums involved are very large: people pay into insurance contracts for up to four decades, to receive funds for a period of typically at least two decades. Multiplying this by the number of people who take out life insurance, it is clear that insurers must hold asset portfolios that are substantial on the scale of the overall economy to back those claims.

Regulatory Angle. Life insurance is an investment product, and an ultra-long-term investment product at that, and it is therefore highly regulated. Given the impact the failure of a life company has on the local population, local regulators tend to be keen to supervise insurers who provide such insurance, even if in the EU they are passporting their services in from another Member State.

5.5.4 Reinsurance

Reinsurance is the insurer's insurance, ie insurance companies protecting themselves against the overall amount of claims they have to pay out becoming too high. This allows insurers to take on risks that would not normally be insurable. For example, because of distribution advantages and regulations many insurance companies' presences are local, eg at a country level, or even at state level in the US. Some claims exhibit a high local correlation, eg damages to property by weather events. Local insurers on their own cannot insure those because of the correlation of losses. However, in the presence of reinsurance, an insurer can lay off the extreme part of the risk to a reinsurer who can in turn pool it over a much larger region, and those risks therefore become insurable.

Regulatory Angle. Reinsurance is a very small market, with only a few dozen important players, who tend to follow an unwritten code of honour in their business. Local insurance regulations apply, but reinsurance is a global market, and many of the reinsurers do their business from a few light-touch locations.

5.6 Financial Advisory

There are a number of retail advisory businesses in the financial services advisory space:

- general investment advice
- pension advice
- tax planning advice
- insurance advice
- mortgage advice.

The first three areas deal with investments, and how to best match investments with an investor's personal situation, expectations, and risk tolerance, taking into account external constraints such as tax and pension legislation. The fourth area can deal either with life insurance—in which case there is a strong investment component—or with risk insurance, in which case it is more about identifying and addressing the risks an individual is facing. The final one is not about investing but about borrowing, notably about getting the most suitable mortgage for the purchase of a property.

A key distinction in all of those segments is between **captive advisors**, also referred to as **tied agents**, who only offer products of the company they represent and who often do not charge a fee, but receive a commission on all contracts they bring in, and **independent advisors**, who are free to offer a wide range of products and services, and who can either be remunerated on a fee basis or a commission basis. In many cases those *advisors* are able to execute or at least facilitate the contracts on which they advise, and in the independent space they are then often referred to as **brokers**. For example, **mortgage brokers**, who are an example of the originators introduced in the section on retail lending, will have access to information about a large number of mortgage offerings from different providers and will assist in a customer's mortgage application process, and **insurance brokers** can execute insurance contracts on the spot. Some **equity brokers** could also be counted in this segment, notably if they provide their clients with research, and if they are able to give investment recommendations.

Finally one should mention **private banking** in this segment, which is described in the asset management section, but which also has a strong advisory offering for customers who do not want to hand over their investment decision to a third party. Often private banking clients also have access to investment research.

Regulatory Angle. Retail advisors are highly regulated, both under general consumer protection rules and more segment-specific rules. For example, the provision of investment advice, and the relationship between investment firms selling those investments on one hand, and tied or independent advisors on the other hand, is regulated under MiFID in the EU, and in other jurisdictions similar rules apply. The other areas are regulated by sector-specific local regulation, which in some cases involves regulation by self-regulatory bodies. In many cases, the classic advisory business model was nominally free for the customer and advisors received commissions from the providers for successful contract closures. In many jurisdictions—notably the EU since MiFID 2—this is no longer allowed because of the skewed incentives it produces.

CHAPTER 6

Wholesale Financial Services Products

I n the previous chapter we have discussed the products in the financial services sector that are mostly targeted at individuals, and at small to medium-sized companies. Here we will discuss the products that remain, and that are targeted at wholesale players in the market. Those products fall into the following categories (see also Figure 6.1):

1. wholesale credit
2. wholesale and specialist asset management
3. primary markets and origination
4. sales, trading, brokerage, and exchanges
5. settlement, custody, and ancillary services
6. advisory and research.

6.1 Wholesale Credit

6.1.1 Large Corporate Credit

The large corporate credit segment serves large corporations, often multinationals that have a presence in multiple jurisdictions. Large corporates are offered the same products as mid-market companies, but in a bigger size. Large corporates in particular tend to engage in more derivative activities, therefore derivatives lines become more important.

Also, the loan documentation becomes more complex: a large corporation consists of a group of companies, and ultimately it is loan companies entering into agreements, not the corporations who themselves do not have a legal identity. It is therefore important to consider which group company

FIGURE 6.1   Classifying Financial Services by Product (Wholesale)

is the actual borrower, which group companies guarantee it, whether there are specific assets that can be pledged, what kind of covenants—like limits on additional borrowing—should be attached to the loan, and which companies should those covenants relate to.

Because of size reasons, single banks are often reluctant or not able to deal with all the financing needs of large corporations who therefore have multiple banking relationships. In principle, corporations could enter into independent loan agreements with each of their banks, but this is impractical, and it can easily violate loan covenants. Instead, banks enter into **syndicated loan** agreements, where a syndicate of banks lends to the company on the basis of a single loan documentation. Syndicated loans are *fungible*, ie they are all treated equally in all respects, and they are *tradeable*, meaning banks can buy and sell them on the secondary market.

Also, large corporates often engage in derivatives business, and in order to do so they need **derivatives lines**. In the section on derivatives I discuss that in many cases derivatives transactions need to be subject to a margining agreement, meaning that whenever, because of market moves, the replacement value of a contract changes, the person whose side gained in value gets cash or other collateral from the side that lost, so that at any given point in time the replacement value of the derivative net of collateral held is zero for both sides. For corporates, there is often no margining agreement in place as their treasuries are not operationally set up to service them. So if a derivatives contract goes against a corporate, one could see that as the corporate 'owing' the margin payment to the counterparty, but being allowed to defer the payment until the maturity date of the derivative contract. In a nutshell, the right to defer margin payment until the maturity is a derivative credit line, and it is being 'drawn' whenever the value of the derivative moves against the corporate. Those lines have no explicit fees associated with them—they are priced into the cost of the derivative itself.

Large corporates can also issue **bonds**, ie loans in security format that are sold directly to the market; I will discuss bonds in the *primary issuance* section below.

Regulatory Angle. As discussed in the section on small corporate credit, in many jurisdictions corporate lending without taking deposits is not or only very lightly regulated. So in principle, very lightly regulated companies could operate in this market. However, because of the size of the loans involved, this area is in practice mostly covered by banks, and therefore prudential regulations apply (Basel internationally; CRD in the EU). To the extent that the loans are in a securities or quasi-securities format, or that they relate to derivatives business, markets regulations apply (MiFID in the EU).

6.1.2 Real Estate, Project and Other Asset Finance

Real estate and infrastructure projects like power stations, toll roads etc. offer very predictable returns and are therefore financed with debt. Lending in this space is known as **real estate lending** or **infrastructure lending** if it relates to the finished object, and as **construction finance** or **project finance** if it relates to the object being under construction.

The loans relating to the finished objects tend to be regular loans, except that they are *non-recourse*, ie if a sponsor has borrowed against multiple objects, those are all financed independently, and financial distress in one of them does not lead to a claim on the other objects of the sponsor. This is an important feature because it allows the objects to be sold independently without having to rearrange the financing due to a change in risk structure. Real estate loans are also often *balloon* or even *bullet* loans because the maturity of the financing is shorter than the end of the economic life of the object, so refinancing is envisaged, but there is a refinancing risk.

When objects are not finished, loan agreements are more complex as the funds are being released subject to milestones being reached. In the event of major breaches the lender can step in, take over the object and arrange for it to either be finished or to be sold to another sponsor.

As in the retails space discussed previously, there are a number of different lending models here: loans can be extended by banks and they can hold those loans on balance sheet; or they can be originated by banks or by non-bank originators and sold to financial investors, typically either a fund or fund-like investment vehicle, or into a securitisation structure.

Regulatory Angle. If those loans are held by banks the usual bank prudential regulations apply (CRD in the EU) and there are in particular capital and liquidity requirements. Funds and securitisation vehicles face little regulatory scrutiny with respect to lending, but as usual in the funds space, the set of regulations appropriate to the fund or securitisation structure applies (AIFMD or UCITS in the EU; also MiFID if they are exchange-traded). Note also the securitisation retention requirements in this case (see section on securitisation).

6.2 Wholesale and Specialist Asset Management

This segment covers the following segments:

- **Hedge funds** or **Alternative investments.** 'Alternative investment funds' is a catch-all name for all fund structures that are not within the mainstream investment universe accessible for retail investor, for example because they employ leverage or derivatives.
- **Private Equity.** Private equity funds invest in large, mature businesses, and they employ significant leverage to achieve higher returns. Often there is a turn-around angle to a private equity investment, ie they purchase loss-making companies and in addition to employing financial engineering to improve the returns they are attempting to improve operational efficiency.
- **Venture Capital.** Venture capital funds invest in start-up businesses, often, but by no means always, in the technology space. Within this segment there are subsegments focusing on **early-stage** and **late-stage** investments, and there are **angels**, who are individuals focusing on pre-VC investing.

The most common structure in the VC and PE space is that of a closed-ended fund with a finite horizon, and little to no secondary market liquidity.

Investments are made with a certain horizon in mind, ie there is a plan—but no guarantee—to liquidate the investments within this period, and to return the proceeds to the investors. Investors who want to leave the fund early are sometimes able to sell their share to others, but this is not guaranteed and will usually be at a steep discount to net asset value. Because of the long lead time of the fund's deals, investments are often made in form of a *commitment*, ie a binding agreement to provide cash once the fund manager demands it. This avoids the drag that large low-yielding cash balances have on a fund-manager's reported returns.

In the alternatives space the structures are more varied, but typically an open-ended approach similar to retail funds is applied, with a notice period in line with the liquidity of the assets, and a possibility to gate the fund—ie temporarily close it for redemptions—in times of market distress.

Whilst I have placed this is in the wholesale segment—ie targeted at institutional investors like insurance companies and pension funds—it is important to mention that those products are often also offered to eligible high net worth (HNW) private investors, typically in a slightly different legal structure or at least in a different vehicle. Also important are **Funds-of-Funds (FoFs)**, which are investment vehicles who invest into other investment fund structures, ie they represent a typically diversified portfolio investment into multiple underlying funds.

Regulatory Angle. All those areas are relatively lightly regulated, and a lot of the regulation that happens in this space happens on the local level. In the EU, AIFMD applies, albeit only at the manager level, and there are exemptions when dealing with sophisticated and/or professional clients. Within AIFMD there are some specific regulations for private equity funds that are of a macro-prudential type, in that regulators want to ensure that private equity activity does not negatively impact the underlying markets, and there are also some safeguards for the employees in the impacted firms in place.

6.3 Primary Markets and Origination

In the **primary markets** and **origination** segment the providers' role is to intermediate between providers of financing, and the companies that need financing. The most important primary markets by product area are:

- equity capital markets (ECM)
- debt capital markets (DCM)
- syndicated loans
- securitisation.

Syndicated loans have already been discussed in the corporate lending section, and on top of the lending-product aspect they have an origination-product aspect and a trading-product aspect.

6.3.1 ECM, DCM, and Syndicated Loans

Equity capital markets are about selling equity securities, ie company shares. This includes **initial public offerings (IPOs)**, when a company is listed on a stock exchange for the first time, and **secondary offerings**, where large blocks of additional shares are being sold in the market. Note that secondary offerings should not be confused with the secondary market which covers the transactions in already-issued securities held by market participants. Another product in that space is the **rights issue**, where existing shareholders are given for free the right, but not the obligation, to purchase additional shares at a discount to where they are currently trading. The greater the discount, the more likely that those rights are taken up. Usually those rights are tradeable, which allows shareholders who don't want to or can't put up additional money not to lose the value associated with those rights, and which increases the uptake.

Debt capital markets are about selling debt securities. They are similar to ECM, but the services provided are more technical. For example, only a group holding company issues equity, but debt can be issued from any company in a group. Then there is the question of what the maturity of the debt should be, whether the coupon should be fixed or floating and at which level it should be set, what covenants should be included, if and where the debt security should be listed and so on. There is also the question of seniority: most debt is **senior debt**, ie high up in the pecking order of creditors in the event of default. There is also **subordinated debt** and **mezzanine debt**, which is lower in the pecking order, and therefore has a higher coupon.

Syndicated loan origination is, as far as the customers are concerned, very similar to DCM, even though it is usually in the corporate lending department as originators often retain some of the originated loans on their own balance sheet.

Regulatory Angle. For large-cap equities and their debt, the players in this market are mostly the large investment banks, and the universal banks with an investment banking franchise. In the past they might have been regulated as an investment firm—or the US equivalent thereof, a broker/dealer—but since the crisis those players have started appreciating the value of having access to central bank liquidity, and therefore have chosen to obtain banking licences. In the mid-cap market there are a number of different regulatory models that are possible; in many cases those business models are anchored in their respective local jurisdiction. In the EU this would typically be one of the different models that fall under the investment firm umbrella that is defined in MiFID.

6.3.2 Securitisation

The key defining characteristics of **securitisations** is that they represent an asset pool, and the ownership of the asset pool is divided into horizontal tranches where losses are distributed in increasing order of seniority. The most senior tranche is akin to senior debt, the most junior one to equity, and the ones in-between to various levels of subordinated or mezzanine debt.

I want to give a simple example of a three-tranche securitisation: one **equity tranche**, one **mezzanine tranche**, and one **senior tranche**. Let's assume the overall pool is $100m, and the tranche sizes are $80m, $15m, and $5m respectively. When the assets in the pool repay, the first $80m goes to the senior tranche, the subsequent $15m to the mezzanine tranche, and everything else to the equity tranche. Or, to put it the other way around: the first $5m of losses are borne by the equity tranche, which also will benefit from all the gains made. The next $15m of losses are borne by the mezzanine tranche, and only if mezzanine and equity are fully wiped out, the senior tranche starts being eaten into. The expected return on those tranches will be commensurate to their risk, so the senior tranche will earn the risk-free rate plus a small premium, the mezzanine tranche a few percentage points more, and the equity returns are typically in the 5–15% per annum range.

Depending on the underlying assets in the pool, securitisations are referred to by different names:

- the term **ABS** (asset-backed security) is a generic term that is used for all type of securities mentioned below, and in particular for those that are based on asset classes not mentioned there (eg *card ABS* for credit card receivables)
- a **CDO** (collateralised debt obligation) is based on all kinds of debt, for example bonds or loans, usually investment grade; it is a generic term in this category
- a **CLO** (collateralised loan obligation) is based on loans, typically high-risk leveraged loans that are related to private equity deals

- a **CBO** (collateralised bond obligation) is based on bonds, often high-risk junk bonds, also related to private equity deals
- a **REMIC** (real estate mortgage investment conduit) is a term used in the US for securitisations based on real estate loans; in Europe the terms **RMBS** (retail mortgage-backed security) for loans to individuals and **CMBS** (commercial mortgage-backed security) for loans in relation to commercial real estate objects are more common.

The asset pools underlying securitisations can either be **static**, meaning asset proceeds are returned to investors as soon as the asset repays or is liquidated, or **revolving**, meaning asset repayments during the reinvestment period are reinvested into fresh assets. Even revolving deals turn static eventually after the reinvestment period is over.

Depending on the asset class, deals are either meant to finance the loan production of an originator—typically in the RMBS/CMBS/card space—in which case the originator usually retains the high-risk/high-return equity tranche, or they are meant to produce high returns for the investors in the equity tranche—typically for CLO/CBO—in which case the whole deal is managed by an asset manager who actively purchases the assets in the market.

Regulatory Angle. Those are securities, so normal securities law applies. They are not usually offered to retail investors, in which case often more simplified rules apply. To the extent that they are listed on an exchange—which they usually are, even if they don't trade— the market regulations apply (MiFID in the EU). To the extent they are rated—which, again, typically they are—the regulations on rating agencies are important (RAR in the EU). Depending on the underlying asset class, there might also be originator risk retention requirements (in the EU those are implemented via requirements on investors via CRD4-CRR for banks and investment firms, AIFMD for fund managers, and SolvencyD for insurers).

6.4 Sales, Trading, Brokerage, and Exchanges

In this segment there are three large sub-segments

- sales and trading in investment banks and broker/dealers
- brokerage
- exchanges.

The last two cover both wholesale and retail markets, albeit with different product offerings in the case of the brokerage segment, and the first one is a wholesale product only.

6.4.1 Sales and Trading

The **sales and trading** segment covers the business of investment banks and broker dealers where they trade with customers, or among each other. At its base this is an intermediation business, and the dealers mostly take positions to facilitate client business. For example, if a client wants to sell an illiquid bond, chances are that no buyer can be found immediately, and a dealer taking it on its own books with a view to selling it later provides a service by offering liquidity to the market. In this case the dealer is often referred to as a market maker, ie a market participant who usually offers two-way prices—bid and offer—at a reasonable spread (the difference between bid and offer) and in a reasonable volume.

At the other end of the spectrum there is the pure proprietary trading business where dealers go out into the market to actively purchase assets that they believe are undervalued. However, this latter is nowadays strongly discouraged by regulators, so dealing tends to happen more towards the client-driven end of the spectrum. There are, however, non-bank dealers that have somewhat stepped into that breach, notably high-frequency trading (HFT) funds, who are willing to buy or sell depending on the flows they see on the various markets they cover.

One way to categorise the dealing activities is by legal format of the asset traded, notably:

• securities and syndicated loans
• foreign exchange
• derivatives and repo.

The first one deals with assets that are traded as standardised packages, and whilst in the era of electronic share certificates this is no longer really the case, it often helps to think of those assets as paper-based share certificates that are physically traded. Foreign exchange, the second one, used to have the peculiarity that dealers would promise to exchange cash against cash. For example, a dealer selling GBP vs USD would make a GBP transfer into a UK bank account, and receive a USD transfer into a US bank account. More recently, however, a large majority of the forex trading is being cleared, and is therefore not much different from securities trading, other than that it is traded 24 hours a day out of the different financial centres around the world.

Derivatives are contracts to exchange cash flows based on the value of an underlying tradeable asset, like for example call options which correspond to the right, but not the obligation, of purchasing a specific asset at a specific price at a specific date in the future. Repurchase agreements (aka repos) are agreements to sell a security and purchase it back at a later date, or economically equivalent secured lending agreements. Both derivatives and repos are discussed in more detail below.

Regulatory Angle. I have already discussed the bulge bracket investment banks in the section on primary issuance, and the same observations hold here, in that in this sector we find the large investment banks or universal banks with investment banking franchise, and they are usually regulated as banks because they require access to central bank liquidity. This means that they are regulated as banks (CRD in the EU), so they have minimum capital requirements based on, inter alia, the amount of trading and trading counterparty risk they are taking, and how risky their operations are. To the extent that smaller firms operate in that market, they might be regulated as investment firms (MiFID for EU).

Securities trading

The **securities trading** segment within the banks and broker dealers is focused on securities that are not liquidly traded on exchanges, and where therefore the balance sheet provided by the dealer makes a difference. A dealer adds value where the requested transaction size is larger than what the liquidity on the exchange can provide. So for illiquid securities, customers might need to go through a dealer for deals of any size; for liquid securities, going through a dealer might only be necessary for very large **block trades**, but even that is today often not necessary because of the existence of the dark pools discussed together with the exchanges below.

Major equities mostly trade on exchanges, which leaves the dealer market for secondary equities and bonds, where 'bonds' includes securities issued by companies and governments as well as securitisation tranches. Whilst they are not technically securities, one should also include the trading of **syndicated loans**, ie loans that are documented in way that they can be traded in smaller pieces.

Regulatory Angle. In addition to the aforementioned rules, the securities law of the jurisdiction is important here. For example, this means that it must be ensured that no trades are based on material non-private information (MNPI). As investment banks also engage in advisory work, this means that there must be organisational Chinese walls in place, separating the private side from the public side. Also, to not dissipate liquidity, some securities must be traded on exchanges—except for very large trades—or on other approved trading venues, and trades must be reported to trade repositories (MiFID in the EU).

Derivatives trading

Derivatives are contracts to exchange cash flows based on the value of one ore more underlying tradeable assets. Typical underlyings are forex, equities, and interest rates. For example, in an interest rate swap one counterparty might contract to pay 1%, times the swap notional of say $100m, and receive a floating rate, eg LIBOR, times the same notional in return, over a period of, say, 3 years. To give another example, an **option** is the right, but not the obligation, to buy an asset, eg a share, at a specific date and a specific 'strike' price. There are also **credit derivatives**, which are more like an insurance contract: the buyer pays a periodic premium, and will in return be compensated for credit losses should the reference name default.

Derivatives can either be **exchange-traded** or traded **OTC** (over the counter), ie directly with a dealing desk. They can also be **cleared** or **bilateral**, the former meaning that the derivative contract is *novated* with a central clearing counterparty (CCP) whilst in a bilateral contract the original counterparties remain the contracting parties. Derivatives can also be **margined** or **not margined**, the former meaning that every change in value leads to a compensation transfer of cash collateral. See the section on clearing below for a more detailed explanation of novation and margin payments.

It is important to understand that margined derivatives can be very different products to unmargined ones. As an example, consider a corporate issuing a floating rate bond—because this is what some investors like to invest in—and swapping it into fixed—because the corporate likes to fix their interest payments in advance. If the bond is long then its present value is quite sensitive to changes in rates. For the sake of argument, if it is a 10-year bond and rates change by 1%, then the value of the bond changes by almost 10%—it is a bit less because of the effects of discounting. Say it is a $100m bond; if the movement is going the wrong way, the corporate would have to post $10m in cash as collateral. In order to be able to do this, the corporate would have to keep a significant amount of the $100m raised as cash, which defeats the purpose of raising the money in the first place. This is why dealers offering unmargined derivatives to corporates—ie providing derivative credit lines as discussed in the section on wholesale lending—is an important product line.

Regulatory Angle. For derivatives there are numerous additional requirements: they must be cleared with a CCP, reported to a trade repository, and in some cases—for highly standardised products where it is important not to dissipate liquidity—they must even be traded on an exchange or another authorised trading venue (MiFID, EMIR in the EU). The market risk of derivatives attracts a capital requirement under prudential regulations (CRD in the EU). Even hedged positions that have no market risk attract a counterparty credit charge, covering the risk that a derivative counterparty might default. This charge strongly depends on the margining in place, and is highest if the counterparty is a corporate that has been granted a derivative line.

Repo and securities lending

A special segment of the securities trading market is the repo market, where *repo* is short for 'repurchase agreements'. Technically, a **repo** is the sale of a security with an agreement to buy it back at a fixed price at a specified later date, the date being typically only a few days in the future. The opposite transaction is referred to as a **reverse repo**. Economically this can be seen as a **secured lending transaction**: the repo side receives cash and hands over the security as guarantee. At the end of the transaction it returns the cash plus interest, and gets the security back. Seen this way, the purpose is often to finance a trading or investment portfolio: the repo side would like to take economic ownership of the asset, but does not want to or can't put up the financing to do so.

Alternatively, a repo transaction can be seen as a **securities lending** transaction: the reverse repo side wants to obtain a specific security, typically to sell it, with the view to purchasing it back later at a lower price— a process also being referred to as *short selling*. They hand over cash as a guarantee that they'll return the security. Note that depending on jurisdiction and underlying asset, legally true-sale repo transactions might be documented as secured lending transactions and vice versa.

Regulatory Angle. In order to significantly engage in the repo trading market, a dealer needs central bank access, and therefore is usually regulated as a bank (CRD in the EU). A key issue specific to the repo market is that repos use a lot of balance sheet for very low-risk items. This means that if a bank has a big repo book when compared to its other assets, the constraint imposed by the leverage ratio— which does not take into account riskiness—starts to bite.

6.4.2 Brokerage

As opposed to **dealers** who can take positions for their own account, **brokers** only intermediate between counterparties. Brokers tend to be highly specialised both along customer and the product dimensions. Traditionally, the broking business used to be based on **voice brokerages**, where customers would phone in with their orders, or brokers would actively phone their customers with trading suggestions. For cost-efficiency reasons, in the retail space this has now mostly moved to **online brokerages**, and in the wholesale space there are a number of dedicated electronic systems in place.

Retail brokerages mostly provide an interface for retail customers to deal on an exchange, or sometimes other trading venues. Whilst the most important type of securities covered here are equities, brokerages often allow the buying and selling of any type of security listed on the exchanges they cover, notably *bonds* and *investment certificates*. Most brokerages cover multiple exchanges, albeit often only exchanges in the country where they are based, meaning that only locally listed securities can be traded. Retail brokers usually offer a number of ancillary services, for example safe-keeping and reporting, and sometimes financing.

In the wholesale markets, brokers not only serve to connect end-customers with dealers, but there are also **inter-dealer brokers** (IDBs) that connect dealers to each other. In some markets that are not covered by exchanges—for example the foreign exchange market—brokers run quasi-exchanges for those asset classes, typically electronically. Also, more complex products, eg complex derivatives, are often intermediated through a broker rather than by dealing desks calling up each other directly. In the wholesale market, brokers provide few ancillary services—once the clients are introduced to each other those clients execute the deal directly between themselves.

I want to briefly mention **prime brokerages** here, which are not really brokerages, but rather a bundle of ancillary brokerage services—eg financing and reporting—offered by investment banks to hedge funds that transact with their dealing desks.

Regulatory Angle. Brokers are generally regulated as investment firms (MiFID in the EU), and, depending on clients, they are subject to things like best-execution rules. Retail brokers, unless they are specifically acting on an execution-only basis, also have fiduciary duties with respect to their clients, and must, for example, ensure that the investments are suitable. There are also best-execution rules in place, meaning that if there are multiple ways to execute a transaction the broker must choose the cheapest one, considering the purchase price plus all applicable charges and fees.

6.4.3 Exchanges

Exchanges are organised market places for securities or derivatives. Their role is to match buyers and sellers, up to the point where they agree on a transaction at a given price. There is no negotiation involved, and all derivatives contracts are standardised. Once a transaction is agreed, the involvement of the exchange is finished, and a *clearing house* takes over to ensure the trade is settled (see below).

Depending on the exchange and the security or derivative in question, there are a number of different ways how exchanges can organise the market-place. The simplest way is *continuous trading*, where buyers and seller continuously submit their orders, and those orders are matched whenever a trade is possible. For example, a buyer might submit a limit order to buy at $101 or less, and a seller one to sell at $100 or more. Those orders can be matched, eg by splitting the difference and executing the transaction at $100.50. Both buyers and seller can leave *market orders* as well, which will be matched with the best available order on the other side. For illiquid securities, this can on occasion be very far away from where the person leaving the order expected it to be.

Continuous trading works best if the securities are highly liquid, so that there are at any given point in time sufficient sellers and buyers available. In particular, market orders are dangerous if there are not enough limit orders around to bracket the possible price range, as someone might just opportunistically jump in at a price very unfavourable for the person who had left the market order earlier. For less-liquid securities, an alternative is periodic *auctions*, eg at the beginning and/or end of the business day. Those compress the daily liquidity into a much smaller time frame, leading to a more reliable price recovery, albeit at the expense of immediacy. Some exchanges also require **market makers**—privileged dealers on this exchange—to always quote two-way prices in a reasonable volume, typically with an exception in times of market turbulence. This improves liquidity on the exchange, but dealers have to step in and take on the risk in the event of an imbalanced market. Given the tightening of capital requirements this business has become much less attractive to banks who used to be a major player in this area.

There is an interesting twist with **derivatives exchanges**. When trading bond futures—contracts to buy or sell bonds at a given point in the future—they are typically defined by the *tenor* of the bonds in question, eg '5 years'. However, for technical and legal reasons, the derivative contracts are defined by the bond maturity, eg '2022'. So after a year, a 5-year contract becomes a 4-year contract and so on. To constantly offer a 5-year contract, periodically a new contract with the desired maturity date is offered on the exchange. In practice the *front contract* attracts by far the largest liquidity, and many investors *roll* their contracts, meaning that they at the same time take a position in the front future and cancel their previous one. Futures contracts are then often the basis for other derivatives contracts, for example calls that give the option to buy that future at a fixed strike, and puts that give the right to sell it.

The same dynamics happen on the commodity futures markets, where contracts are for forward delivery of, say, oil of a certain quality at a certain location. Those contracts almost always get closed out before the final maturity date, as few players want to deal with the actual physical delivery of the commodity.

Lastly, there are **multilateral trading facilities** (MTFs), which are similar to exchanges, but typically smaller in scope, and not universally accessible. Sometimes they have obtained certain waivers and are therefore not subject to the same reporting requirements, in which case they are usually referred to as **dark pools**. Specifically, on an exchange all trades are published with a very short delay. Dark pools can report with a more significant delay, allowing, for example, the wind-down of large positions more easily. Broker/dealers, who run most of the dark pools, are subject to a best-execution rule, implying that they can only route trades to the dark pool if it offers an execution better than the best price available for this volume on an exchange.

Regulatory Angle. Exchanges—and to some extent other trading venues—are both highly regulated, and also a source of regulations in terms of the listing requirements that they impose on the securities they list. In terms of regulation, exchanges must be highly transparent with respect to the trades that are executed on exchange, and they must provide non-discriminatory access to their services based on objective criteria. For other venues this holds, albeit in a slightly weaker form. Exchanges are in some instances granted a monopoly in the sense that if a security is listed on an exchange then it might not be allowed to trade it off exchange. In the EU, the key regulation governing exchanges is MiFID. Related is EMIR, which deals with CCPs and information repositories that are discussed in the next section.

6.5 Settlement, Custody, and Ancillary Services

6.5.1 Clearing and Settlement

As discussed above, the purpose of exchanges and other trading facilities is to match buyers and sellers of securities or derivatives. An issue that arises is that the two sides of the deal don't know who their respective counterparty is before they commit to a deal, and they therefore cannot assess whether they trust their counterparty to deliver on their side of the bargain. To alleviate this issue, those trades are cleared in the associated **clearing house**, also referred to as central counterparty or CCP, that guarantees both parties' respective performance to each other.

Securities clearing and novation

The guarantee provided by a clearing house involves a process called **novation**, where the clearing house inserts itself between the two counterparties. For example, if A commits to sell a security to B for a certain price, then after novation A will sell the security to the clearing house, and the clearing house will sell the security to B, both transactions happening at the same price. Importantly, even if A or B defaults, the clearing house is still responsible to deliver on the other side of the deal.

In practice, a securities clearing house typically has a number of **clearing members**—who often jointly own the clearing house—through which all transactions are processed. All clearing members have sufficient collateral deposited with the clearing house that if they default on their obligation, that collateral is enough to indemnify the clearing house against any losses incurred. End-customers do not deal with the clearing house directly, but they go through a clearing member of their choice. To look at the process in detail, assume customer A goes through clearing member CMA, and customer B through CMB. If A does not deliver on its side of the trade, CMA is still on the hook as far as the clearing house is concerned, and in the unlikely event that CMA defaults, the clearing house can use the collateral CMA posted to ensure delivery to CMB and eventually B. So here CMA and CMB take the risk that their respective customers default, and it is up to them to ensure that that risk is at commercially acceptable levels, and commensurate with the fees they earn.

Regulatory Angle. For securities clearing houses the same regulations as for derivatives clearing houses apply, except that there is not usually a requirement to post a variation margin as the clearing period is only a few days. See the next section on derivatives CCPs for details.

Derivatives clearing, novation, and margining

In principle, **derivatives clearing** and **derivatives novation** is the same concept as in the corresponding securities markets. This means that the clearing house, also referred to as **central counterparty (CCP)**, steps between the two contracting parties. However, the key difference is that whilst a securities clearing operation only lasts for a very short period of time—a few days at most—derivatives need to be intermediated for the whole duration of the underlying contract, for example for 10 years for a 10-year swap. The purpose of this novation is to build a firewall between the derivatives counterparties so that a default of one player can no longer cascade through the entire market—as long as the clearing house is safe, the market is fully insulated.

The key mechanism by which a CCP is kept safe is using margin payments, more precisely variation margins and initial margins. I have already discussed variation margin payments before, in the discussion of derivative credit lines, but I'll repeat it here for completeness: any derivative contract has a current fair value. For example, the right to buy an asset now that is currently worth $110 at a price of $100 has an intrinsic value of $10. If the right is to buy the asset not now but in the future, then this has to be adjusted for the option value, and for interest rates, but ultimately this option will have a present value that can be calculated. Margining means that the counterparty for whom the net present value is negative—ie that in all likelihood owes money in the future—must post cash or other collateral with the other counterparty so that at any given point in time, the present value of the derivative and the present value of the collateral exchanged cancel each other out. Variation margin is adjusted as needed, and apart from a delay in posting margin, and possibly valuation issues post margin payments, the credit risk of either side is zero.

Derivatives CCPs are privileged counterparties in the sense that they are meant to be kept particularly safe. So on top of the variation margin that two regular counterparties would exchange, there is also the so-called 'initial margin', which protects the CCP against losses in the period between a change in market values and when it receives the collateral, and against valuation errors. This makes a difference for the contracting counterparties: if, say, a contract would previously be in the money by $50m, then one counterparty would have posted $50m in collateral, and the other one would have received it, so net/net the collateral requirement goes away. If a clearing house is involved, there is an initial margin of, say, $10m for each side. This means that now net one side must post $60m in collateral whilst the other one receives only $40m. The net overall collateral requirement of the two counterparties together is therefore $20m, which is exactly the amount in initial margin required by the CCPs.

Regulatory Angle. The use of derivative CCPs for derivatives traded in the OTC (ie, non-exchange-traded) market has become mandatory after the crisis, giving a tremendous boost to something that was prior to that a marginal business. They are subject to relatively uniform standards, which in the case of the EU are mostly within EMIR. They are subject to some conduct and market structure regulation—mostly about giving access on a non-discriminatory basis—but the main regulatory concern here is prudential: CCPs are the proverbial basket in which the regulator chose to collect all those previously dispersed eggs, so now it really has to watch this basket. If any one of the big CCPs were to go down this, at least in the short term, could impact the market as much as the Lehman default did.

Ultimately the centre of the regulatory concern is about the amount of margin held, in that at every given point in time it should be sufficient to cover potential losses in the event of of counterparty default. This is a complex problem: first, it requires adequate modelling of market risks, in particular correlations during times of distress, which is notoriously difficult. Second, it is an IT and operations problem: not only must the IT systems be able to handle all daily transactions in a timely intra-day manner, they also must be able to perform intra-day revaluations, possibly very quickly in the event of large market moves. Then the systems must be able to communicate margin requirements to all impacted counterparties very quickly, reconcile the margin payments received with those requested, and in turn handle margin payments to the customer to whom they are owed by the CCP. Finally, if margin payments have not come in at the cut-off time, the systems must ensure that the affected contracts of the offending counterparty are terminated and replaced by equivalent ones before markets can move so much as to completely deplete the margins. Having systems and processes in place that are able to do that is a tremendously complex task, and arguably convincing the regulators that all technical and operational risk have been taken care of is even more difficult.

6.5.2 Trade Repositories and Other Reporting Entities

Trade repositories are information service providers that collect trade information about all reportable derivatives trades—which includes all trades that are done on an exchange and/or cleared with a CCP—and make it publicly available in an aggregate format, and to the regulators with trade level granularity if requested. Fundamentally, this is not a complex task, but the data volume is tremendous, and the data is not always clean. In particular, currently every trade is reported twice, and data reconciliation is often a difficult and labour-intensive task because of slight differences in the reported fields that need to be manually adjusted.

There are also a number of regulatorily-required reporting services providers, notably **approved publication arrangements (APAs)**, who publish trade reports on behalf of investment firms, **approved reporting mechanisms (ARMs)**, who report details of transactions to regulators or ESMA on behalf of investment firms, and **consolidated tape providers (CTPs)**, who collect trade reports from various venues and consolidate them into a continuous electronic live data stream.

Regulatory Angle. Trade repositories in the EU are regulated under EMIR. Interestingly, they are not regulated locally, but directly by ESMA. They are less critical than CCPs in the case of market distress. Nevertheless, to the extent that regulators require adequate information due to periods of market turbulence, repositories must be able to both process new trade information and create up-to-date reports in a timely manner. APAs, ARMs, and CTPs are in the EU described and regulated under MiFID.

6.5.3 Custodians and Registrars

Historically, securities were physical pieces of paper, and trading securities involved exchanging those pieces of paper against the agreed-upon amount of cash. This, by the way, explains why settlement was, and for historical reasons often still is, a few days after the trade happened: the seller had to go back to his safe deposit box, retrieve the securities certificate and physically and safely transport it to the place of settlement.

This arrangement was rather cumbersome—and dangerous, because in transit papers could be stolen, destroyed, or lost—and markets developed a better solution: **custody**. Custodians can either offer **individual safe deposit** or **collective safe deposit**. In the former, the securities that belong to a given client are kept physically separated. In the latter, all securities belonging to the custodian's clients are kept in one big pile in the safe, and ownership is established using a ledger run by the custodian. The difference between the two deposit types becomes important if the custodian defaults and securities are missing, either because of operational issues at the custodian, or due to counterparty default when securities are lent to third parties.

When a security is traded and both counterparties are using the same custodian, changing ownership of the security is as easy as changing a ledger entry in the case of collective deposits, or moving a certificate from one package into another in the case of individual deposits. If the counterparties use different custodians it is up to the custodians to arrange for the handover of the certificates, which still is significantly more efficient and safer than having the counterparties arranging the exchange themselves, especially if the security is liquidly traded and only the net exchange of security certificates has to take place.

Most securities give the owner the right to recurrent payments, either dividends or coupons. Historically those were literally coupons that needed to be *clipped* off the corresponding certificate and that would allow whoever could present it to collect the payment. Again, custodians would usually take care of this, ie they would physically detach all the coupons and credit the owners' accounts with the cash they received. Finally, sometimes issuers need to get in touch with the owners of the securities they issued. They'd do that through the financial press, but, again, custodians would often also provide the service of notifying their customers of the events that concern them, for example annual shareholder meetings or rights issues.

Nowadays most shares are held electronically, meaning that there are no share certificates, but there is a central and authoritative ledger run by a **registrar** that contains the information regarding who owns how many of which securities. This ledger might either contain the name of the end customer who owns the security—that's the equivalent of an individual deposit—or it would contain the name of the custodian with whom the end customer has an account, which is the equivalent of a collective deposit. Issuers who want to contact their investors can in this case simply go through the registrar, who either notifies the investors directly, or notifies the custodian who in turn notifies the investors.

Regulatory Angle. Custodians and registrars are regulated locally, typically in the regulations that also set the requirements for investment management businesses. They tend to be what one would expect them to be, ie requirements to have processes in place that ensure that they are performing their duty in a competent manner, customer assets are safe in cases where this is relevant, and possibly things like the eligibility of people to hold key positions within those companies.

6.6 Advisory and Research

6.6.1 Investment Banking Advisory

Investment banking advisory is mostly about advising companies on **mergers & acquisitions** therefore this whole area is often referred to as **M&A**. However, this sells the business short, as the bankers in the advisory business tend to advise companies—and sometimes governments—on a wide range of finance-related issues.

> **Regulatory Angle.** The major advisory businesses tend to be regulated as banks as they usually also have a capital markets franchise and therefore need central bank access. Smaller advisors can be regulated as investment firms (MiFID in the EU). Customer-facing staff are in many jurisdictions required to take an exam showing adequate knowledge, and be registered with the appropriate regulator.

6.6.2 Broker Research and Ratings

Broker research, also referred to as **sell-side research**, is research produced by investment banks or broker/dealers and provided to their clients. Traditionally research has been provided for free, with a general understanding that this would lead to increased deal flow. However, in some jurisdictions the possibility of doing this is being restricted, leading to a reduction in research resources within the banks and broker dealers, and an emergence of paid-for research shops. The biggest research segment is **equities research**, where research analysts follow certain industry sectors, meet the companies, and in general opine on the fair valuation of the respective stocks. There is also **credit research**, that covers the bond issuance for the same companies. More generally, many trading operations will have some associated research staff. For example there are **FX strategists** for the fx markets, and **structured finance analysts** covering the structured finance markets. Also there are generally economists in the investment banks who provide a more high-level **economic research**.

> **Regulatory Angle.** Companies providing investment advice are regulated as investment firms, and investment research is an ancillary service (MiFID in the EU). One key focus of the regulations since the early 2000s has been to align incentives between the analysts and their investors, as during the dot-com bubble it emerged that some companies put pressure on their analysts to provide positive reports, and in particular some analysts' public views were not the same as the ones they expressed in private. Also, under the latest regulations in the EU, it is expected that research is being paid for explicitly, as opposed to being a free service provided to, say, brokerage clients, putting pressures on this business model.

Rating agencies are similar to sell side analysts in that they opine on securities and issuers. The important difference is that ratings agencies only opine on fixed income products, ie bonds paying a coupon, not equities representing company ownership, and they express their opinion by assigning letter grades representing the credit quality of the respective security. The highest grade is triple-A (AAA or Aaa, depending on the agency), and it goes down via AA/Aa, A/A, to BBB/Baa, which is the lowest so-called *investment grade rating*. Below that are the *sub-investment grade ratings* BB/Ba, B/B, CCC/Caa, CC/Ca, and C/C. There is also a D rating for securities that are in default. The three major rating segments are

- company debt ratings
- sovereign debt ratings
- structured finance (ABS) ratings.

Whilst they all use the same grading system, ratings in different segments are not easily comparable, ie 'triple-A rating' has a very different meaning in the corporate, sovereign, and structured finance world.

Regulatory Angle. Rating agencies are now usually subject to direct regulation (RAR in the EU). Also, ratings are a cornerstone of most prudential regulatory frameworks, eg Basel (CRD in the EU).

PART II

Selected Regulations in Detail

After having discussed regulations on a more general level I am now getting into the nitty-gritty of what regulations actually look like. In order to avoid duplication—a lot of the regulation in this space is reasonably harmonised internationally, especially when looking at it from a slightly higher level—I had to choose a jurisdiction. Out of the two obvious choices—the United States and the European Union—I chose the EU. The reason for this is that I believe the EU regulatory framework is slightly cleaner in that responsibilities are more clearly assigned. In the US there is always the tension between state-level law and federal law, and there is also the issue of agencies with overlapping competences. In principle a similar tension exists in the EU between what is coming out of Brussels, and Member State law. In most areas of financial services, however, by now a fair amount of convergence has been achieved, in particular also because of the very powerful drive to ensure companies established in one Member State can passport their services into all other countries in the Single Market with minimal additional hurdles, so this body of law is a very good starting point to understand what a consistent and comprehensive set of financial services regulations looks like.

By necessity the summaries provided will omit a lot of the detail—after all I am summarising about 2,000 pages of regulations into a bit more than 100 pages. However, every piece of information given here is linked back to the article in the legislation where it comes from, and the entire European Union legislative body is available on the Internet, so anyone wanting to understand the details can go back and look at the actual legislation.

1. Alternative Investment Fund Manager Directive
2. Anti Money Laundering Directive
3. Bank Recovery and Resolution Directive
4. Cross-Border Payments Regulation
5. Consumer Contracts Directive
6. Consumer Credit Directive
7. Capital Requirements Directives
8. Deposit Guarantee Scheme Directive
9. Distance Marketing in Financial Services Directive
10. European Market Infrastructure Regulation
11. Electronic Money Directive
12. General Data Protection Regulation
13. Market Abuse Regulation
14. Mortgage Credit Directive
15. Markets in Financial Instruments Directive
16. Packaged Retail and Insurance-based Investment Products Regulation
17. Payments Services Directive
18. Rating Agencies Regulation
19. Undertakings for Collective Investment in Transferable Securities Directive
20. Unfair Commercial Practices Directive

Alternative Investment Fund Manager Directive

Alternative Investment Fund Manager Directive—The directive regulating alternative investment fund managers

Summary

This directive is regulating alternative investment fund managers (AIFMs; eg managers of hedge, private, and real estate funds). It also regulates the underlying AIFs and their depository service providers, albeit indirectly as it only has jurisdiction over the managers and how they market to their customers.

Relevance for Fintech Companies

As opposed to UCITS funds, alternative funds are not usually targeted at retail investors, so for Fintech companies targeting consumers this directive is probably of secondary importance.

References

- Directive 2011/61/EU (AIFMD)
- Directive 2009/65/EC (UCITS 4)
- Directive 2004/39/EC (MiFID1)

The Alternative Investment Fund Managers Directive is 2011/61/EU. It relies on a number of other directives, notably 2009/65/EC (UCITS 4) and 2004/39/EC (MiFID1).

1.1 General

This directive regulates Alternative Investment Funds (AIFs), ie investment funds that do not fall under the UCITS Directive 2009/65/EC, in the EU. Typical representatives of this class would be hedge funds, private equity funds, and venture capital funds. The directive does not actually regulate the funds themselves, but rather their managers, referred to here as alternative investment fund managers (AIFMs). AIFs are only regulated indirectly in that non-compliance AIFs with this regulation means that AIFMs have to resign from managing and marketing them. It regulates both EU and non-EU entities: whenever either the AIFM or the AIF or the customer is in the EU, it is very likely that this directive applies (Arts 1, 4). There are a number of important exceptions, however, notably pension schemes, or smaller managers not open to external investors (Arts 2, 3).

1.1.1 Authorisation

Every AIF within the scope of this directive must have one and only one AIFM, and that AIFM is in charge of compliance with this directive with respect to all AIFs it is managing. Only authorised AIFMs can manage AIFs, and managing AIFs and performing the ancillary activities listed in Annex I and Article 6 are the only activities an AIFM is allowed to perform (Art 6).

EU AIFMs must apply for authorisation in their home Member State. AIFMs must notify their regulator of all changes—including those regarding their AIFs—and only if the regulator does not object to those changes can they be implemented (Arts 7, 10). Authorisation can be withdrawn (Art 11). In order to qualify for authorisation, AIFMs have to inter alia satisfy a minimum capital requirement, and both management and dominant owners have to be suitable for their respective roles. Authorisation of an AIFM in one Member State is passported into all other Member States (Arts 8, 9). ESMA keeps a public register of all authorised AIFMs within the EU (Art 7).

1.1.2 General Requirements

AIFMs have to adhere to a number of general principles. In particular, they must treat investors fairly, and preferential treatment of some investors is only acceptable when it is disclosed in the relevant AIF's rules. AIFMs who also offer discretionary portfolio management cannot invest in their own AIFs unless this has been agreed with the customer (Art 12). AIFMs must have remuneration policies for key staff in place in line with this directive and ESMA guidance (Art 13, Annex II). AIFMs must manage conflict of interest at all levels where it may arise (Art 14). They must have a risk management structure that is functionally and hierarchically separate from the operational units. Risk management systems and procedures must be documented and reviewed at least annually (Art 15). There must be maximum levels of leverage at each AIF individually (Art 15).

All AIFs must employ an appropriate liquidity management system, and must conduct regular liquidity stress tests. In particular, they must ensure that redemption terms offered to the AIF's investors are commensurate with the liquidity profile of the assets. Unlevered closed-ended funds, which by design don't run liquidity risk, are exempt from those requirements (Art 16). AIFMs must support securitisation retention requirements (Art 17), they must employ at all times *adequate and appropriate human and technical resources*, and they must ensure that appropriate personal-transactions policies are in place (Art 18).

All AIFs must be periodically valued. The absolute minimum valuation frequency is once per year. Otherwise it depends on the fund's assets—more-liquid assets require more-frequent valuation—and its subscription and redemption conditions. It must be ensured that inflow and outflow are recorded at fair valuations (Art 19). The valuation must either be performed by an external valuer, or internally, provided it is done in a unit that is independent from the operational units and does not have conflicts of interest, eg vis-à-vis remuneration (Art 19).

AIFMs can sub-contract functions where it is justifiable for objective reasons. By and large, the sub-contractors employed must satisfy the same authorisation and registration requirements as the top-level AIFMs. Sub-delegation is possible provided the top-level AIFM consents. Delegation does not release an AIFM from its responsibilities vis-à-vis its customers (Art 20).

1.1.3 Depositaries

Every AIF must appoint a single depositary as custodian of its assets. The depositary must be a regulated entity eligible to be a depositary under the UCITS 4 directive, for example a bank or an investment firm. For non-EU AIFs, and for some AIFs holding long-dated illiquid assets, slightly more relaxed rules apply. Conflicts of interest should be avoided, so the AIFM cannot act as a depositary, and neither can a prime broker who is also acting as a counterparty unless the depositary function is functionally and hierarchically separated. The depositary must be located in the same Member State as the AIF for EU AIFs. For non-EU AIFs it can either be in the same country, or in the home/reference member state of the AIFM managing the AIF. If a depositary is established in a third country there must be regulatory cooperation agreement in place between that country, and every country where the fund is being marketed. That country cannot be listed as non-cooperative by the FATF, and it must comply with the OECD Model Tax Convention (Art 21).

Depositaries must ensure that the AIF's cash flows are properly monitored. Assets that can be held in custody—including physical custody—must be held in custody by the depositary, in segregated accounts. For assets that cannot be held in custody—eg because they are established via a contractual relationship rather than as bearer securities—the depositary must verify ownership, and maintain a register. The depositary must ensure that dealing in, operations on, and valuation of the shares and units they hold in custody is done appropriately and according to applicable law. A depositary must not delegate their duties other than the actual custody of the assets. If they do delegate, the depositary remains liable to AIFs and their investors for losses caused by delegates, except where there is an agreement to the contrary between the depositary and the AIF or the AIFM. Depositaries must provide to the regulators all information necessary that those might need with respect to the relevant AIFs and the AIFMs (Art 21).

1.1.4 Transparency

AIFMs must prepare an annual report for every AIF they manage. This report must be provided to their regulators and—on request—to their investors. This report must include at least audited basic financials (balance sheet, income statement), as well as an activities report, a material changes report, and a remuneration report (Art 22).

Before investors invest in an AIF, the AIFM must provide them with a specific set of information in relation to this investment (Art 23). AIFMs must also report directly to their regulators information that is relevant with respect to market integrity. This includes general information on positions taken, concentrations and illiquid exposures, leverage, and results of stress tests employed (Art 24).

1.1.5 Rules for Specific Types of Funds

This regulation singles out and addresses two areas of concern where funds could negatively impact the functioning of the markets, and the overall economy more generally: highly leveraged funds and—to use the term commonly employed rather than the legal term used in the regulation—private equity funds.

The concern with highly leveraged funds is that they—either on their own or in concert with others who are running similar strategies—lead to the creation of bubbles. When on the way up excessive leverage leads to large rises in assets that suddenly turn, and where the downwards movement is accelerated by highly leveraged players who have to liquidate their positions before the value of the assets falls below the amount of debt outstanding against them.

We have discussed above the reporting requirement under Article 24 where AIFs have to report to their regulator information about positions, concentration and liquidity risk, results of stress tests, etc. It is the regulators' responsibility—together with ESMA and ESRB in order to ensure a pan-European or even global view—to look at this data in aggregate, and to identify areas of the market where there is a risk of unsustainable leverage building up.

Where those areas are identified, regulators can implement a number of measures, including limiting the leverage that specific AIFs are allowed to employ. The authority to do this rests solely with the fund regulators; ESMA can only issue recommendations, and expect regulators to follow them on a comply-or-explain basis (Art 25).

Regulators are also concerned about private equity funds, which, loosely speaking, are AIFs that purchase controlling stakes in unlisted large companies; SMEs are specifically excluded (Art 26). Under this directive, whenever an AIF, or a group of AIFs acting as a consortium, changes its stake (upwards or downwards) that brings it to cross one of the thresholds (10%, 20%, 30%, 50%, 75%) the home regulator must be notified.

If an AIF acquires control—individually or jointly—then also the company in question and its identifiable shareholder must be notified, and the company board must be asked to inform the employee representatives (Art 26). The relevant AIFM in this case has to provide some additional information, notably information that is interesting for the employees, including future plans that the acquirer has with respect to that company (Arts 27, 28).

1.2 Authorisation to Market

The conditions under which an AIFM can market an AIF to a professional investor depend on the country of residence of the AIFM, the country of residence of the AIF, and the country of residence of the investor. This allows for a number of different permutations, which are dealt with in 10 articles: six for AIFMs based in the EU (Arts 31–36) and four for AIFMs based in third countries (Arts 39–42). There are also two articles that deal with third-country AIFMs in general (37, 38). Those 10 articles are repetitive as they represent different combinations of the same elements, and to understand them it is better to discuss those principles than to go through them individually.

The first principle is that the procedures for AIFMs that are resident in the EU (in their 'home Member State') and for third-country AIFMs that are authorised in the EU (in their 'reference Member State') are very similar. In particular, whilst the former always go through their home regulator, the latter always go through the regulator in their reference Member State. In the following I will only refer to home regulators, with the understanding that this might also indicate the regulator of the reference Member State.

The second principle relates to the residence of the AIFs. There are three options: they can be in the home Member State, they can in a Member State other than the home Member State, or they can be in a third country that is not part of the EU. We take those three cases in turn.

1.2.1 AIF Domiciled in Home Member State

First, we consider the case where the AIF is in the home Member State of the AIFM.

> **Investor in same Member State as AIF**. The AIFM provides its home regulator with a notice according to Annex III. Unless the AIFM is not compliant with the regulations, it should be authorised to market the AIF to professional investors within 20 days (Art 31 for EU funds, Art 39 for non-EU funds).
>
> **Investor in different Member State than AIF**. The AIF provides its home regulator with a notice according to Annex IV. Unless the AIFM is not compliant with the regulations, the home regulator should forward the notice to the host regulator within 20 days, from which point onwards the AIFM is authorised to market the AIF to professional investors there (Art 32 for EU funds, Art 39 for non-EU funds).

1.2.2 AIF Domiciled in Another Member State

Now we consider the case where the AIF is in the EU, but in another Member State than the home Member State of the AIFM. In this case, the AIFM has to notify its home regulator that it wants to manage an AIF in another Member State, either directly or via a branch. Unless the AIFM is not in compliance with this regulation, the home regulator approves this request within 1 month in the case of direct management, or 2 months in the case of a branch (Art 33 for EU funds, Art 41 for non-EU funds).

At this point the AIFM has to follow the aforementioned processes—notably notification to its home regulator (not the regulator of the Member State where the AIF is located) under Annex III for marketing in the same Member State as the AIF (not AIFM), and notification under Annex IV for marketing in another Member State—and within 20 days those notices should be forwarded and the fund should be available for marketing.

1.2.3 AIF Domiciled in a Third Country

If the AIF is established in a third country, then first there must be a cooperation agreement between the regulator in the country where the AIF is located, and the home regulator of the AIFM. Second, between the third country and every EU country where the AIF is meant to be marketed there must be an agreement compliant with the OECD Model Tax Convention.

Provided all this is in place, the AIFM gives Annex III notice to its home regulator to be allowed to market the AIF in its home country, and Annex IV notice to its home regulator to market in another EU country. In both cases, after 20 days the AIFM should be allowed to market the fund, assuming compliance with the regulations (Art 35 for EU AIFMs, Art 40 for non-EU AIFMs).

1.2.4 Special Cases

The cases we have considered above were the regular cases that followed the rules, but there are some special cases to consider.

EU AIFM marketing non-EU AIF to non-EU customers. In the case where an EU-based AIFM is marketing a non-EU-based AIF to non-EU-based professional investors, the rules as far as the EU is concerned are pretty simple; they mostly care about there being a cooperation agreement between the regulator in the AIFM's home Member State and the third country where the AIF is located (Art 34).

AIFM marketing non-EU AIF in its home MS. In the case where an AIFM is marketing a non-EU-based AIF to investors in its home/reference Member State, instead of demanding a process according to Article 35 or 40, Member States can require simplified rules that mostly require supervisory cooperation between the home regulator and the regulator in the country where the AIF is located (Art 36 for EU AIFMs, Art 42 for non-EU AIFMs).

1.2.4 Retail Investors

Member States can allow AIFMs—locally domiciled or not—to market AIFs—again, locally domiciled or not—to retail investors within their territory. This regulation imposes no other requirements in this case other than that ESMA has to be informed, and that Member States cannot treat AIFs domiciled in another EU country and being marketed cross-border any worse than those domiciled locally (Art 43).

1.3 Interaction with Regulators

Each Member State must designate a regulator which will be responsible for prudential supervision of AIFMs. Where AIFMs operate on a cross-border basis, the split of responsibilities between home and host regulator is defined in the directive. Host regulators must not discriminate against AIFMs authorised in other Member States vis-à-vis locally authorised AIFMs. In the event of non-compliance, regulators (including host regulators, if there was no successful intervention of the AIFM's home regulator) have the right to take appropriate measures, including asking AIFMs to cease managing certain AIFs, or to cease marketing them. Disagreements between regulators are mediated by ESMA (Arts 44, 45). Regulators must have the powers necessary to perform their regulatory duty (Art 46). ESMA has mostly powers to engage at a systemic level and to issue guidelines. It also has some specific responsibilities in the case of non-EU AIFMs (Art 47).

Regulators have the right to impose penalties, as well as any other measures the Member State may consider suitable, on the AIFMs they oversee. Those penalties and measures might be publicly disclosed, and ESMA will draw up an annual report in this respect (Art 48). Decisions—or failures to reach a decision within 6 months—can be appealed to the local courts (Art 49).

Regulators have a duty to cooperate and to exchange data (Arts 50–54) including following the relevant data protection regulations (Art 51). Disputes among regulators are settled by ESMA (Art 55).

The functions an AIFM has to perform when managing an AIF are described in Annex I, and general remarks with respect to remuneration policy are in Annex II. Annexes III and IV contain the information that has to be provided when an AIFM intends to market an AIF in its home Member State/another Member State respectively.

Anti Money Laundering Directive

Anti Money Laundering Directive—The regulations dealing with the avoidance of money laundering and terrorist finance in the EU

Summary

The Anti Money Laundering Directive establishes the regime that virtually all legal and natural persons dealing with substantial assets have to follow to combat money laundering and terrorist financing. The key requirement under this regime is for institutions to perform a due diligence on their customers before they enter into a relationship, mostly establishing their identity and—where appropriate—that of the ultimate beneficiaries. It also obliges companies to monitor the relationship on a risk-appropriateness basis and report concerns to the respective authorities.

Relevance for Fintech Companies

The anti money laundering and combating terrorist financing regulations are relevant for a large number of companies in the Fintech space—essentially everyone who is involved in transferring money and making payments, and who owns the customer relationship in this space. Not all cases are clear-cut: AISPs and PSPs who just operate bank APIs can probably rely on those banks complying with the relevant regulations. On the other hand, a business operating a payment card that can be replenished with cash in retail outlets and that can be used in a variety of places, and where the cash can possibly be refunded (eg the Japanese public transport payment cards) is probably subject to those regulations.

There are some exclusions in this regulation, eg around gift cards and shop cards, and about items that can be directly charged to a mobile phone bill, but the rules around this are pretty tight, especially with respect to the maximum monetary amounts that are allowed for the exception to apply, so even those businesses should at the very least be familiar with the exact rules for the exceptions.

References

- Directive EU 2015/849 (AML 4)
- Directive 2005/60/EC (AML 3)
- Directive 2006/70/EC (AML3 Impl)
- Regulation EU 2015/847 (TrInfo)
- FD 2002/475/JHA (Terrorism)
- Directive 2013/36/EU (CRD4-CID)
- Regulation 575/2013 (CRD4-CRR)
- Directive 2009/138/EC (Solvency 2)
- Directive 2004/39/EC (MiFID1)
- Directive 2002/92/EC (Insurance Mediation)

The Anti Money Laundering Directive 2015/849 (AMLD 4) is the latest revision of the anti money laundering directives of the EU. It repeals the previous third revision of the directive 2005/60 as well as the associated implementation directive 2006/70. Regulation 2015/847 on the information accompanying transfers of funds is related, as is the Framework Decision on combating terrorism 2002/475/JHA. The directives and regulations 2013/36/EU (CRD4-CID), 575/2013 (CRD4-CRR), 2009/138/EC (Solvency 2), 2004/39/EC (MiFID1) define the entities that are subject to those regulations.

2.1 Definition and Scope

The purpose of this directive is to ensure that the EU's financial system is not used for the purposes of money laundering (ML; also AML for anti money laundering) or terrorist financing (TF; also CTF for combating terrorist financing). Thereby, money laundering is defined as any of the following activities provided it is pursued intentionally (Art 1):

1. the conversion or transfer of property, knowing that such property is derived from criminal activity or from an act of participation in such activity, for the purpose of concealing or disguising the illicit origin of the property or of assisting any person who is involved in the commission of such an activity to evade the legal consequences of that person's action

2. the concealment or disguise of the true nature, source, location, disposition, movement, rights with respect to, or ownership of, property, knowing that such property is derived from criminal activity or from an act of participation in such an activity

3. the acquisition, possession or use of property, knowing, at the time of receipt, that such property was derived from criminal activity or from an act of participation in such an activity

4. participation in, association to commit, attempts to commit and aiding, abetting, facilitating and counselling the commission of any of the actions referred to in the previous points

Or, to make the point shorter albeit less precise, *money laundering* means helping to convert the proceeds of criminal activity into assets that appear to come from legal activities.

Terrorist financing in the context of this directive is defined as follows (Art 1):

'terrorist financing' means the provision or collection of funds, by any means, directly or indirectly, with the intention that they be used or in the knowledge that they are to be used, in full or in part, in order to carry out any of the offences within the meaning of Articles 1 to 4 of Council Framework Decision 2002/475/JHA.

The directive applies to a number of obliged entities, notably credit institutions and other financial institutions, and a number of professions that are traditionally related to the acquistition or exchange of assets like lawyers, notaries, or estate agents. Notable entities included are *providers of gambling services* and anyone trading in goods to the extent that it involves payments in cash of over €10k in aggregate terms (Art 2).

Credit institutions in the context of this article are entities commonly referred to as banks, as defined the CRD4-CRR Regulation 575/2013 (Art 3):

'credit institution' means an undertaking the business of which is to take deposits or other repayable funds from the public and to grant credits for its own account (Art 4.1.1).

'Financial institutions' covers a large range of entities. First, it covers those which carry out activities listed in the Annex I to the CRD4-CID Directive 2013/36/EU (Art 3). Those are defined in Annex I of CRD4-CID:

• lending of all kinds (Point 2)
• financial leasing (Point 3)

- payment services (Point 4)
- issuing and administering other means of payment (Point 5)
- guarantees and commitments (Point 6)
- trading for own account or for account of customers (Point 7)
- participation in securities issues and related (Point 8)
- investment banking advisory (Point 9)
- money broking (Point 10)
- portfolio management and advice (Point 11)
- safekeeping and administration of securities (Point 12)
- safe custody services (Point 14)
- issuing electronic money (Point 15).

It also covers insurance companies offering life insurance, as defined in Solvency 2 2009/138/EC, Article 13.1, and investment firms as defined in Article 4.1.1 of MiFID 2004/39/EC. Finally, it applies to collective investment undertakings, and insurance intermediaries as defined in Article 2.5 of IMD 2004/39/EC (Art 2). If necessary, Member States can extend the scope to other areas (Art 4).

2.2 Implementation

Both the Commission and the Joint Committee of EBA, EIOPA, and ESMA periodically issue opinions and guidelines (Art 6). Member States assess the risks of ML and TF within their jurisdiction and develop measures to mitigate them. They also establish a designated authority that has responsibility to coordinate AML and CTF measures with other Member States (Arts 7, 8). The Commission is compiling a list of high-risk third countries where they consider that the AML/CTF regime is insufficient and in respect of which special transaction rules apply (Art 9).

Anonymous accounts or passbooks are forbidden, and there are measures in place to prevent misuse of bearer shares and bearer warrants (Art 10). Customer due diligence measures must be applied by obliged entities when (Art 11):

1. establishing a relationship
2. carrying out occasional transactions of €15k or more
3. carrying out occasional transfers of €1k or more
4. trading in goods for cash of €10k or more
5. providing gambling services of €2k or more (stake or winnings).

They also must be applied every time where there is a suspicion of ML or TF, and when there are doubts about previously obtained customer identification data. Where appropriate, series of linked transactions are to be considered as one transaction as far as the threshold amounts are concerned (Art 11). Member States may allow obliged entities to forego some due diligence measures for electronic money instruments that satisfy certain conditions, including that both monthly transaction volume and maximum amount stored do not exceed €250 (Art 12).

Obliged entities must apply the following customer due diligence measures on a risk-sensitive basis (Art 13):

- establishing the customer's identity based on documents, or information obtained from a reliable source
- identifying the beneficial owner, and—where different—verifying that person's identity as well
- understanding the purposed and intended nature of business relationship.

Risk assessment has to take a number of specific points into account (Annex I). Obliged entities also must monitor the customer relationship on an ongoing basis, including scrutinising transactions to ensure that they are in line with the customer profile previously established. They also have to be able to demonstrate to the relevant authorities that their measures are appropriate (Art 13). Except in circumstances where the risk of ML or TF is low, customer verification has to take place before any transactions are being carried out (Art 14).

In low-risk areas it is sometimes possible to carry out simplified customer due diligence procedures (Arts 15–17). On the other hand, when dealing with the aforementioned high-risk third countries, or in other cases of higher risk, enhanced customer due diligence measures have to be applied. This includes examining complex and unusual transactions and transaction patterns, especially if they have no apparent economic purpose (Art 18). Similarly, special rules apply to politically exposed persons and their relationships, for example the requirement to obtain senior management approval, to establish the sources of their wealth and funds, and to generally conduct enhanced, ongoing monitoring of those relationships (Arts 20–23). Relationships with shell banks—banks that have no appropriate physical presence (Art 3)—are forbidden (Art 24).

Whenever an entity is working with an institution in a third country—whether this country is considered high risk or not—it must perform due diligence on that institution, document respective responsibilities with respect to AML/ATF obligations, and obtain senior management sign-off (Art 19).

Obliged entities can rely on the contributions of third parties (except those located in high-risk third countries) for their due diligence process. However, the responsibility remains with the obliged entities (Arts 25–29).

Where an obliged entity knows or suspects that a certain transaction is related to ML or TF, it must refrain from carrying out said transaction until it has been reported to the relevant FIU (see below), and that FIU has authorised the firm to execute the transaction. There is an exception where not carrying out the transaction is impossible, or where it is likely to frustrate efforts to pursue the beneficiaries of that operation, in which case the FIU must be informed immediately afterwards (Art 35). The fact that a transaction has been reported must not be communicated to the customer in question (Art 39).

Obliged entities have to retain all due diligence records as well as all transaction records, in a format suitable for judicial proceedings, for at least five years after the relationship has ended. After that point, personal data must usually be deleted (Art 40). General data protection rules apply, and the processing of the due diligence data for commercial purposes is prohibited (Arts 41, 43). The entities must have systems and processes in place to respond fully and speedily to enquiries from their FIU (Art 42).

If obliged entities are part of a group, they must implement group-wide policies and procedures compliant with this regulation, including in third countries wherever this is legally possible (Art 45). Entities must ensure—on a basis proportionate to the risk incurred—that their employees are aware of their duties under this regulation, and must organise training in this respect (Art 46).

To the extent that this is not already required by other pieces of applicable legislation, obliged entities must be registered or authorised, and their management must pass a fit and proper test, which in particular excludes people with a prior relevant criminal record (Art 47). They must be adequately monitored for compliance with those regulations (Art 48). Breach of obligations can be sanctioned (Arts 58–62).

2.3 Obligations of All Companies

Whilst the previous part of the regulations applied to companies in financial services only, this part deals with all companies, and in fact mostly with companies that are potential financial service customers. The key requirement here is that all entities incorporated in the EU must hold information about their beneficial ownership, ie who is or are the natural persons who ultimately benefit. It must also hold information details of beneficial interests held. All this information must be disclosed to obliged entities during the due diligence process, and it also must be held in a central register that is accessible to everyone having a legitimate interest. Obliged entities, however, are not allowed to solely rely on that central register for their due diligence process (Art 30).

Similar provisions apply to trusts (Art 31).

2.4 Financial Intelligence Units and Cooperation

All Member States establish what is called a Financial Intelligence Unit (FIU), which is an institution that receives all reports on suspicious activities, analyses them, and distributes the intelligence gathered to the appropriate entities concerned. It is responsible for both operational analysis of individual incidents and the strategic analysis of system-wide trends (Arts 32–34). Disclosure under this regulation—if done in good faith—is not considered a breach of a contractual or legal obligation to not disclose those facts (Art 37), and individuals who disclose such information (*whistleblowers*) must be protected from negative consequences of such disclosure, in particular in relation to discriminatory employment actions (Art 38).

The various official actors involved in this space (FIUs, other national competent authorities, ESAs, the Commission) interact according to specified guidelines (Arts 49–57).

2.5 Information Requirements on Transfers of Funds

The related regulation 2015/847 on the information accompanying transfers of funds decrees that—unless equivalent information can be derived from the context—all transfers either starting or ending in the EU must be accompanied by the payer's name, account number, and, importantly, either address or official personal document number (eg passport number) or customer identification number or date and place of birth. Intermediaries must have systems in place that detect missing information, and are obliged to hold up transfers if it does not comply with those regulations. This supplements the AML regulations by blocking transfers that have not been subject to the appropriate processes.

Bank Recovery and Resolution Directive

Bank Recovery and Resolution Directive—The directive defining the resolution and recovery process of failing banks in the EU

Summary

This directive deals with mechanisms to support the recovery of financial institutions, or their resolution (winding down) if recovery is not possible. It contains a number of implementation measures, notably the establishment of a dedicated resolution authority (which usually is not the regulator) and the requirement of institutions to prepare recovery plans for themselves, and the authorities to prepare individual resolution plans for the institutions.

It defines a number of tools the resolution authority can use, notably the *sale of business tool*, the *bridge institution tool*, the *asset separation tool*, and the *bail-in tool*. The first three are dealing with breaking up the institution, typically in to a good and a bad part, and the latter allows losses to be attributed to the different liabilities so that the institution becomes viable again. It also defines two second stage tools, the *public equity support tool* and the *temporary public ownership tool*, that allow the state to take a direct stake in the institutions. Finally it establishes the European system of financing arrangements which is a fund supported by the covered entities that governments can use in the resolution process.

Relevance for Fintech Companies

Technically the BRRD applies to financial institutions (banks) and investment firms so it might or might not technically apply to Fintech companies. Also the main concern here are systemically important companies which many Fintech companies are not (yet) be. However, insolvency will always be a regulatory concern when dealing with start-ups, and therefore especially the business continuity arrangement here are probably highly relevant.

References

- Directive 2014/59/EU (BRRD)
- Directive 2013/36/EU (CRD4-CID)
- Regulation EU 575/2013 (CRD4-CRR)

The Bank Recovery and Resolution Directive is 2014/59, and it relies in a number of areas on directive 2013/36 and regulation 575/2013 (together the CRD 4 package).

3.1 Definition and Scope

This directive deals with bank resolution and recovery, ie how to either wind down failing banks or ensure that they can recover in the shortest possible time so that their ability to lend is not more impaired than absolutely necessary. 'Bank' here is understood in a wider sense, including banking and mixed groups, and big local branches (Arts 1, 2). Every country must designate a resolution authority that is given the necessary powers under this directive. This can be the central bank or the regulator, or it can be some independent public authority associated with the finance ministry, given that provision of taxpayer money is often involved (Art 3).

The requirements under this directive depend on the size and importance of the institution within the financial systems of the countries in which they are operating. Small institutions can be subjected to a simplified set of obligations, at the discretion of the regulator. On the other hand, large institutions—in particular those that have more than €30bn in assets, or where those assets constitute more than 20% of a Member State's GDP—are subject to additional obligations (Art 4).

3.2 Preparation

Every institution must draw up a recovery plan. If a bank is subject to consolidated supervision at the group level, then the recovery plan is to be drawn up at the group level as well. Recovery plans must be updated annually or when there are significant changes, like changes to the company structure. Companies must not assume extraordinary public support in their plans, and they have to identify the assets that could be used to obtain financing at the central bank. They must define objective trigger indicators—based on either systemic or company-level stress—for the various recovery options proposed in the plan (Arts 5, 7, 9).

The recovery plan is submitted to the regulator (not the resolution authority) for assessment. The regulator has 6 months to perform this assessment. If the plan is found to be unsatisfactory, the company has another 2–3 months to submit a new plan. If this is still found to be unsatisfactory, then the regulator can ask that the company make changes to its business that address the deficiencies in the plan. If this is found to be inadequate, the regulator can impose specific changes, for example require it to reduce risk (solvency or liquidity), or to recapitalise, or change the strategy, structure or governance (Arts 6, 8).

The resolution authority (not the regulator) draws up the resolution plan, possibly with the assistance of the institution, and shares it with the company and the regulator (Arts 10–14). A resolution authority must then assess the *resolvability* of an institution (Arts 15, 16; Annex C), and if it finds it not to be resolvable then it can demand that changes be implemented which are similar in nature but more far-reaching than those the regulator can impose. The changes required can be substantial, including divestment of business and change of the group structure (Arts 17, 18), leading in particular to more pressure for companies to operate locally through subsidiaries, ie independently viable legal entities.

So to step back for a moment and to summarise the above: the company draws up a *recovery plan* allowing it to become viable again in the event of distress. This plan is assessed and approved by the *regulator*. The *resolution authority* draws up the *resolution plan*, specifying what happens if the recovery plan fails.

To strengthen resilience of specific entities within a group of companies, other group companies can enter into a support agreement. Support agreements must be entered voluntarily and gain shareholder approval, and cannot be a condition for gaining approval of the recovery plan. They might, however, make approval of the recovery plan easier, and allow for a risk profile in that entity that would otherwise not be possible. They must be approved by all relevant entities responsible for both the group and the relevant constituent companies, and certain conditions must be fulfilled, including disclosure (Arts 19–26).

3.3 Execution

When a company gets into distress—in particular when it reaches some of the triggers in its recovery plan—it gets into what is called the *early intervention phase*. In this case the regulator has a number of options. For example, they can require management to put in place some of the measures in the recovery plan, or remove members of management that have been found unfit. They can also require changes in strategy, or in the legal or operational structure of the company, or they can appoint a temporary administrator replacing the entire management, and they also can prepare to put a resolution plan in place (Art 27–30).

Either after the above actions were not sufficient to address the problems, or immediately if a number of conditions are fulfilled (eg institution likely to fail; resolution in public interest; no alternative private sector measures available), the resolution authorities can set in motion the resolution plan (Arts 31–33). In this case, the resolution should be based on a number of key principles (Art 34):

- the shareholders bear the first losses, then creditors in order of priority under normal insolvency proceedings; importantly, no creditor suffers greater losses than they would have suffered under normal insolvency proceedings
- management is replaced except where retention is necessary to achieve the resolution goals, and where appropriate, legal action is taken against management and others responsible
- covered deposits are protected, and safeguards are respected.

Resolution authorities appoint a *special resolution manager* who—under the control of the resolution authority—has the powers of both the institution's shareholders and the management. This appointment cannot last longer than one year (Art 35). Before proceeding there must be a valuation:

> *Before taking resolution action or exercising the power to write down or convert relevant capital instruments, resolution authorities shall ensure that a fair, prudent and realistic valuation of the assets and liabilities of the institution is carried out by a person independent from any public authority, including the resolution authority, and the institution (Art 36).*

This valuation is important, as it will be the basis for apportioning losses to the different stakeholders. It has to follow certain specific requirements. If those requirements are not fulfilled it must be considered provisional, and an *ex-post definitive valuation shall be carried out as soon as practicable*. Decisions taken based on a provisional valuation are valid, but the regulator can, for example, adjust the amount of consideration an acquirer paid if the provisional and definitive valuations differ (Art 36).

This directive defines a number of specific resolution tools that the resolution authorities can use either individually or in combination (Art 37):

- **Sale of business tool.** Using the sale of business tool, either the institution's shares, or (part of) its assets and liabilities can be sold to a third party, on *commercial terms having regard to the circumstances* (Arts 38, 39).
- **Bridge institution tool.** The bridge institution tool is similar to the sale of business tool, except that the purchaser is not a private sector third party, but a state-sponsored bridge institution, with a view to either winding it down or selling it later (Arts 40, 41).
- **Asset separation tool.** Using the asset separation tool, some or all of an institution's assets and liabilities can be sold into an asset management vehicle (Art 42).
- **Bail-in tool.** When the bail-in tool is used, certain creditors' claims on the institution are reduced, taking into account their priority in the event of insolvency. Some creditors—eg insured depositors, covered bond holders, employees with respect to some claims—are protected (Arts 43, 44). When this tool is used, a number of detailed and highly specific rules apply (Arts 46–55).

For the bail-in tool to work, an institution needs a sufficient amount of bail-in-able liabilities. In order to ensure an institution has those, institutions need to satisfy a certain Minimum Required own funds and Eligible Liabilities (MREL) (Art 45). Eligible liabilities are roughly defined as *all capital securities with a remaining maturity of more than one year, plus all debt instruments that are subordinated to deposits, excluding covered bonds* (Art 45.4). The amount of the MREL is determined by the regulator on an individual basis (Art 45.6). Note that terminology here is often confused: MREL in market lingo can refer to the requirement, or to the underlying instruments as a class, or to one specific instrument in the class.

In addition to the resolution tools described above, the directive also defines government financial stabilisation tools, which shall only be used as a last resort when the other tools have failed *to avoid a significant adverse effect on the financial system* and using them is in the *public interest* (Art 56):

- **Public equity support tool.** The public equity support tool allows Member States to provide capital to institutions under all possible forms, ie CET1, AT1 and T2 (Art 57).
- **Temporary public ownership tool.** The temporary public ownership tool allows memberships to temporarily transfer ownership of an institution (via its shares) to either a nominee, or a company that is 100% state-owned (Art 58).

Independently of resolution actions—but possibly in conjunction with them if appropriate—resolution authorities have in the event of distress the power to write down capital securities, or to convert them into other, lower-ranked ones (Art 59). This power is subject to certain rules and procedures (Arts 60–62).

In order to be able to fulfil their duty, the resolution authorities must be vested with a number of powers that are described in detail in the regulation (Arts 63–72), and a number of important safeguards (Arts 73–80) and procedural obligations (Arts 81–84) apply. In particular, a second independent valuation has to be carried out that determines what would have happened under normal bankruptcy proceedings without any resolution actions or state support, and the No Creditor Worse Off (NCWO) principle applies, meaning that no equity holders and creditors can be worse off under resolution than they would have been under insolvency (Arts 73–75).

Concerned parties have a right of appeal through the courts system; however, lodging an appeal does not entail automatic suspension, and decisions of the resolution authority are immediately enforceable (Art 85). Whilst under resolution, some other proceeding—notably bankruptcy proceeding—cannot be brought against an institution (Art 86). The directive contains a number of provisions regarding how to deal with cross-border resolution of groups, both within the EU (Arts 87–92), and when third countries are involved (Arts 93–98).

3.4 Ancillary Regulations

The directive also establishes the *European system of financing arrangements*, which consists of the respective national financing arrangements. Those financing arrangements are meant to financially support resolution proceedings if and when they arise. They can lend to each other, which is important when used in a cross-border context. Their respective minimum available funds are 1% of covered deposits, to be reached by the end of 2024, raised from the relevant institution in accordance with an established key. Contributions can also be requested ex-post if the amounts raised ex-ante prove to be insufficient (Arts 99–107).

The next paragraph is interesting, in that it directs Member States to change their insolvency law—that is most likely different from the law that implements the BRRD—in order to rank deposits in insolvency in a certain way, so as to ensure that their insolvency ranking is in line with their ranking in the event of resolution, notably bail-in. Importantly, deposits not covered by a deposit protection scheme—including the portion of deposits above the limit—must rank junior to protected deposits (Art 108). If the bail-in tool is being used, and if covered deposits would have been written down according to the tool's criteria, then the relevant protection scheme is to contribute the corresponding amount (Art 109).

The remainder of the regulation deals with penalties, specific provisions and other technical matters, such as the amendment of other regulations (Arts 110—132). It has a number of annexes, notably one on information to be included in recovery plans (Annex A), information that resolution authorities require to draw up the resolution plan (Annex B), and what a resolution authority must consider when assessing resolvability (Annex C).

Cross-Border
Payments Regulation

Cross-Border Payments Regulation—The regulation
establishing price levels for transfer within the Single Euro
Payments Area (SEPA)

Summary

This regulation mostly applies to payments in Euro between the different Member States, and it requires that the fees charged for EUR cross-border payments are not higher than those for EUR national payment. It also requires that if a bank account accepts national direct debits it must also accept cross-border direct debits.

Relevance for Fintech Companies

This is a very small directive, but it is important in that it restricts the value that payment service providers can bring in respect of cost improvement in the EUR payments space. In particular in Eurozone countries where national payments are free, cross-border EUR payments must be free as well, leaving no margin for new entrants to enter this particular market for cost reasons.

References

- Regulation EC 924/2009 (Cross-Border Payments)

    The Cross-Border Payments Regulation is 924/2009.

4.1 Definition and Scope

The regulation covers cross-border payments in the EU, ensuring that charges for cross-border payments are the same as those for the same currency within a Member State. For obvious reasons this is most relevant for cross-border payments denominated in EUR, but non-Euro countries can opt into those regulations should they want to (Art 1). For the purpose of this regulation, a payment is considered *cross-border* when the payer's and the payee's payment service provider are located in a different Member State (Art 2).

The central provision in that regulation is Art 3.1:

> *Charges levied by a payment service provider on a payment service user in respect of cross-border payments of up to EUR 50,000 shall be the same as the charges levied by that payment service provider on payment service users for corresponding national payments of the same value and in the same currency*

ie for payments up to €50k, charges for cross-border payments must be the same as charges for corresponding national payments. Thereby the definition of *corresponding* is to be clarified by the local regulator (Art 3).

Payment service providers must communicate to their clients which IBAN and BIC they should use to make and receive payments. This information should also be found on statements. Whoever initiates a payment must do so by communicating the appropriate IBAN and BIC, otherwise additional charges might be levied (Art 4).

Where a consumer account is reachable via national direct debit, it must also be reachable by SEPA direct debit, meaning that consumers that can pay their local bills this way shall also be able to pay cross-border bills originating in that manner (Art 8). Note that there is no obligation that would require bills payable by national direct debit also be payable by cross-border direct debit.

Member States must establish complaints procedures and out-of-court complaint and redress procedures for payment users vis-à-vis their payment service providers (Arts 10, 11). Member States who do not have the euro as national currency can opt into those regulations (Art 14).

Consumer Contracts Directive

Consumer Contracts Directive—The regulation dealing with unfair terms in consumer contracts

Summary

This directive defines unfair terms in consumer contracts, and establishes that those shall be ignored, and/or interpreted to the benefit of the consumer where ambiguity is present. A non-exhaustive list of unfair terms in provided in the Annex.

Relevance for Fintech Companies

This regulation is relevant for all companies that are dealing with consumers, including start-ups.

References

• Directive 1993/13/EEC (CCOD)

  The Consumer Contracts Directive is 1993/13/EEC.

5.1 Definition and Scope

This directive addresses unfair terms in contracts between sellers or suppliers and consumers (Art 1) where consumers are defined as a *natural person acting for purposes which are outside his trade, business, or profession* (Art 2). A contractual term is considered unfair if it has not been individually negotiated, and contrary to the requirement of good faith causes a significant imbalance to the detriment of the consumer. Any term that has been drafted in advance is to be considered not individually negotiated, and the fact that some terms have been individually negotiated does not preclude the other ones from being subject to this directive (Art 3). A non-exhaustive list of examples of terms considered unfair is provided in the Annex.

The price level is not relevant for the assessment as to whether an agreement is unfair, unless the communication around that price level was unclear or misleading (Art 4). Where the definitions of terms are ambiguous they must be interpreted in the most favourable way for the consumer (Art 5). To the extent that this is possible, contracts containing unfair terms remain binding, with the unfair terms removed (Art 6).

Avoiding those regulations by choosing a non-EU jurisdiction shall be prevented (Art 6), and consumer watchdogs and similar organisations can represent consumers in court, in particular in order to establish precedents (Art 7).

Consumer Credit Directive

Consumer Credit Directive—The regulation dealing with consumer credit, in particular its marketing, and the calculation of APRs

Summary

This regulation specifies what the requirements are when consumer credit is marketed, and in particular which information must be present to allow consumers to compare different products. The list of required information is long but not surprising—it contains things like the identity of the counterparties and their regulators, a full schedule of cash flows, and a detailed breakdown of charges. A key figure to be reported is the annual percentage rate (APR), and detailed and specific instructions of how to compute it are given.

Relevance for Fintech Companies

This short regulation is relevant for Fintech companies that operate in the space of consumer lending, whether it be as lenders, advisors, or intermediaries.

References

- Directive 2008/48/EC (CCRD)
- Directive 2014/17/EU (MCD)

The Consumer Credit Directive is 2008/48. A related directive is the Consumer Mortgage Credit Directive 2014/17.

6.1 Definition and Scope

This regulation addresses certain aspects of marketing and providing credit to consumers in the EU (Art 1), notably the requirement to provide sufficient information before a contract is agreed, including an annual percentage rate of charges (APR). Consumers in this context are *natural persons who are acting for purposes which are outside their trade, business, or profession* (Art 3).

In the context of this regulation, creditors are defined as *natural or legal persons who grant credit in the course of their trade, business, or profession* (Art 3), which is interesting because on the face of it this definition might not include some lenders on peer-to-peer lending platforms. The platforms themselves, however, almost certainly fall under the definition of credit intermediary, which means that the provisions here apply to them.

There are important exceptions in terms of credit agreements where this regulation does not apply, for example most kinds of secured credit, including mortgages, loans below €200 or above €75k, leasing agreements without obligation to purchase the asset, some overdraft facilities, some cost-free or subsidised credit agreements, margin loans, and loans extended by pawnbrokers (Art 2).

6.2 Information to Be Provided Before Concluding an Agreement

Advertisements. Whenever an advertisement of a credit product contains any figures relating to the cost of credit to the consumer it must also contain a certain set of standard information. This set is as follows (Art 4):

• borrowing rate and any charges included
• total amount and duration of credit
• APR (in most cases)
• total amount payable.

In the case of instalment purchases, the total amount of instalments must also be indicated, as must the cash price be if the same product or service were not being bought under a credit agreement.

Pre-contractual information. Before a contract is concluded, the creditor and/or the intermediary have to *provide the consumer with the information needed to compare different offers in order to take an informed decision on whether to conclude a credit agreement.* The information must be provided on paper or another durable medium, the set is defined in detail in the regulation (Art 5.1, or 6.1 for overdraft facilities), and it must be provided by means of the Standard European Consumer Credit Information form (SECCI form) (Annex II). There can be no other information provided on that form, but additional information can be provided in a separate annexed document (Arts 5, 6).

An exception is the case where *an agreement has been concluded at the consumer's request using a means of distance communication which does not enable the information to be provided* in which case the SECCI form has to be provided *immediately after the conclusion of the credit agreement* (Art 5.3).

Another exception is *suppliers of goods or services acting as credit intermediaries in an ancillary capacity* (Art 7).

6.3 Credit Assessment and Credit Databases

Before extending credit—and when the total amount of credit is being changed subsequently, or the creditor obtains additional information impacting the creditworthiness of the consumer—there must be a credit assessment. This assessment must be at least based on the data provided by the consumer, and possibly on consultation of relevant databases (Art 8). If a credit application has been rejected based on information obtained from a database, the creditor must inform the consumer immediately and free of charge of the result of the consultation, and the particulars of the database consulted. Databases must be available for cross-border access on a non-discriminatory basis (Art 9).

6.4 Information to Be Provided with Agreements

When entering into a credit agreement, all contracting parties must have received a copy of the agreement on paper or another durable medium. This agreement must contain a certain set of information (Art 10.2, or 10.5 for overdraft facilities; also 10.3-4). Consumers must be informed of changes in borrowing rates before the change enters into force, except in the case where the rate is based on external reference rates, in which case a reporting period can be agreed (Art 11). In the case of overdraft facilities, consumers must be provided with period statements containing a specified set of information (Art 12). If accounts overrun—ie overdrafts are granted without a specific agreement in place—similar terms apply (Art 18).

6.5 Consumer Rights Under Credit Agreements

Withdrawal. Consumers have the right to withdraw within 14 days from the later of where they enter into a contract or receive the full documentation. In this case they must repay the funds received, plus any interest due, within 30 days of cancellation (Art 14).

Cancellation of Open-Ended Agreements. Unless agreed otherwise, open-ended credit agreements can be cancelled by the consumer without notice, and by the creditor with two months' notice. If a consumer notice period is agreed, it cannot be longer than one month. In any case, cancellation must be free of charge (Art 13).

Linked Credit Agreements. If a credit agreement is linked to the purchase of goods or provision of services, and if the consumers exercise their right of withdrawal from this contract, they are no longer bound by the linked credit contract either (Art 15). Also, where a consumer has a right to pursue remedies against a provider of goods or services because those have not been supplied, or only supplied in part, or are not in conformity with the contract, then the consumer has the right to pursue remedies against the creditor. In some jurisdictions this requires that the consumer has unsuccessfully pursued his remedies against the supplier first. In others, creditors are joint and severally liable right away (Art 15).

Early Repayment. Consumers are always allowed to repay credit early. If the repayment is during a time where the borrowing rate under the agreement is fixed, the creditor is in some cases entitled to fair and objectively justified compensation. This compensation, however, cannot be more than 1% of the repaid amount, and not more than 0.5% if the remaining term of the credit agreement is less than a year (Art 16).

6.6 Annual Percentage Rate of Charge (APR)

The APR figure is to be computed using the formula in Annex I as the discount rate that makes the net present value of all cash flows—including relevant charges—of the product zero. For products where those cash flows depend on consumer choice, key assumptions are given, eg maximum possible drawdown at the earliest possible date, lowest possible repayment dates. Note that in the presence of fixed charges those assumptions have a tendency to *lower* the APR, ie customers that borrow less or repay earlier might actually face higher APRs.

Capital Requirements Directives

Capital Requirements Directives—The set of EU directives and regulations that transposes the Basel 3 Accord

Summary

The Basel 3 Accord is a global standard for the prudential regulation of banks. It was transposed into EU law in 2013 as CRD 4, consisting of a directive (the Credit Institutions Directive or CID) and a regulation (the Capital Requirements Regulation or CRR).

Relevance for Fintech Companies

The CRD regulations only directly affect Fintech firms authorised either as banks or as investment companies, which many early-stage firms can usually avoid, eg by using authorised institutions to hold client funds in escrow, rather than holding client deposits. Even if CRD applies, the large majority of the regulations in here will be irrelevant for Fintech firms, as they'll be applying the standardised and simplified approaches rather than the advanced internal model-based approaches that many large institutions use.

However, even if those regulations do not apply directly, Fintech executives should be aware of them to the extent that their business touches product areas that this regulation covers (eg taking deposits, lending, running a securities or derivatives trading book). To the extent that a Fintech company offers products and services that are similar in kind, the chances are that regulators will have that framework in their mind when talking to that company, and assessing whether and under what conditions they should be allowed to do their business.

Also, Fintech companies should be mindful that a lot, if not all, of the wholesale counterparties they are working with are subject to this regulation, so the services that are being provided to them—and the prices at which they are being provided—will be shaped by the constraints imposed by this framework.

The key areas that Fintech companies should be aware of if they touch their business model in any way are the following:

- Standardised Approach for credit risk and market risk capital requirements
- principles behind operational risk capital requirements, and the Basic Indicator and Standardised Approaches
- securitisation capital requirements, and rules imposed on the originator
- liquidity requirements, notably the Liquidity Coverage Ratio (LCR) and the Net Stable Funding Ratio (NSFR) and the principles behind it
- large exposure rules, and possible exceptions
- capital requirements under the leverage ratio framework
- transparency rules ('Pillar 3 reporting').

If Fintech companies are subject to minimum capital requirements— or where they feel they could overcome regulatory reluctance if they were better capitalised—they might also look into the definitions of own funds to see whether there are some types of capital that are easier to raise than others.

References

- Directive 2013/36/EU (CRD4-CID)
- Regulation EU 575/2013 (CRD4-CRR)
- Directive 2010/76/EU (CRD3)
- Directive 2009/111/EC (CRD 2)
- Directive 2009/83/EC (CRD 2)
- Directive 2009/27/EC (CRD 2)
- Directive 2006/49/EC (CRD1-CAD)
- Directive 2006/48/EC (CRD1-BD)
- Directive 2004/39/EC (MiFID1)

The Basel 2 Accord was implemented in two directives, jointly and confusingly named the Capital Requirements Directives (CRD): 2006/48 (Banking Directive) and 2006/49 (Capital Adequacy Directive). In 2009, CRD 2 (aka Basel 2.5) was implemented in Directives 2009/27, 2009/83, and 2009/11.

In 2010, CRD 3 introduced some more amendments in directive 2010/76.

Basel 3 was finally implemented in CRD 4 as directive 2013/36 (Credit Institutions Directive) and regulation 575/2013 (Capital Requirements Regulation). To a large extent CRD 4 is a roll-up of the changes made to CRD, so CRD 4 repeals the previous directives (it does keep some of the annexes, however). MiFID 2004/39 is a related directive.

7.1 General Background on Basel and CRD

Starting from Basel 2, the implementation of the Basel Accords into EU law is done via the so-called Capital Requirements Directives. The counting, however, is slightly confusing

- CRD 1 corresponds to Basel 2; it consists of two directives, the Capital Adequacy Directive and the Banking Directive.
- CRD 2 corresponds to amendments made to Basel 2 in 2009, immediately after the crisis—often referred to as Basel 2.5—which in particular introduces the liquidity requirements, modifies the definition of capital, and increases a number of capital requirements, notably for market risk; it is contained in three separate directives.
- CRD 3 corresponds to some more amendments made after the crisis in 2010, notably in respect of remuneration policy, resecuritisations, and trading book capital requirements.
- CRD 4 corresponds to Basel 3. To a large extent it is a roll-up of the previously made changes into a consistent regulatory rule set.

The CRD 4 is contained in the Credit Institutions Directive (CID), and the Capital Requirements Regulation (CRR). As a reminder, Regulations are directly applicable law, and directives must be transposed by the Member States. Since CRD 1, Member State legislation has converged to the extent that now the largest part of CRD 4 is codified as part of a Regulation. The CRR is divided into parts, titles, chapters, and sections. The CID is significantly smaller, and there is no separation into parts, so it is divided into titles, chapters, and sections.

The CRD 4 regulation applies to *institutions*, which it defines as credit institutions and investment firms (CID 1). Credit institutions—commonly referred to as banks—are defined as follows (CRR 4):

Credit institution means an undertaking the business of which is to take deposits or other repayable funds from the public and to grant credits for its own account

The definition of investment firms is taken from MiFID, where it is defined as a company providing investment services or activities on a professional basis (CRR 4, MiFID 4). Investment services are defined as most services related to buying, selling, managing, or advising on investments in securities, derivatives, or fund units (MiFID Annex 1A, 1C), so it covers for example broker-dealers, investment banks, fund managers, and trading facilities.

7.2.1 Authorisation Requirements (CID Title 3, 8–27)

Credit institutions must obtain authorisation before commencing their activities (CID 8), and only credit institutions are allowed to take deposits (CID 9).

The minimum capital requirement is €5m, possibly €1m at the discretion of the Member State (CID 12). Branches of institutions authorised in another Member State neither require local authorisation nor are they subject to local capital requirements (CID 17). An application for authorisation must set out the types of business envisaged, and the structural organisation (CID 10). An application cannot be refused because there is no economic need for that institution (CID 11). There are certain requirements as to the directors and large shareholders of an institution (CID 13–14). Applications must be decided in not more than six months after they have been submitted complete (CID 15). There are certain requirements in the event of acquisition or divestiture (CID 22–27).

7.2.2 Passporting (CID Title 5, 33–46)

Title 5 (CID 33–46) deals with passporting, ie the right of an institution authorised in one country to provide the services for which they are authorised all over the Single Market without having to establish locally regulated subsidiaries, either by establishing a branch, or by providing services cross-border (CID 33). Only activities actually carried out in the home Member State can be passported (CID 34).

In order to establish a branch (*right of establishment*), an institution has to apply to its home regulator who has to either approve and forward this application to the relevant host regulator, or refuse it within a period of three months (CID 35). The host regulator then has another two months to prepare for the supervision of the passported branch, at the end of which the branch can commence its activities (CID 36). In order to provide services on a cross-border basis (*freedom to provide services*), an institution has to apply to its home regulator, who has to either approve and forward this application to the relevant host regulator, or refuse it within a period of one month (CID 39).

Host regulators can ask branches established in their territory to report to them periodically for statistical or supervisory purposes (CID 40). Generally regulation is responsibility of the home regulator, but there are mechanisms regarding how host regulators can intervene, including taking emergency measures (CID 41–45).

7.2.3 Third-Country Relationships (CID Title 6, 47–48)

Title 6 (CID 47–48) deals with relations to third countries. Branches of third-country institutions cannot be accorded a more favourable treatment than those of institutions who have their head office in a Member State. The EU can agree with third countries that branches of institutions headquartered and supervised there are accorded identical treatment throughout the Single Market (CID 47). The EU can also agree on a basis for consolidated supervision for groups headquartered in a third country (CID 48).

7.2.4 Prudential Supervision (CID Title 7, 49–142)

Title 7 (CID 49–142) is the largest title of this directive, occupying more than half of its entire volume. It deals with the details of prudential supervision of banks and investment firms.

The first chapter (CID 49–72) establishes the key principles of regulation, including interaction between home and host regulators, information exchange with other regulatory bodies more generally (CID 55–61), and regulation of so-called significant branches (CID 51).

The second chapter (CID 73–110) deals with the regulatory review process, ie the regulatory dance where regulated firms provide information to their regulators, and the regulators respond. One key chapter in here is chapter 1 (CID 73) on the Internal Capital Adequacy Assessment Process (ICAAP), which is the main Pillar 2 report that institutions have to provide to their regulator, where they both quantify and describe the risks they are taking, and how they are mitigated.

The other important chapter is chapter 3 on the regulator's response to ICAAP, namely Supervisory Review and Evaluation Process (SREP). The other chapters deal with the internal processes the institutions must have in place (CID 74–96), with supervisory measures and powers (CID 102–107), and with where in a group hierarchy those regulations apply (CID 108–110).

7.3 Capital Requirements Overview

Under the Basel framework, capital requirements are for credit risk, market risk, and operational risk. For historical reasons—the first Basel Accord focused on credit risk—capital requirements are often expressed as Risk Weighted Assets (RWAs), where an asset with a risk weight of 100% is deemed to have the risk of an *average* loan, and the capital requirement is a certain percentage of it (historically 8%; now different).

Over time, additional risk categories have been added, notably the residual undiversified risk of large exposures (the remainder of the credit risk framework assumes that only systemic risk components matter), the CVA risk that I'll explain in the section below, and the settlement risk related to trade settlement. Also, special rules have been added for transferred credit risk, ie mostly the risk of purchased securitisation tranches.

All those risk figures are added together, and the result is one single capital requirement figure for the overall institution. In addition to this there is a second, parallel measure called the leverage ratio, which only looks at balance sheet risk, but takes a mostly unweighted view. As of this regulation the measure is only being observed, but there seems to be strong consensus to make the leverage ratio a binding backstop at a level of 3%.

More detailed information on this topic is provided under the three following headings:

- the first one looks at credit risk, which is by far the largest topic, and it includes large exposure and transferred credit risk
- the second one looks at the other components of risk that enter the RWA calculations, notably market and operational risk, as well as CVA and settlement risk
- the third one looks at the leverage ratio, which is an independent way of looking at capital requirements that is different from the RWA-based approaches discussed above.

7.3.1 Types of Own Funds (CRR Part 2, 25–88)

A company's capital is also referred to as *own funds*, so the terms *capital requirements* and *own funds requirements* are equivalent. The second part of the CRR (CRR 25–88) deals with the definition of those own funds, ie Tier 1 capital (aka T1)—consisting of Common Equity Tier 1 capital (CET1), Additional Tier 1 capital (AT1)—and Tier 2 capital (T2).

CET1 capital (CRR 26–50) is the most important component of capital, and it is mostly what people usually refer to as equity, ie shares of the company that express a residual ownership interest once all liabilities are paid, and that typically control the entity as well.

AT1 capital (CRR 51–61)—which is the second component of T1 capital—is technically debt, albeit debt on which payments can be cancelled or where the principal can be written down without causing a default event. T1 capital and AT1 capital in particular is therefore also often referred to as going-concern capital as it provides a buffer against losses when the company is still a going concern.

Finally, T2 capital (CRR 62–71) is gone concern capital, meaning that if an interest or principal payment is missed this is a default even for the entire company. It is subordinated debt, meaning that in the event of default it protects the senior debt holders, in the sense that losses in the event of default are borne by T2 holders (and T1 holders before them), and only if both T1 and T2 are fully exhausted do senior debt holders start incurring losses.

7.3.2 Initial Capital Requirements of Investment Firms

Investment firms are regulated under the CRD, and they are subject to initial capital requirements according to the rules of Title 4 (CID 28–32). By default the capital requirement is €730k (CID 28), but for some lower-risk firms it can be lower at €125k (CID 29), or even as low as €50k for local firms (CID 30), or firms not authorised to hold client assets (CID 31).

7.4 Capital Requirements for Credit Risk

7.4.1 Credit Risk

Title 2 of Part 3 deals with credit risk (CRR 107–302) and it is by far the largest title here—it takes up more than half of the entire part. After the chapter on general principles (CRR 107–110) it deals with the Standardised Approach for Credit Risk. For all but the largest institutions—including the majority of Fintech companies, at least for the time being—this will be the most important approach to use.

The Standardised Approach is dealt with in chapter 2 (CRR 111–141). Its Section 1 (CRR 111–113) is about general principles. The most important information is in Section 2 (CRR 114–134), which contains the risk weights for the different asset classes and ratings. The last two sections (CRR 135–141) define how external ratings provided by rating agencies (formally: ECAIs) are to be used in this process.

The third chapter (CRR 142–191) is about the Internal Ratings-Based Approach or IRBA, which allows the larger and more sophisticated banks to estimate some of the risk parameters that go into the regulatory provided risk models. There is a section on what conditions institutions must fulfil in order to be allowed to use IRBA (CRR 142–150), one on how to calculate credit exposures (CRR 151–157), one on expected loss or EL (CRR 159–159), one on Probability of Default (PD), Loss Given Default (LGD), and maturity (CRR 160–165), one on exposure values (CRR 166–168) and finally a large section on the requirements that an IRB institution has to fulfil (CRR 169–191).

The fourth chapter (CRR 192–241) is about the impact of credit risk mitigation on capital requirements, and the fifth chapter (CRR 242–270) deals with the capital requirement for securitisations. The last chapter finally deals with the capital requirement for counterparty credit risk, ie the risk that derivatives counterparties default whilst their position is *out-of-the-money*, meaning that under the derivative they in net present value terms owe money to the institution in question.

7.4.2 Large Exposures (CRR Part 4, 387–403)

Part 4 (CRR 387–403) deals with large exposures, ie exposures of counterparties—or group of related counterparties—to which the aggregate exposure is large when compared to an institution's capital base. Note that in some cases this can apply intra-group as well, restricting a group's ability to move funds raised in one jurisdiction into another one. It can also be relevant for institutions that receive customer funds in the regular course of their business, but who have no lending business and therefore have to place their funds in the market. This last situation does not technically cover the typical Fintech situation where funds are kept in third-party escrow, but it is nevertheless to be kept in mind, and Fintech companies should be mindful when growing, as to whether reliance on a single provider of escrow accounts creates too much of a concentration risk.

An exposure (CRR 390–391, 400–401) to a client—or a group of connected clients—is defined as being *large* if it is bigger than 10% of an institution's capital base (CRR 392), typically corresponding to a few percent of an institution's balance sheet size, and large exposures must be reported (CRR 394). The large exposure limit after taking credit mitigation into account is 25% of eligible capital, but at least €150m (CRR 395). Under some circumstances institutions are allowed to breach those limits, provided they satisfy higher capital requirements (CRR 395.5, 397). There are special rules for mortgage exposure (CRR 402), and guaranteed exposure (CRR 403).

7.4.3 Transferred Credit Risk (CRR Part 5, 404–411)

Part 5 (CRR 404–411) deals with exposures to transferred credit risk, mostly via securitisations. The back story here is that part of the issue in the crisis was that certain securitised assets—notably highly rated tranches of subprime securitisations—were found to be riskier than investors had previously assumed, and to avoid this happening again the regulators have put certain rules in place.

The more straightforward requirement imposed here is that investing institutions should have the skills necessary to assess the risk of the assets that they are investing in (CRR 406). More interestingly, there is an indirect requirement imposed on the originators of securitisations, notably a retention requirement where they have to retain at least 5% of the risk they originate (CRR 405) and certain minimum origination standards (CRR 408–409). This is enforced via requirements on the purchasers of those securities, notably increased capital requirements (CRR 407), meaning that it impacts originators regardless of whether they fall under the remit of those regulations or not.

7.5 Capital Requirements for Non-credit Risk

7.5.1 Market Risk

Market risk—ie the risk that the aggregate trading position of an institution causes losses—is dealt with in Title 4 of Part 3 of the CRR (CRR 325–377). There is a market risk standardised approach that specifies the risk charge for every position depending on its type, possibly taking into account hedging, which is detailed in chapters 1 to 4 of this title (CRR 325–361). More sophisticated institutions can also use internal models to calculate the market risk capital requirements for part or all of their trading book, which is described in chapter 5 (CRR 362–377). The calculation splits out the specific risk and the general risk of any position, whereby the former is the diversifiable risk that a specific entity defaults or loses significant equity value, whilst the latter is the non-diversifiable market risk (CRR 362).

The market risk calculation is based on the Value-at-Risk (VaR) concept, ie on the maximum amount an institution could lose at a certain confidence level over a certain loss horizon. Technically the VaR figure is a 99% confidence 10-day holding period figure calibrated to average market conditions, and there is also a stressed VaR figure, which is the same but with risk parameters calibrated to a period of stress (CRR 365). The capital requirement is the sum of the regular and the stressed VaR figure, each multiplied with a factor that is between 3 and 4, based on the back-testing results of the model (CRR 366) and subject to a certain lookback period (CRR 364).

7.5.2 Operational Risk

Operational risk—ie the risk that operational failures cause large losses— is dealt with in Title 3 of Part 3 (CRR 312–324). There are three different approaches, the Basic Indicator Approach, the Standardised Approach, and the Advanced Measurement Approach.

Under the Basic Indicator Approach (BIA) the own funds requirement is 15% of the relevant indicator—typically a gross income figure—averaged over a period of three years (CRR 315–316).

Under the Standardised Approach (SA) (for operational risk), companies must divide their income into business lines according to the table in CRR 317, apply the corresponding weighting factors that range from 12% to 18% and add them up, so instead of using a constant 15% like under the BIA the weighting factor is slightly more differentiated according to the operational risk of the business (CRR 317–318). Alternatively, for some lending business lines, the outstanding loan notional can be used, where the corresponding interest income is imputed as 3.5% of the outstanding notional (CRR 319). Firms wanting to use the SA must satisfy certain requirements (CRR 320).

Finally, there is an Advanced Measurement Approach, where sophisticated institutions can use their own internal models to calculate operational risk capital requirements (CRR 321–324).

7.5.3 Settlement Risk

Settlement risk is the risk associated with the settlement of financial transactions, eg when a stock is purchased against cash. It is dealt with in Title 5 of Part 3 of CRR (CRR 378–380). There are two types of settlement risk: the first is when the settlement is delayed, but there is procedural ensurance that funds are only paid out when the security is delivered, in which case the risk is only due to a variation in price of the underlying asset. The more serious risk in this context is the *free delivery risk*, where one side has already delivered on its obligations while the other side has not.

7.5.4 Credit Valuation Adjustment (CVA)

Credit Valuation Adjustment (CVA) risk, ie the risk that a counterparty will default on its obligations under a derivative transaction, is dealt with under Title 6 of Part 3 CRR (CRR 381–386).

To give an example, if an institution has a contract to purchase a stock for $100 at a given date in the future, and the stock is at $105, then—ignoring interest and dividends—this institution is essentially owed $5, and there is a credit risk associated with this. However, if there is volatility, this risk is bigger than just the $5 outstanding: assume for example that the stock could go up or down by $10, with equal probability. In this case the institution is either owed $15, or nothing (in fact it owes $5, but this does not matter), so the *expected* credit risk is ($15 + $0)/2 = $7.5, which is bigger then the current amount of $5. On the other hand, if there is a margining agreement in place where whenever the value of the stock changes the difference is settled in cash (in this case: the institution would be handed $5 by their counterparty) the credit risk greatly reduces because it is only restricted to the periods between collateral calls.

The CRR provides two methods for calculating the credit risk for those types of situations, an Advanced Method (for CVA): (CRR 383), and a Standardised Method (for CVA) (CRR 384), both of which are fairly complex.

7.6 Leverage Ratio

Part 7 (CRR 429–430) deals with the leverage ratio capital requirements. Those are similar to regular capital requirements in that they require a certain minimum amount of capital to be held against an institution's assets. The difference is that whilst regulatory capital requirements are based on Risk Weighted Assets (RWAs), where riskier assets are given a higher weighting, the leverage ratio is based on unweighted assets, ie all assets count the same, regardless of their risk, with the caveat that some assets are entirely excluded from the leverage ratio calculations.

The leverage ratio is defined as the ratio of an institution's *capital measure* divided by its *total exposure measure*. The former is defined as its total Tier 1 capital (including Core Tier 1 and Alternative Tier 1 capital), and the latter is defined in more detail in the regulation. It includes off-balance sheet obligations, in particular credit derivatives, as well as repo and similar transactions allowing some netting. Most items have a weighting factor of 100%, but there are a few where this factor is lower (CRR 429). The CRR only establishes a reporting requirement, and posits that the regulator takes it into account in its supervision activities, but it does not have a hard limit (CRR 430). The minimum ratio is probably being set to 3% by regulation currently in progress.

7.7 Liquidity Risk

Part 6 (CRR 411–428) deals with liquidity risk limits and liquidity reporting. Those requirements have been established as a response to the financial crisis where it was shown that even apparently solvent banks—ie those which had sufficient capital resources to meet their net obligations—could run into difficulties because of liquidity constraints. Those requirements are still somewhat experimental as it is unavoidable that banks take liquidity risks: one of their functions is to intermediate between savers who prefer their savings to be liquid, and borrowers who need loans on a long-term basis, and too-tight liquidity requirements can seriously impede the ability of banks to lend.

In this context, the regulators look at two indicators, *liquidity coverage ratio (LCR)* and *net stable funding ratio (NSFR)*. The former is comparing the liquidity inflows and the liquidity outflows under stressed conditions on a short time horizon (CRR 412), whilst the latter is looking at the same on a longer-term horizon (CRR 413). Contrary to the situation with capital requirements, a breach in one of the liquidity requirements first and foremost triggers a daily reporting requirement to the regulator, and the preparation of the liquidity restoration plan which the regulator has to approve (CRR 414). Institutions report not only headline numbers, but also a very detailed breakdown of both sides of the respective requirement equation. As usual, regulators responsible for consolidated group supervision are charged with informing the other ones (CRR 415).

7.7.1 Liquidity Coverage

For the calculation of the liquidity coverage situation, the relevant time horizon is 30 days (CRR 420), and there are specific rules how to calculate the outflows for the different types of liabilities contributing to the outflows (CRR 420–424). They key here is to make some behavioural assumptions—most of them supplied in the regulation—eg treating insured retail deposits differently from uninsured ones (CRR 421). Balancing the outflows are the inflows (CRR 425) and importantly the liquid assets that can be sold in a stressed scenario to create additional inflows, and that are enumerated in the regulation to the extent that they are eligible in the liquidity calculation (CRR 416). There are certain associated operational (CRR 417) and valuation requirements (CRR 418). Specific rules apply for currencies where the supply of eligible liquid assets is severely limited (CRR 419).

7.7.2 Net Stable Funding

For the net stable funding ratio there are similar requirements defining the balance sheet items *providing* net stable funding, which must be reported separately for buckets of less than 3 months, 3–6 months, 6–9 months, 9–12 months, and finally greater than a year (CRR 427), and those that *require* stable funding (CRR 428).

7.8 Pillar 3 Disclosure

Part 8 (CRR 431–455) deals with institutions' disclosure requirements, meaning the so-called Pillar 3 requirements to disclose certain information publicly. The reporting requirement for all institutions is specified in Title 2, and Title 3 has additional requirements applicable to some institutions (CRR 431; Title 2 is CRR 435–451, Title 3 is CRR 452–455). Institutions might be allowed to not disclose some of the required information either because of immateriality or because it is proprietary or confidential (CRR 432). Disclosure must happen at least annually, together with the annual report (CRR 433), and there are some requirements as to the means of disclosure (CRR 434); in practice most institutions publish those reports on their website.

The following topics must be covered in the Pillar 3 report by all reporting institutions (Title 2):

- risk management objectives and policies (CRR 435)
- scope of application (CRR 436)
- own funds (CRR 437)
- capital requirements (CRR 438)
- exposure to counterparty credit risk (CRR 439)
- capital buffers (CRR 440)
- indicators of global systemic importance (CRR 441)
- credit risk adjustments (CRR 442)
- unencumbered assets (CRR 443)
- ECAIs (rating agencies) (CRR 444)
- market risk (CRR 445)
- operational risk (CRR 446)
- equities not included in the trading book (CRR 447)
- interest rate risk outside the trading book (CRR 448)
- securitisation positions (CRR 449)
- remuneration policy (CRR 450) Leverage (CRR 451).

The following reporting requirement only apply to some institutions (Title 3):

- IRB approach for credit risk (CRR 452)
- credit risk mitigation techniques (CRR 453)
- Advanced Measurement Approaches for operational risk (CRR 454)
- internal market risk models (CRR 455).

7.9 Other

7.9.1 Scope and General Provision

Part 1 of the CRR (CRR 1–25) contains general provisions, including definitions of many entities and products in the financial services space (CRR 4). It also deals with the question at which level(s) in a group those rules apply on an individual or a consolidated basis (CRR 6–24). Similarly, Title 1 of the CID (CID 1–3) defines the scope of the directive, and contains a definition section that largely refers to the one in the CRR.

7.9.2 Regulators

Title 2 of the CID (CID 4–7) establishes a requirement for Member States to designate one or more regulators (CID 4–5), and to cooperate within the Single Market (CID 6–7).

7.9.3 Delegated and Implementing Acts, Transitional Provisions (CRR Part 9, 456464)

Delegated and implementing acts are in Part 9 (CRR 456–464), and transitional provisions are in Part 10 (CRR 465–520). Note that in particular the latter section is very large, but as of 2018 the large majority of these provisions have lapsed.

7.9.4 Regulatory Disclosures and Technical Provisions (CID Title 8, 143–144)

Title 8 (CID 143–144) deals with disclosures by the competent authorities (aka regulators).

7.9.5 Technical Provisions (CID Title 9–11, 145–165)

The other titles are of a technical nature: Title 9 deals with delegated and implementing acts (CID 145–149), Title 10 deals with amendments to (CID 150), and Title 11 contains transitional and final provisions (CID 151–165).

Deposit Guarantee Scheme Directive

Deposit Guarantee Scheme Directive—The directive establishing uniform Deposit Guarantee Schemes in the EU

Summary

This directive establishes common standards for deposit guarantee schemes within the EU. In particular, it defines which deposits are covered and which are not, what the coverage levels are, and operational details like the timeframe within which customers have to be reimbursed.

It also establishes the requirement that deposit-taking institutions must join a DGS, and it deals with the applicable split of contributions to be made to that scheme.

Relevance for Fintech Companies

This directive is potentially important for all entities holding customer deposits. It will probably not apply to a large number of Fintech companies—taking deposits in many cases also implies being regulated as a bank, eg under the Basel 3/CRD regulations which can be tedious—but for some business models it is important to understand the exact nature of the exceptions, and to ensure that the company stays within the relevant parameters.

Also, companies must understand that funds that are not subject to deposit protection can be very fickle and disappear at the first sign of trouble, so regulators might want companies to be either be prepared for that, or to ensure that their funds are held in segregated accounts with a third party where they are bankruptcy-remote with respect to the Fintech company in question, and ideally protected by a deposit protection scheme.

References

- Directive 2014/49/EU (DGSD 2)
- Directive 2014/59/EU (BRRD)
- Directive 2002/58/EC (Data Processing)
- Directive 2009/14/EC (DGSD Amendment)
- Directive 94/19/EC (DGSD 1)

The Deposit Guarantee Scheme Directive 2 2014/49 is a recast of the previous directive DGSD 94/19, which in turn had previously been amended by directive 2009/14. The Directives 2002/58 (data processing) and 2014/59 (bank resolution) are related.

8.1 Definition and Scope

A deposit guarantee scheme (DGS) is an institutional framework that guarantees deposits at banks or similar institutions, which are then often referred to as insured deposits. The guarantee typically has a cap, and sometimes a first loss and/or percentage deductible. For example, a scheme might pay out *90% of the losses above €1,000 with a maximum pay-out of €18,000.*

There are a number of public policy reasons why protection schemes are desirable:

- Many depositors, in particular small ones, can ill afford to lose all or even significant parts of their savings.
- Many depositors are either not able to adequately assess the creditworthiness of a bank, or doing so would be excessively expensive for them.
- If deposits are not insured there is a risk of a bank run—everyone trying to withdraw deposits at once—when there are rumours that a bank is in financial difficulties.

We have seen in the financial crisis, when depositors *did* actually run on Northern Rock in the UK, that the risk of bank runs is real, even when deposit protection schemes are in place (the one in force in the UK at that time had deductibles, and quite a low maximum amount). The current DGSD enacted in 2014 is a response to the events in that crisis, essentially recasting the old 1994 directive and the 2009 amendment that was made during the crisis and that significantly increased the minimum protection that had to be offered under schemes.

This directive relates to *statutory* and *officially recognised* deposit guarantee schemes; there are a number of schemes in the market that are not recognised—eg some top-up schemes that provide additional protection—and that are not subject to this regulation (Art 1).

Each Member State must make sure that there is at least one recognised DGS within its territory. This does not necessarily have to be a local scheme, cross-border schemes are acceptable. Any bank—technically, any credit institution as defined in the CRD 4, 2013/36—must be part of a deposit protection scheme (Art 4).

There are a number of deposits which are not eligible for deposit protection, for example those made by entities active in the financial sector (banks, investment and pension schemes, insurance companies, etc) and by public authorities. Member States can have derogations for SME pension schemes and local authorities with a budget of below €500k (Art 5).

The coverage level must be at least €100k and there can be no deductible.

Some deposits must be protected above that amount for a limited period of time (3–12 months), for example deposits relating to a private residential real estate transactions (Art 6). The coverage level is to be understood per-customer per-institution. This means if a customer has multiple accounts with the same bank, those are aggregated. For joint accounts the amount is apportioned to the account holders; for example for a joint account where both owners do not have other accounts the coverage level is €200k.

Note that this per-customer per-institution basis can be misleading from a customer point of view: what matters is the legal entity that takes the deposits, not the brand under which it operates. In particular, if a Fintech company holds their customers' funds with a high-street bank then, if that bank gets in trouble, a customer's direct holdings at this bank and his indirect holdings via the Fintech company are aggregated for the purpose of calculating the cap.

Repayments from the DGS should be made at most 7 working days after the event. This requirement is being phased in until 2024, however, and as of 2017 the time horizon is 20 working days (Art 8). DGSs are financed by contributions from their members, often after the fact, and the regulation allows DGSs to raise annual contributions of up to 0.5% of an institution's covered deposits. Contributions must be proportional to the amount of covered deposits, but the risk profile of the institution can be taken into account at the discretion of the Member State (Art 13). Schemes must have raised at least 0.8% of the covered deposits amount in advance by mid-2024 (Art 10).

Whilst DGSs would usually use their funds to repay depositors, they can also use them to support a failing bank if this is cheaper (Art 11). Also, if the *Bail-in Tool* of the BRRD is used, then the DGS is being asked to contribute according to the write-down that depositors would have received (Art 11; Art 109 BRRD).

Branches—ie offices without own legal personality—in other Member States are ultimately the responsibility of the DGS in the country where the institution is incorporated. However, initially the disbursements to depositors are being made by a DGS in the host Member State, which will ultimately be reimbursed by the one in the home Member State (Art 14). For branches of institutions resident in third countries, the local regulator must ensure that an equivalent DGS is in place and that covers the losses in the country of the branch. Where this is not the case, the branch can be required to join a host country DGS (Art 15).

Member States, DGSs and deposit-taking institutions are required to provide certain information to depositors and the public (Arts 16, 17).

Distance Marketing in Financial Services Directive

Distance Marketing in Financial Services Directive—
The regulation establishing certain requirements in respect
to marketing financial services by means of distance
communication, notably information requirements, and a
right of withdrawal

Summary

This short directive is applicable whenever financial services are marketed to consumers by means of distance communication. It establishes specific information requirements ahead of closing a contract, and certain withdrawal rights for the consumers. It also addresses unsolicited communications and tacit renewals.

Relevance for Fintech Companies

This directive is relevant for Fintech companies to the extent that they are marketing their services to consumers.

References

- Directive 2002/65/EC (DMFSD)
- Directive 1993/13/EEC (CCOD)

Distance Marketing in Financial Services Directive is 2002/65. A related directive is the Consumer Contracts Directive 1993/13/EEC

9.1 Definition and Scope

This short directive regulates the marketing of financial services via means of distance communication—ie in particular via telephone and the Internet —to consumers (Art 1). Hereby consumers are defined in the usual manner as *natural persons* who are *acting for purposes which are outside their trade, business or profession*. Financial services are defined as *any service of a banking, credit, insurance, personal pension, investment or payment nature* (Art 2).

9.2 Information Requirements

The key requirement of this directive is that prior to concluding a financial services contract the consumer must be provided with a specific set of information concerning the supplier of the service, the service provided, the contract itself, and possibilities of redress if need be (Arts 3, 4). If the contract is agreed to via telephone a much-reduced set of information is sufficient, provided the required information is supplied at a later stage (Art 3.3). The information must be provided on paper or another durable medium (Art 5). In the case of repeated interactions, the information only has to be provided either before an initial framework agreement is executed, or—if no such framework agreement exists—before the first agreement is executed, and thereafter at least once per year (Art 1).

9.3 Withdrawal and Renewal

In most cases, consumers must have an unconditional right of withdrawal free of charge from financial services contracts concluded by means of distance communication for a period for 14 calendar days, and 30 days for certain life insurance and pension products. There are some important exceptions, in particular with respect to the sale or purchase of financial instruments and foreign exchange transactions and short-term contracts, and possibly property-related transactions depending on Member State discretion. If another distance contract is attached to a cancelled financial services contract, then this contract will be cancelled free of charge as well (Art 6). When services are cancelled the payment required under the contract can be at most proportional to the services provided and there can be no penalty element (Art 7).

In the case of a distance contract where a fraudulent card payment is made, there must be a means of cancelling that payment and having the money returned (Art 8).

Whilst tacit renewal of contracts might be allowed depending on the Member State in question, chargeable financial services are subject to certain restrictions, and absence of a reply cannot be interpreted as consent (Art 9).

9.4 Other

Unsolicited communications by automated calling systems without human intervention and via fax are only allowed after prior consent. Depending on the Member State, unsolicited communications by other means either require prior consent, or at least no prior objection. They must not entail costs for consumers (Art 10).

The exact nature of the sanctions for non-compliance is left with the Member States. Usually they include that the consumer may cancel the contract at any time, free of charge and without penalty (Art 11). Consumers cannot waive their rights (Art 12), and there should be an out-of-court redress procedure (Art 14). In many Member States the burden of proof that information requirements have been complied with falls on the supplier, and contractual terms that would shift this burden back to the consumer are considered unfair terms under the Consumer Contracts Directive 1993/13 (Art 15).

European Market Infrastructure Regulation

European Market Infrastructure Regulation—The directive
regulating central counterparties and trade repositories, and
establishing clearing and reporting requirements

Summary

After the crisis, intransparent derivative exposure at banks has been seen
as one reason impeding the recovery. Regulators decided that most derivative exposure of banks should be intermediated by tightly supervised
clearing houses, regardless of whether it came from derivative exchanges
or from the OTC market. They also put in place a reporting requirement
for all derivatives trades, regardless of whether they cleared or not.

   This regulation establishes the details of those clearing and reporting requirements. It also defines the authorisation process for clearing houses, and the registration process for trade repositories, and it
describes the ongoing supervision of both.

Relevance for Fintech Companies

EMIR is directly relevant only for companies active in the derivatives
space, so for the standard Fintech company operating in the consumer space it is not particularly important. However, the technical
challenges behind the clearing and reporting obligations imposed by
EMIR are enormous, and they provide ample opportunity for Fintech/
Regtech companies operating in this space.

> ### References
>
> • Regulation EU 648/2012 (EMIR)
>
> The European Market Infrastructure Regulation (EMIR) is 648/2012.

10.1 Definition and Scope

The European Market Infrastructure Regulation (EMIR) deals with issues related to derivatives contracts, notably (Art 1):

• clearing and bilateral risk management requirements for OTC derivatives
• reporting requirements for derivatives contracts generally
• rules on central counterparties and trade information repositories

Derivatives in this context are financial contracts like swaps, options, and futures. *OTC* stands for 'over the counter', meaning a derivative contract that is negotiated directly between two counterparties (dealer/customer or dealer/dealer) and not on a *derivatives exchange*. *Trade repositories* are institutions that gather and make available information about all derivatives transactions in the market, both OTC and exchange-traded.

ESMA is required to publish a number of items related to this regulation on their website, including contracts eligible for clearing obligations, and authorised CCPs and repositories (Art 88).

10.2 Central Counterparties

Central counterparties (CCPs) are the equivalent of securities-markets clearing houses, but for derivatives contracts—they get inserted in the contract between the two counterparties in a process called *novation*. Once this is done, the legal counterparty for both sides is the CCP, so they no longer have a default risk against their original trading counterparty. They of course now have default risk against the CCP, but this is being dealt with by margining, which makes the CCP a highly secure entity.

Margining means that CCPs require all derivatives trades to be over-collateralised on both sides of the transaction, meaning that every counterparty is owed money by the CCP at all times in net-present value terms. To give an example, if the transaction is such that in net present value terms A owes

$5m to B, then the clearing house would, say, demand $6m in collateral from A and $1m from B so that not only the current liability is protected, but there is some protection against market moves. If markets move, then the clearing house will demand additional collateral from one of the counterparties, and return the same amount to the other side. If a counterparty does not post sufficient collateral after a move, the clearing house closes out the contract, and goes out to the market to replaces it. The other side is not impacted by that— once a contract has been novated, any relationship to the original counterparty is broken.

The entire process of novation is also often referred to as *clearing*, so a *clearing obligation* for certain transactions means that they *have* to be novated with a clearing house. In other words, if there is a clearing obligation for a certain derivatives transaction then counterparties are *not allowed* to keep facing each other during the life of the contract; they both must face a clearing house instead.

EMIR establishes a clearing obligation for a large number of transactions (Art 4). This obligation depends on (a) that particular class of derivative being cleared on a recognised clearing house—not all possible contracts are—and designated by ESMA as being subject to clearing obligation (Art 5), and (b) the type counterparties facing each other. The rules are slightly complex, but essentially the only exemptions to clearing obligation are

- intra-group transactions, which includes transactions between some loosely associated companies, eg the savings bank associations in Germany (Art 3.3)
- transactions involving one or two private counterparties, neither of which exceeds a certain clearing threshold in terms of the amount of business they do, ie light users of derivatives (Arts 4, 10).

ESMA keeps a public register of all classes of derivatives subject to clearing (Art 6). A CCP that is clearing certain contracts must clear them on a non-discriminatory basis regardless of where they have been traded (Art 7). Vice versa, all trading venues must provide CCPs with the relevant data they need to perform their clearing operation (eg price feeds) on a non-discriminatory basis (Art 8). All trades must report to trade repositories, and it is the responsibility of both the counterparties and the CCP to do so (Art 9).

Where contracts are not cleared via a CCP—either because of the counterparties involved, or because of the underlying instrument—there must be certain risk mitigation techniques in place. At the very minimum, there must be a timely confirmation of all trades, and formalised processes dealing with reconciliation and possible disputes in this respect. If a financial counterparty is involved, it must provide a daily mark-to-market, or mark-to-model if no market prices are available. Financial counterparties must have procedures for collateral exchange in place as if the contract was cleared in a clearing house, but non-financial counterparties must only engage in collateral exchange if they exceed the aforementioned clearing threshold. Also, many intra-group transactions (as defined above) are exempt (Art 11).

CCPs that are legally resident in a Member State mostly apply for authorisation to their home regulator, ie the regulator in the country where they are incorporated, who then organises a *college* of all supervisors concerned to review the application (Arts 12, 18). Third-country CCPs can also operate in the Single Market under certain conditions, provided they are authorised by ESMA (Art 25). Prior to this being possible, the Commission must have established that the third country in question has a regulatory framework that is equivalent. Equivalence can—and must, under certain circumstances—be withdrawn with 30 days' notice (Art 13). Once a CCP is authorised, it is authorised across the entire Single Market. Whether it is EU-resident or from an equivalent third country does not make a difference here (Art 12).

CCPs are subject to minimum capital requirements, with the absolute minimum being €7.5m (Art 16). They must have a robust governance structure in place, and shall be subject to frequent independent audits (Art 26). This structure must include effective conflict-of-interest procedures (Art 33), business continuity plans (Art 34) and risk management procedures (Art 49). There are certain requirements that senior management, the board members, and shareholders with significant influence must fulfil (Arts 27, 30). There is a requirement to establish a risk committee (Art 28), and for adequate record-keeping (Art 29). Regulators must be updated of any significant changes, and acquisitions especially must be pre-cleared (Arts 31, 32). CCPs can outsource some of their tasks to third parties, but the CCP itself remains responsible for ensuring that all rules and regulations are followed (Art 35).

CCPs must admit clearing members on a non-discriminatory basis. They must verify on an ongoing basis that clearing members do not pose a risk to its financial stability, and they must reject—or terminate as the case may be—clearing members if they don't meet the requirements (Art 37).

A CCP must be transparent about the services it provides, and about the associated prices and fees (Art 38).

There are some rules about segregation of assets and adequate record keeping as to asset ownership. In particular, clearing members are obliged to offer their clients individual asset segregation, and this segregation must also be respected by the CCP (Art 39).

CCPs must measure exposure and credit to its members—and other CCPs where applicable—on a near real-time basis (Art 40). CCPs shall hold margin covering at least 99% of the possible moves over a time period commensurate to the time it takes them to obtain additional margin. They must be able to execute intra-day margin calls (Art 41). They must also maintain a pre-funded CCP default fund that socialises losses due to insufficient margin to all clearing members. The default fund must at least be able to cover the losses if the largest clearing member defaults (Art 42). A CCP must also have sufficient pre-funded financial resources to cover losses that exceed those mitigated by margins and the default fund (Art 43), and it must have adequate liquidity arrangements (Art 44). There are certain requirements as to what CCPs can accept as collateral and where they can invest their funds. For non-financial counterparties, bank guarantees can be an acceptable collateral (Arts 45, 46).

CCPs may enter into interoperability agreements with other CCPs provided certain conditions are met. This allows, for example, counterparties to a derivatives trade to each deal with the CCP of their choice, instead of having to agree on a common CCP (Arts 51–54).

10.3 Trade Repositories

Trade repositories that are legally resident in a Member State must register with ESMA (not their local regulator). After successful registration, they gain the right to operate across the Single Market (Arts 55–61). Registered trade repositories are subject to ongoing ESMA supervision, including examination of records and on-site visits (Arts 62, 63). ESMA can delegate some supervisory responsibilities to local regulators (Art 74). It can impose fines and penalties (Arts 64–69). It can also issue public notices, and withdraw registration (Art 73).

Trade repositories from countries recognised as equivalent by the Commision can apply for recognition with ESMA and can—once they have been recognised—act like repositories resident in the EU (Arts 75–77).

Trade repositories must have robust governance structures in place. They must grant access to their services in a non-discriminatory manner and must be transparent about services offered and fees. If a repository offers ancillary services, they must be operationally separate from the reporting business (Art 78). They must be operationally reliable, and must have a business continuity and a disaster recovery plan in place (Art 79). They also must have robust data protection policies in place, and can only use the data they have received for commercial purposes if the relevant counterparties have consented (Art 80).

A trade repository shall regularly, and in an easily accessible way, publish aggregate positions by class of derivatives on the contracts reported to it. It also must make their data available to a number of relevant authorities including ESMA, ESRB and the regulators overseeing trading venues and CCPs (Art 81).

Electronic Money Directive

Electronic Money Directive—The directive regulating electronic money (ie non-cash payment systems) within the EU

Summary

The Electronic Money Directive establishes the regulatory regime for electronic money, ie electronic cash replacements. A typical example that falls under this regulation is a payment card, but the directive is deliberately vague so as to not exclude functionally equivalent schemes that operate in an unforeseen manner. However, it deliberately excludes narrow network systems like store cards or store-specific gift cards.

Relevance for Fintech Companies

The Electronic Money Directive is highly relevant in the Fintech start-up space as it is the basis for a large number of new payment-related business models.

References

- Directive 2009/110/EC (e-money 2)
- Directive 2005/60/EC (AMLD 3)
- Directive 2006/48/EC (CRD 1)
- Directive 2007/64/EC (PSD 1)
- Directive 2000/46/EC (e-money 1)

The e-money Directive 2 is 2009/110/EC. It repeals the first e-money directive 2000/46/EC, and it amends the Anti Money Laundering Directive 2005/60/EC as well as CRD 1 2006/48/EC. It relies on PSD 1 2007/64/EC for some definitions.

11.1 Definition and Scope

The Electronic Money Directive (EMD) deals with private sector providers of services for money-like payment solutions, also referred to as electronic money (Art 6). Those providers are generally referred to as *electronic money institutions* or, in the more restricted form if a waiver (Art 9, Art 1) has been granted, as *electronic money issuers* (Art 2). Those institutions are the only ones that are allowed to issue electronic money (Art 11), which is being defined here as

electronically, including magnetically, stored monetary value as represented by a claim on the issuer which is issued on receipt of funds for the purpose of making payment transactions [...], and which is accepted by a natural or legal person other than the electronic money issuer (Art 2)

The canonical example for electronic money is a current account together with a payment card, but the directive is deliberately vague about implementation details so as to not stifle innovation. Importantly, the money can be 'stored' both on the instrument and on a server, so the end user is not necessarily in possession of an electronic device. The directive, however, does specifically *exclude* what it refers to as limited-network instruments, such as store or petrol cards or childcare vouchers.

The directive requires that e-money providers must be authorised, and that there is a prudential regulation scheme in place, notably that there is an ongoing minimum capital requirement. There are a number of different ways of computing capital, notably methods A–C of the Payments Services Directive (PSD 2) and an additional method D which is simply *2% of the e-money held* (Art 5).

E-money is not considered a deposit, which means that it is not protected by deposit protection schemes, and the associated regulations do not automatically apply here (Art 6). E-money providers are not allowed to loan out the funds except in direct connection with the payments business. Instead, they must be held in safe investments (Art 7). Institutions are allowed—but not obliged—to pay interest, but this interest cannot depend on the duration for which the funds are held (Art 12), and funds cannot be locked in—they must be redeemable at any point in time, in full or in part, at par value. Only a small, cost-based redemption fee is allowed (Art 11).

Authorisation is passported across the Single Market. Third-country providers can also be given access to local markets, but it cannot be on better terms than providers operating under the Single Market passport. Third-country providers need separate authorisation for every country in which they want to operate (Art 8).

There must be an out-of-court procedure for the settlement of disputes between the providers and their customers (Art 13).

General Data
Protection Regulation

General Data Protection Regulation—The regulation
establishing common standards for data protection and
privacy in the EU

Summary

This regulation is about data controllers (those who collect and own
data), data processors (those who work with the data), and their relationship with data subjects (those whose personal data is being stored
and processed).

Key obligations of controllers and processors are to keep the data
safe, accessible, and accurate, and to adequately inform data subjects
and seek their consent if necessary before data is processed. Key
rights of data subjects are to access or correct their data, to prevent it
being used for certain analysis or in a certain context, and to have it
erased (*right to be forgotten*).

Relevance for Fintech Companies

This directive is almost universally relevant for companies doing business in the EU, and especially for Fintech companies that deal with
sensitive data of individuals, regardless of whether those individuals
are their customers, or whether they are a service provider to someone else owning the customer relationship.

Companies must understand whether they are considered a data
controller or a data processor under this regulation, and if the answer
to at least one of those questions is yes—which for a large majority
companies it will be—then they must ensure that they comply with

the applicable parts of this regulation. Fines for non-compliance can be very high at up to the bigger of €20m or 4% of turnover.

References

- Regulation EU 2016/679 (GDPR)
- Directive 2002/58/EC (PrivacyECommsD)
- Directive 95/46/EC (GDPD)

The General Data Protection Regulation is 2016/679. It replaces the previous General Data Protection Directive 95/46. A related directive is the one with regard to privacy in electronic communications 2002/58.

12.1 Definition and Scope

The General Data Protection Regulation (GDPR) is meant to ensure that data protection does not create an impediment to the free movement of data within the EU (Art 1). One of its main purposes is to define the rules that protect a natural person's data. This person is referred to as data subject. Other key actors are the *data controller*, ie the entity collecting and owning the data, and the *data processor*, ie the entity analysing the data, which might or might not be the same as the controller (Art 4).

The regulation applies mostly to electronically held personal data, with some exceptions (Art 2), and where either controller or processor is established in the EU, regardless of whether the processing takes place in the EU or not. It also applies to controllers or processors not established in the EU where it relates to (a) offering paid or unpaid goods or services in the EU or (b) monitoring data subjects' behaviour to the extent that behaviour takes place in the EU (Art 3).

12.2 Definition of Data

For the purpose of this regulation, personal data is defined as (Art 4):

any information relating to an identified or identifiable natural person

where the definition of '*identifiable natural person*' is very broad (Art 4):

one who can be identified, directly or indirectly, in particular by reference to an identifier such as a name, an identification number, location data, an online identifier or to one or more factors specific to the physical, physiological, genetic, mental, economic, cultural or social identity of that natural person.

The regulation also defines *'special personal data'* as (Art 9):

personal data revealing racial or ethnic origin, political opinions, religious or philosophical beliefs, or trade union membership, and the processing of genetic data, biometric data for the purpose of uniquely identifying a natural person, data concerning health or data concerning a natural person's sex life or sexual orientation.

12.3 Pre-requisites of Data Collection—Purpose and Consent

Personal data must be (Art 5):

- processed lawfully, fairly and in a transparent manner in relation to the data subject (*'data lawfulness, fairness, and transparency'*)
- for specified, explicit and legitimate purposes, and not further processed in a manner that is incompatible with those purposes (*'purpose limitation'*)
- adequate, relevant and limited to what is necessary in relation to the purposes for which it is processed (*'data minimisation'*)
- accurate and, where necessary, kept up to date (*'data accuracy'*)
- kept in a form which permits identification of data subjects for no longer than is necessary for the purposes for which the personal data are processed (*'storage limitation'*)
- processed in a manner that ensures appropriate security of the personal data, including protection against unauthorised or unlawful processing and against accidental loss, destruction or damage (*'data integrity and confidentiality'*).

Compliance with the above rules is the responsibility of the controller (*'data accountability'*).

Data processing is only lawful if at least one of the following conditions applies (Art 6):

1. the data subject has given consent
2. for performing a contract
3. to comply with the controller's legal obligations
4. to protect vital interests of data subject or another natural person

5. to perform a task in the public interest/under official authority
6. where there is a legitimate interest by the controller that is not overridden by the interests of the data subject.

The conditions 3–5 above are clarified in EU or Member State law, and may be subject to additional provisions (Art 6). If a controller wants to process data for other reasons than those for which it was originally collected he has to take into account a number of specific provisions (Art 6.4).

The term 'consent' in this context is defined as (Art 4):

any freely given, specific, informed and unambiguous indication of the data subject's wishes by which he or she, by a statement or by a clear affirmative action, signifies agreement to the processing of personal data relating to him or her.

Where processing is based on consent, the controller must be able to prove that consent was given. If consent is requested in a communication that also concerns other matters, eg other terms and conditions, then it must be presented *in a manner that is clearly distinguishable, in an intelligible and easily accessible form, using clear and plain language.* Data subjects cannot consent to terms that infringe this Regulation. They have the right to withdraw consent at any time, and *it shall be as easy to withdraw as to give consent.* Finally, when assessing whether content was freely given, it is important to consider whether the data requested is necessary for the performance of the contract (Art 7). Children can only consent from the age of 16; below that, parental consent is necessary (Art 8).

By default, processing of special personal data as defined above is by default prohibited. There are, however, a number of exceptions to this, for example when the data subject has given explicit consent to this and was allowed to give such consent under applicable local law, when the data subject has already made such data manifestly public, or for other specified public interest reasons (Art 9). Similarly, processing of data relating to criminal convictions is subject to specific rules (Art 10).

Communication by the data controller to their customers in this context must be in a *concise, transparent, intelligible and easily accessible form,* and it must use *clear and plain language, in particular for any information addressed specifically to a child.* Information must be provided *without undue delay* and in any case within one month of a request. If the controller decides to not take action upon receipt of a request, he has inform the person making the request within the same time frame of the reason for doing so. Where requests are unfounded or excessive—in particular because of their repetitive character—the controller can either charge a reasonable fee, or deny the request. The burden of demonstrating that a request is excessive rests with the data controller. Where a data controller has doubts regarding the identity of the person making the request, he may request additional information necessary. If icons are used to identify eg data categories, those icons must be machine-readable (Art 12).

12.4 Information Requirements

Where personal data is collected directly from the data subject, they have to be provided with specific information at the time the information is requested (Art 13). A similar slightly different information has to be provided—subject to certain exclusions—to the data subject if the data has been collected from third-party sources. In this case, the information must be provided at the latest in the first communication with the data subject, when the data is disclosed to a third party, or one month after the data has been collected, whichever of those is earlier (Art 14).

Any data subject has the right to know whether a controller holds their personal data, and—if this is the case—obtain specific information about the data held, as well as a copy of the data itself (Art 15). Where data is incorrect or incomplete, the data subject has a right to have it amended (Art 16). Under certain circumstances a data subject has the *right to be forgotten*, ie the right that a controller erases all their personal data (Art 17). Under certain circumstances the data subject can also require the controller to restrict processing of the subject's data, usually until certain conditions are fulfilled (Art 18). Controllers must forward those requests to processors as appropriate and feasible (Art 19).

12.5 Rights of the Data Subject

Where a data subject has provided data to a controller, they are entitled to receive it back in a *structured, commonly used and machine-readable format* and they have the *right to transmit the data to another controller*, without hindrance by the controller from whom the data has been received.

Data subjects have, in situations where the data processing is based on points 5 or 6 above, the right to object to such processing, with the burden of proof of legitimacy falling on the data controller. In cases where data processing is used for direct marketing, it must cease when the data subject complains. Those rights must be brought to the data subject's attention (Art 21).

Data subjects usually have the right to object to fully automated decision making in cases where the decision has significant impact, one important exception being if it *is necessary for entering into, or performance of, a contract between the data subject and a data controller* (Art 22). There are a number of specific public policy reasons that—if enshrined in local law—restrict the rights of data subjects vis-à-vis processing of their personal data (Art 23).

12.6 Data Controller Requirements

Data controllers must implement and document measures to fulfil their specific responsibilities under this regulation. Those measures must be updated regularly (Art 24). In particular, they must implement appropriate technical and organisational measures—examples mentioned are data minimisation and pseudonymisation to fulfil those responsibilities. An approved certification mechanism can be used to demonstrate compliance (Arts 25, 42). Joint controllers must all implement the necessary measures. In addition, they must have an explicit arrangement in place which defines their respective responsibilities. Data subjects can choose against which controller to exercise their rights (Art 26). Generally, controllers and processors not resident within the EU must appoint a local representative, located in one of the Member States where the data subjects reside (Art 27). Every controller must keep a specified log of all data processing activities under their responsibility (Art 30).

Processors can only engage subprocessors after explicit consent by the controller, and it is subject to similar requirements to those for engaging processors. In any case, the ultimate master processor retains full liability vis-à-vis the controller and the data subject (Art 28). A processor can only process data under specific instruction from the controller (Art 29). A processor must take appropriate steps—eg encryption, pseudonymisation, regular back-ups—to ensure a level of data security and availability that is appropriate considering risks and their possible impact (Art 30). Data breaches must always be reported to the regulator, and usually to the impacted customers (Art 31).

In particular where new technologies are used, and the impact is possibly large—eg large-scale processing of special data as defined above, or systematic monitoring of a publicly accessible area on a large scale—an impact assessment must be performed prior to processing (Art 35). If the assessment indicates that the processing would result in high risk unless special measures are taken, the controller must consult with their supervisor prior to processing, inter alia to discuss the appropriateness and effectiveness of such measures (Art 36).

Both controllers and processors can—and in some cases must—designate a *data protection officer* whose role and responsibilities are described in the regulation (Arts 37–39). Member States and supervisors must encourage the drawing up of codes of conduct, the implementation of which is monitored by appropriate institutions (Arts 40, 41). Member States, supervisors and the Commission encourage the establishment of data protection certification mechanisms and of data protection seals and marks for the purpose of demonstrating compliance with this regulation. Those certificates are voluntary and available via a transparent process (Arts 42, 43).

12.7 Transfer to Third Countries

Data can only be transferred to third countries if specific conditions are fulfilled (Art 44). If data is transferred to a third country that has been subject to an *adequacy decision* by the Commission then no additional steps have been taken—such transfers are always lawful (Art 45). Where such a decision is not available, data may only be transferred if certain specific safeguards are fulfilled (Arts 46, 47). Third-country court orders are only recognised or enforceable if they are based on an international agreement, eg a mutual legal assistance treaty (Art 48). There are a number of derogations that allow third-country data transfer even if the above conditions are not fulfilled, eg explicit consent by the data subject, it being necessary for the performance of a contract with the data subject, or public interest reasons (Art 49).

On a technical note, if a data processor no longer requires the identification of a data subject they are not obliged to maintain, acquire or process additional information in order to identify the data subject for the sole purpose of complying with this Regulation (Art 11).

12.8 Role of Supervisors

Controllers and processors must cooperate with the supervisors when asked to do so (Art 31). Supervisors must cooperate internationally (Art 51). Member States establish one more multiple supervisors according to a specific set of criteria (Arts 52–59). Where multiple supervisors are involved they operate under the direction of a lead supervisor (Arts 60–62).

The EU establishes the *European Data Protection Board* (Arts 68–76) that *ensures the consistent application of this regulation* throughout the EU (Arts 63, 67, 70). It does this inter alia by issuing opinions (Art 64), and by putting in place a dispute resolution mechanism between national supervisors (Art 65).

Data subjects have the right to lodge complaints with a supervisory authority. It is their choice whether they want to lodge at the place of their habitual residence, their place of work, or place of the alleged infringement (Art 77). Every legal or natural person—data subjects or others—have a right to appeal supervisory decisions in the court of the country where the supervisor is established. Data subjects also have the right to appeal to a court if the supervisor does not handle a complaint within three months (Art 78).

Notwithstanding other settlement mechanisms, data subjects have a right to bring proceedings against controllers and processors in court, either in a country where said controller or processor has an establishment, or—unless it is against a public authority—the country of the data subject's habitual residence (Art 79). Data subjects have the right to mandate certain not-for-profit organisations to represent them in court (Art 80). If there are proceedings against the same controller or processor because of the same issue in multiple Member States then every court except the first court contacted can either suspend its proceedings for the duration of that first trial, or can order those proceedings to be consolidated in cases where this is possible (Art 81).

12.9 Liability

Controllers and processors are liable for damages that flow from an infringement of this regulation, and have to compensate data subjects and others for material damages caused. If controllers and processors are jointly responsible for an infringement they are jointly and severally liable vis-à-vis a data subject, ie the data subject can demand compensation for the full amount from each of the controllers and processors involved, who then apportion the payment among themselves as they see fit (Art 82). Controllers and processors are also subject to substantial fines and penalties, the amount of which depends on a number of specific criteria such as previous fines, whether negligence was involved, whether the impact was mitigated, etc. Depending on the breach, administrative fines can be up to 4% of worldwide revenues or €20m, whichever is larger (Arts 83, 84).

12.10 Specific Situations

The regulation deals with the protection of data in a number of specific situations, notably in relation to *freedom of expression and information* (Art 85), *public access to official documents* (Art 86), *national identification numbers* (Art 87), and *in the context of employment* (Art 88). Finally there are some *safeguards and derogations relating to processing for archiving purposes in the public interest, scientific or historical research purposes or statistical purposes* (Art 89). The remainder of the regulation deals with technical details (Art 90–99).

Market Abuse Regulation

Market Abuse Regulation—The regulation dealing
with inside information, insider dealing, and market
manipulation and abuse

Summary

This regulation defines inside information, which is price-sensitive
information in relation to financial instruments. It prohibits unlawful
disclosure of such information, as well as insider dealing, ie dealing
on the basis of insider information. It defines and prohibits market
manipulation and abuse, and it establishes the regulatory framework,
powers, and sanctions with respect to all of the above.

Relevance for Fintech Companies

The rules with respect to inside information only apply to companies
whose shares are publicly traded, which means that they will not be
relevant to the large majority of start-ups. The interesting question in
this context is, however, whether they apply in the space of crypto
tokens. This regulation does not apply to currencies, and only in a very
limited sense to commodities (it does, however, apply to derivatives in
respect of both, as well as contracts for differences). It appears—and
this like everything else in this book is not legal advice—that it also
does not apply to bitcoin and other crypto tokens. One could, however, make a case that exchanges that trade crypto tokens should be
considered MTFs, in which case one might also want to consider the
tokens subject to the regulations here.

Regardless of whether those regulations apply or not, a lot of the
requirements here are best practices, and a company active in this

space might want to consider complying with them to the extent that it makes sense in their specific context, as this could make current and future regulatory interaction significantly easier.

References

- Regulation EU 596/2014 (MAR)
- Directive 2014/65/EU (MiFID2)
- Regulation EU 600/2014 (MiFIR)
- Directive 2003/6/EV (MAD)

The Market Abuse Regulation is 596/2014. It repeals the previous Market Abuse Directive 2003/6. Related directives are 600/2014 (MiFIR), and 2014/65/EU (MiFID2).

13.1 Definition and Scope

The regulation establishes a common regulatory framework on insider dealing, the unlawful disclosure of inside information and market manipulation (aka market abuse), as well as measures to prevent market abuse. Its purpose is to ensure the integrity of financial markets in this respect (Art 1). It applies to financial instruments that are traded on a regulated market, or on a Multilateral Trading Facility (MTF), or on an Organised Trading Facility (OTF), all as defined in the MiFID2/MiFIR regulations. It also applies to financial instruments *the price or value of which depends on or has an effect on the price or value of a financial instrument* referred to above (Art 2). The term 'financial instrument' is also defined in MiFID (Art 3). The definition there is as follows (Annex 1C of MiFID2):

- transferable securities
- money market instruments
- units in collective investment
- undertakings
- most derivative contracts
- contracts for differences
- emission allowances.

Note: Articles 12 and 15 not only apply to financial instruments as defined above, but also apply to spot commodity contracts and benchmarks (Art 2).

All trading venues referred to above must report the respective securities they list to their regulator, who in turn must report them to ESMA, who then publishes a list of all financial instruments covered under this regulation on its website (Art 4).

There are a number of exemptions where this regulation does not apply, notably to certain buybacks (Art 5), and to certain public-sector market activities (Art 6).

13.2 Inside Information

The regulation defines inside information as (Art 7.1a):

Information of a precise nature, which has not been made public, relating, directly or indirectly, to one or more issuers or to one or more financial instruments, and which, if it were made public, would be likely to have a significant effect on the prices of those financial instruments or on the price of related derivative financial instruments.

There are a number of additional definitions relating to commodity derivatives and emission allowances. There is also an additional definition of inside information that applies to people or companies that are involved in executing orders for other market participants (Art 7.1d):

For persons charged with the execution of orders concerning financial instruments, it also means information conveyed by a client and relating to the client's pending orders in financial instruments, which is of a precise nature, relating, directly or indirectly, to one or more issuers or to one or more financial instruments, and which, if it were made public, would be likely to have a significant effect on the prices of those financial instruments, the price of related spot commodity contracts, or on the price of related derivative financial instruments.

So to summarise, inside information is certain price-sensitive information about either a financial instrument, or the order-flow relating to a financial instrument.

13.3 Insider Dealing

The regulation also defines insider dealing as acting on insider information, for example by buying or selling an instrument, or cancelling or amending an order. Insider dealing only applies when a person ought to know that they possess inside information, except in a number of specific cases (eg management, shareholder, related professional) where it is always assumed that that person ought to know (Art 8).

There are, however, a number of exemptions where actions are not considered insider dealing, for example (Art 9):

- when a company has established effective *Chinese walls* between the actual people holding the inside information and those taking the dealing decisions
- in certain circumstances, where the company is a market maker, or where it relates to decisions prior to the inside information having become known
- when it is related to a public takeover or merger, or stake building, or where the inside information is only relating to one's own trading intentions.

13.4 Unlawful Disclosure

The regulation defines unlawful disclosure as disclosing inside information to another person, except where the disclosure is made in the normal exercise of an employment, a profession, or duties. Onward disclosure to a third person by a person who has obtained inside information—and who ought to know that it is inside information—is also considered unlawful disclosure (Art 10).

There are specific rules in place in the case of market sounding, ie the communication of information, prior to the announcement of a transaction, in order to gauge the interest of potential investors (Art 11).

13.5 Market Manipulation

The regulation defines market manipulation inter alia as any behaviour that is likely to give false or misleading signals as to the supply or demand for or the price of a financial instrument, or is likely to secure the price of a financial instrument at an abnormal or artificial level. It is not market manipulation if this has been done for legitimate reasons, or if it is to conform with accepted market practice. Other types of market manipulation are the placing of an order which employs a form of deception or contrivance and the dissemination of information and rumours that can affect the market or market benchmarks, provided the person knew or ought to have known that the information was false or misleading (Art 12).

There is a process under which regulators in cooperation with ESMA can establish certain practices as accepted market practices, in which case those are not considered market abuse. Accepted market practices are published on ESMA's website once established (Art 13).

13.6 Requirements, Prohibitions, and Fines

Legal and natural persons must not engage in insider dealing, or induce another person to engage in insider dealing, or unlawfully disclose inside information (Art 14), and must not engage or attempt to engage in market manipulation (Art 15).

Fines. Maximum fines set by Member States in relation to breaching Articles 14–15 are at least €5m for natural persons, and €15m or 15% of annual turnover, whichever is larger, for legal persons (Art 30).

Any operators of a trading venue, and any person professionally arranging or executing transactions, must establish effective arrangements, systems and procedures aimed at preventing and detecting insider dealing, and market manipulation. Any suspicious activity must be reported to the regulator without delay, who then reports it further as need be (Art 16).

An issuer must inform the public as soon as possible of inside information which directly concerns that issuer, and this disclosure must not be combined with the marketing of its activities. Under some circumstances—especially for financial stability reasons—disclosure can be delayed, provided the regulator agrees, and the confidentiality of that information is ensured. As soon as information starts leaking out, it must be disclosed (Art 17).

Fines. Maximum fines set by Member States in relation to breaching Articles 16–17 are at least €1m for natural persons, and €2.5m or 2% of annual turnover, whichever is larger, for legal persons (Art 30).

An issuer must keep up-to-date insider lists that identify which person has access to insider information from which date (Art 18). Managers must notify the issuer of own-account transactions, who in turn must inform the regulators. There is a closed period of 30 calendar days before results announcements where a manager is not allowed to conduct any transactions on its own account (Art 19).

Persons who produce or disseminate investment recommendations or any similar item must make sure that it is objectively presented, and they must disclose conflicts of interest (Art 20). There are also specific rules with respect to disclosure in the media (Art 21).

Fines. Maximum fines set by Member States in relation to breaching Articles 18–20 are at least €500k for natural persons, and €1m for legal persons (Art 30).

13.7 Regulators

The regulators are appointed by the Member State (Art 22) and have a number of specific powers, including requesting access to all kinds of data, suspending trading, and carrying out on-site inspections, except at private residences. Persons must be free to disclose information in this respect to the regulators without prejudice to other confidentiality requirements in place (Art 23).

Regulators cooperate with ESMA (Art 24), among each other (Art 25), and also may cooperate with third-country regulators (Art 26). The regulator has certain requirements with respect to professional secrecy (Art 27), data protection (Art 28), and also vis-à-vis third countries (Art 29).

Regulators can also apply a number of sanctions, including public warnings, disgorgement of profits made or losses avoided, withdrawal of authorisation, and the imposition of fines (Art 30). There are a number of specific considerations regulators shall take into account when deciding on sanctions (Art 31), and regulators report annually to ESMA (Art 33) and publicly (Art 34).

Regulators put in place secure arrangements to allow for persons to report infringements of this legislation, and those who report infringements are protected as whistleblowers (Art 32).

Mortgage Credit Directive

Mortgage Credit Directive—The regulation dealing with consumer mortgage credit, in particular its marketing, the calculation of APRs, and the requirement to perform an income-based credit assessment

Summary

In many jurisdictions, mortgage lenders—here referred to as creditors— are already subject to regulation, so the main focus in this directive is on credit intermediaries and their appointed representatives. It also establishes an authorisation and regulation requirement for non-bank mortgage lenders.

The directive defines the European Standardised Information Sheet (ESIS), which is the key informative document that consumers must receive before entering into a credit agreement. It also establishes some more rules on pre-contractual information, use of credit databases, foreign currency and variable loans, and arrears and foreclosure.

Relevance for Fintech Companies

This directive is relevant for all Fintech companies operating on the consumer mortgage space, be it lenders, intermediaries, or advisors.

References

- Directive 2014/17/EU (MCD)
- Directive 2008/48/EC (CCRD)
- Directive 2003/25/EC (UCPD)

> The Mortgage Credit Directive is 2014/17/EU. A related and very similar directive dealing with consumer credit other than mortgage credit is the Consumer Credit Directive 2008/48/EC.

14.1 Definition and Scope

This directive deals with consumer mortgage credit regulating lenders, intermediaries, and advisors in this space (Art 1). It does not prevent Member States from implementing more stringent customer protection rules (Art 2). It leaves a large number of options for Member States, and therefore in some cases local rules might be less stringent than the ones described here.

The scope of the directive is mainly *credit agreements which are secured either by a mortgage or by another comparable security on residential immovable property* or on land. There are important exceptions, however. For example it does not apply to most equity release products, and many subsidised or employer-sponsored credit agreements. Depending on jurisdiction, it might or might not apply to buy-to-let mortgages and some other optional cases (Art 3).

The definition of a consumer and creditor are exactly the same as in the Consumer Credit Directive, ie *natural persons who are acting for purposes which are outside their trade, business, or profession* and *persons who grant credit in the course of their trade, business, or profession* respectively, as is the definition of credit intermediary. The directive acknowledges that in some jurisdictions lenders are not necessarily banks (aka credit institutions), and non-bank lenders are somewhat awkwardly referred to a 'non-credit institutions' (Art 4). Credit institutions are regulated already because of other regulations, and this directive also requires non-credit institutions to be subject to authorisation and regulation (Art 35).

In every Member State there must be a regulator responsible for this directive, and if it is not the same as the one looking after banks then the two must cooperate. On the European level the responsible agency is EBA (Art 5). Non-credit institutions must also be subject to supervision (Art 35). Member States should also promote measures that support the education of consumers in relation to responsible borrowing and debt management (Art 6).

14.2 General Requirements

Everyone involved in the mortgage process must behave honestly, fairly, transparently, and professionally, taking account of the rights and interests of the consumers, and the activities must be based on information about the consumer's circumstances and any specific requirement made known by a consumer and on reasonable assumptions about risks to the consumer's situation over the term of the credit agreement (Art 7).

Remuneration policies must not impede compliance with this regulation, they must promote sound and effective risk management, and must not encourage risk-taking that exceeds the level of tolerated risk of the creditor. The remuneration strategy must not prejudice the ability to act in the consumer's best interest, and in particular remuneration must not depend on sales targets (Art 7).

Member States can forbid creditors to pay commissions to credit intermediaries, and they can prohibit or impose restrictions on payments from customers to creditors or intermediaries prior to the conclusion of an agreement (Art 7).

Information to consumers must be provided free of charge (Art 8).

Staff must possess and keep up to date an appropriate level of knowledge and competence. Regulators will provide detailed guidance on what this requirement entails. In the case of businesses that operate cross-border, it is the guidance in the host Member State that is relevant, implying that companies operating in multiple jurisdictions must fulfil different requirements in different Member States. Supervision in this respect is responsibility of the host regulator in the case of branches, and of the home regulator in the case of cross-border provision (Art 9).

Except for a number of well-defined exceptions, tying is not allowed, but bundling is. This means that whilst mortgage products can be sold together with other products, possibly at a discount, they must be available as stand-alone products as well (Art 12).

In general, consumers should have a right of early repayment. However, this right can be subject to the existence of a legitimate interest on the part of the consumer during periods in which the borrowing rate is fixed, to avoid consumers cancelling their contracts with the sole purpose of taking advantage of lower rates. In the event of early repayment, creditors are only entitled to fair and objective compensation which can be further limited by the Member State (Art 25).

14.3 Credit Intermediaries and Appointed Representatives

Apart from a number of small exceptions, advice can only be provided by creditors, credit intermediaries, or appointed representatives. Advisors must make it clear to their potential customers whether they are tied and only consider a small range of products available in the market, or whether their advice covers the entire market, or at least a large proportion of it (Art 22).

Credit intermediaries are subject to authorisation and regulation, and there must be a public register of authorised legal and natural persons. An exception to the authorisation requirement is where those activities are *carried out in an incidental manner in the course of a professional activity and that activity is regulated* in another way. Minimum requirements to be authorised are professional indemnity insurance, good repute and a clean police record, and to be appropriately knowledgeable and competent. If a credit intermediary has a registered office, it must be in the same Member State as its head office. If it has no registered office, its head office must be in the Member State in which it carries on its main business (Art 29). Authorisation can be withdrawn, if it is not used, renounced, has been obtained by irregular means, the requirements are no longer fulfilled, or there have been serious infringements (Art 33).

Credit intermediaries that are tied to only one creditor can obtain automatic authorisation through their creditor, who in this case remains fully responsible for their actions (Art 30). Similar rules hold where a credit intermediary appoints representatives, where again the appointing credit intermediary remains responsible (Art 31).

Credit intermediaries are passported to operate throughout the Single Market after going through a short application process with their home regulator. Some restrictions apply, for example they cannot *provide their services in relation to credit agreements offered by non-credit institutions to consumers in a Member State where such non-credit institutions are not allowed to operate.* Similarly, appointed representatives are not allowed to operate via a passport in Member States that do not allow appointed representatives (Art 32).

Supervision is mostly the responsibility of the home regulator. Tied intermediaries might be supervised directly, or as part of the supervision of the creditor to whom they are tied. Credit intermediaries providing services in more than one Member State are always subject to direct supervision. Similar provisions apply to representatives appointed by credit intermediaries. Where intermediaries operate through branches, the host regulators are responsible for specific aspects of the regulation (Art 34).

14.4 Pre-contractual Requirements

All advertising and marketing communication must be fair, clear, and not misleading and must not raise false expectations regarding availability or cost of credit (Art 10). Whenever advertising contains an interest rate indication it must contain a standard set of information defined in the regulation, including the annual percentage rate charge (APRC) (Art 11). Also, creditors—and where applicable credit intermediaries—must make a specified set of information on the products they offer available to their customers, either on paper, or on a durable medium or in electronic form (Art 13).

The APRC is calculated in accordance with the formula given in Annex I as the discount rate that makes the net present value of all cash flows zero, with certain rules as to how to treat cash flows that are not yet known (Art 17).

Once the discussion with a customer has progressed further, and the creditor or the credit intermediary has obtained some information regarding the customer in question, they must provide them with more detailed and personal information on what is called the European Standardised Information Sheet (ESIS), which is laid out in Annex 2. The ESIS must be provided *without undue delay after the consumer has given the necessary information* and *in good time before the consumer is bound*, typically at least 7 days (Art 14). Credit intermediaries and appointed representatives are also subject to specific information requirements (Art 15), and both creditors and intermediaries must provide adequate explanations to their customers both on the core credit products and ancillary services (Art 16). If the customer communication is via telephone, simplified rules apply (Art 14.10).

14.5 Credit Assessment and Credit Databases

Before concluding a credit agreement, and also before substantially increasing the amounts offered, the creditor must make a *thorough assessment of the creditor's creditworthiness*. This assessment must not predominantly rely on the value of the underlying asset but must be based on the customer's ability to repay the loan. The assessment must follow well-established and documented processes (Art 18). To the extent that this assessment relies on information provided by the customer, the information provided must be verified. However, the information required must be limited to data relevant for the credit assessment process (Art 20).

Where credit reference databases are consulted, the customer must be informed in advance of this fact. Where the credit decision has been rejected, the consumer must be informed without delay, and if this rejection was based on an automated process, the customer must be made aware of this. Also, where the rejection is based on a database consultation, the customer must be made aware of this, together with the result of the consultation and particulars of the database used (Art 18). Local credit reference databases must be made available to creditors throughout the Single Market on a non-discriminatory basis (Art 21).

Property valuations must follow standards established by the Member States. Appraisers can be internal or external to the creditor, but they must be sufficiently independent from the underwriting process so that they can provide an impartial and objective valuation. The valuation process must be documented and the documentation retained (Art 19).

14.6 Foreign Currency and Variable Rate Loans

A foreign currency loan is defined as a loan denominated in a currency which is not the national currency of the country where the consumer is resident, or which is different from the currency of the underlying asset. In this case there must be a mechanism in place to limit the foreign currency risk the customer is running, for example the right to convert the loan into either the currency of the asset, or the currency of the country of residence. If a conversion is offered it must be offered at the prevailing exchange rate, unless agreed otherwise in the credit agreement. Before entering into a foreign currency loan the consumer must receive adequate warnings as to the risk incurred, including in the ESIS. In the event of currency fluctuations of 20% or more, customers must be warned in writing on a regular basis of the particular risks of this situation (Art 24).

If the rate used in a loan is variable then the indexes or reference rate used must be *clear, accessible, objective and verifiable* by both the customers and the regulators, and historical records of the index or reference rate must be maintained (Art 25). Consumers must be made aware of changes in their borrowing rate before that change takes effect. If a public reference rate is used, it is sufficient if creditors periodically inform customers (Art 27).

14.7 Arrears and Foreclosure

Creditors should exercise reasonable forbearance before foreclosure proceedings are initiated. Member States may require that default charges are *no greater than is necessary to compensate the creditor for costs it has incurred as a result of the default*, or must at least impose a cap on such charges. Member States can allow no-recourse agreements, ie agreements where the full liability can be discharged by handing over the mortgaged asset. There should be an incentive to obtain the best price for a foreclosed asset.

14.8 Other

Each Member State must ensure that there are appropriate sanctions in place to induce compliance with this regulation (Art 38), there must be an extrajudicial dispute settlement procedure in place that customers can use (Art 39), and consumers cannot waive the rights conferred upon them in relation to this Directive (Art 41).

Markets in Financial Instruments Directive

Markets in Financial Instruments Directive—The regulation establishing the requirements in respect of selling, making markets in, and advising on, financial instruments in the EU

Summary

This directive defines investment firms, which are most firms whose business relates to the sales, trading, and advice in relation to financial instruments. This includes wholesale players like broker-dealers and investment banks that choose to not apply for a banking licence, infrastructure players such as exchanges, and players providing execution and advice in the retail space. All those firms require authorisation in their home Member State, and they can then passport across the entire Single Market.

The two biggest sections in this regulation deal with investor protection and the functioning of markets respectively. On the investor protection side, the rules distinguish between retail clients, professional clients, and eligible counterparties, in increasing order of sophistication. The applicable rules are very detailed, and a lot of focus is on ensuring that the incentives are aligned, eg by forbidding kick-back payments. On the markets side, the rules distinguish between regulated exchanges, MTFs, and OTFs which serve different customer segments. A strong emphasis here is on transparency and reporting, in particular also granular position reporting to the regulators to help them identify systemic risks.

Relevance for Fintech Companies

Together with PSD2, this regulation is probably the most important piece of regulation as far as Fintech companies are concerned, and a lot of the niche Fintech players that go for a licence that can be passported across the EU and that choose not to apply for a banking licence will probably either be regulated as a payment services provider or an investment firm—or both, as this still might be less burdensome than being regulated as a bank.

The primary services covered under this directive are:

• reception, transmission, and execution of trading orders
• portfolio management and investment advice
• underwriting and placement of financial securities
• operating of trading facilities.

A more complete list (plus ancillary services) can be found in Annex 1A. Everyone offering at least one of those services will have to seek regulation under this directive, which means that most of the investment-related Fintech models will be caught. It might not yet apply in some peer-to-peer areas but arguably this is only a question of time. Similarly, application to crypto assets is as of yet unclear as currencies are not considered financial instruments. However, even if a business is not currently regulated under this directive it should probably know the main provisions and adhere to them where appropriate, if only as a means to avoid more detailed regulatory scrutiny.

References

• Directive 2014/65/EU (MiFID2)
• Regulation EU 600/2014 (MiFIR)
• Directive 2004/39/EC (MiFID)
• Directive 2006/73/EC (MiFID Implementation)
• Regulation EU 648/2012 (EMIR)
• Directive 1997/9/EC (ICSD)
• Directive 2014/49/EU (DGSD2)
• Regulation 596/2014 (MAR)

The original MiFID directive is 2004/39/EC. A number of articles in this directive specified that more specific implementation measures needed to be defined, which were published in the Implementation directive 2006/73. After the crisis a number of aspects of MiFID were found to be wanting, so it was repealed and replaced with the MiFID 2 directive 2014/65, and the associated MiFIR regulation 600/2014. The EMIR regulation 648/2012 is related, as are the Investor Compensation Scheme Directive 1997/9/EC, the Deposit Guarantee Scheme Directive 2014/49/EU, and the Market Abuse Regulation 596/2014.

15.1 Definition and Scope

15.1.1 Technical Introduction

MiFID 2 comes as a package with its associated regulation, MiFIR (note: it is not MiFIR 2 as the previous MiFID did not have an associated regulation).

Because of this split into a directive and a regulation as well other legal drafting reasons the structure of the texts is hard to follow and I have reorganised the material into a structure that mixes the two texts along subject lines, which makes it easier to understand the purpose of the regulation at a high level. When providing references, I distinguish between MiFID and MiFIR. For example, 'Art R1' refers to Article 1 of the Regulations, and 'Art D2' refers to Article 2 of the Directive.

15.1.2 Scope of the MiFID Regulations

The range of application of this directive is very wide: it applies to all investment firms and banks that operate in this area, as well as to some other market participants. There are also notable areas where it does not apply, for example to insurance undertakings, or to some companies or people operating for their own account, or to some locally operating firms that are authorised locally and that back their services with investment firms, or to some firms operating in commodities in energies market, for example if they are related to producers. Also, not all parts apply to everyone, so whether or not a certain provision applies to a given entity should always be checked against the legal language (Arts D1–2, R1).

Most importantly, the Directive covers authorisation and operating conditions for investment firms, regulated markets, and data reporting service providers (Art D1). The Regulation provides uniform requirements across the entire Single Market, for example with respect to public and regulatory reporting, derivatives trading and clearing, and third-country equivalence (Art R1).

15.1.3 Definition of Investment Firms

The definition of investment firms itself covers a large range of very different entities, providing for at least one of the following services (Art D4, Annex D1A):

• reception, transmission, and execution of trading orders
• portfolio management and investment advice
• underwriting and placement of financial securities
• operating of trading facilities.

They might also offer ancillary services, for example (Annex D1C):

• safekeeping and other custody and collateral management services
• lending and foreign exchange services, to the extent that it is related to a financial transaction with that particular investment firm
• investment banking advisory, eg on mergers and acquisitions, capital structure, industrial strategy
• investment research and financial analysis.

They cannot offer only those ancillary services. So, for example, an investment firm can offer custody, but a pure custodian is not an investment firm, and neither is a pure investment research shop, or an M&A boutique that is only providing advice (Art D6).

In the context of this directive, the term *financial instrument* is defined as follows (D4.15, Annex D-1C):

• transferable securities
• money market instruments
• units in collective investment undertakings
• most derivative contracts
• contracts for differences
• emission allowances.

15.2 Authorisation and General Requirements

15.2.1 Regulators and Regulatory Sanctions

Member States must designate a regulator. This regulator must have a range of powers, including the power to impose sanctions. Those sanctions must include temporary or permanent withdrawal of the authorisation, and monetary fines. If there is a cap on sanctions it must be at least the bigger of €5m, 10% of annual revenues, or twice the benefit received from the infringement. Sanctions must be reported, and can be published. Regulatory actions can be appealed in the court system (Arts D67–87).

15.2.2 Authorisation

All EU investment firms must be authorised, with slightly more lenient authorisation conditions applying to MTFs or OTFs. The authorisation is limited to the services mentioned in the application, and any extension of services is subject to a new authorisation requirement. Any authorisation can be passported across the whole Single Market (Art D6). Local regulators and ESMA keep a public register of all authorised investment firms (Arts D5–8).

15.2.3 Pre-authorisation Requirements

There are certain requirements that managers and significant shareholders of an authorised investment firm must fulfil (Arts D9, 10) and any acquisition or significant change in ownership must be pre-cleared with the regulator (Arts D11–13), who has 60 days to do so (Art D12). Investment companies must fulfil the obligation with respect to membership in an investor compensation scheme under ICSD or—if they provide structured deposits—in a deposit guarantee scheme under DGSD2 (Art D14). Thereby structured deposits are defined as deposits where the principal amount is protected but the interest is linked to, for example, some equity market performance (Art D4). There is a minimum capital requirement for investment firms (Art D15). For regulated markets, very similar rules apply (Arts D44–46).

15.2.4 Ongoing Requirements

Investment firms other than regulated markets must fulfil a number of organisational requirements, most of which are to do with a general duty of running the firm responsibly (Art D16). There are a number of notable requirements, however:

- Firms that *manufacture financial instruments* must have an approval and a review process in place; those processes must identify a target market, assess the risks to this target market, and ensure that the instrument's distribution strategy is consistent with reaching this target market (Art D16.3).
- Distributors and firms recommending those financial instruments must ensure that they have been provided all the relevant information referred to above by those who *manufacture* them (Art D16.3).
- There are extensive record-keeping requirements (for seven years), including for phone calls and other electronic communications, and regardless of whether those specific communications did lead to a client order or not (Art D16.6–7).
- Investment firms must not comingle client funds with their own, and can only use a client's financial instruments they hold on their own account— eg for a securities lending transaction—with the client's express consent (Art D16.89).

There are specific rules that firms that pursue an algorithmic trading strategy must follow, as well as those investment firms that provide them with direct electronic market access (Art D17).

15.2.5 Passporting

If firms want to passport their authorisation into another Member State they they apply to their home regulator, who then coordinates with the relevant host regulator or regulators (Art D34). Firms can operate in the host Member State via a branch, or using tied agents (Art D35). Host regulators must ensure that firms using a passport enjoy the same level of access to regulated markets and CCPs as local firms do, and—as a general rule—cannot be asked to fulfil more stringent requirements (Arts D35–37). Also host regulators cannot require firms to use local CCP or settlement mechanisms (Art D38).

Host regulators can ask for specific periodic activity reports from institutions who use a passport to operate in their jurisdiction. Those reporting requirements cannot be more stringent than those imposed on locally authorised firms (Art D85). In certain cases where there is a risk to local financial stability and the home regulators have been informed but their response is insufficient, host regulators can take measures to address those issues (Art D86). Regulators can and shall cooperate with third-country regulators and other public entities as need be (Art D87).

15.2.6 Local Authorisation of Third-country Firms

A local regulator can authorise third-country firms to operate in the local market. However, this authorisation does not entail permission to operate in other Member States. The operations must be conducted through an adequately capitalised branch. The third country in question must have an agreement with the Member State in place with respect to the OECD Model Tax Convention. There is, however, no need for a formal establishment of equivalence between the regulatory regimes (Arts D39–43).

Where a client initiates on its own exclusive initiative, the provision of investment services by a third-country firm, that firm does not require authorisation. However, unless authorised, that firm cannot market other products or services to that client (Art D42).

15.2.7 Equivalence When Covering Non-retail Investors

There is an EU-wide equivalence regime that allows investment firms to offer their products and services to eligible counterparties and professional investors but not to retail investors (see the section on investor protection below for definitions). Under this regime, in a first step, the Commission must officially establish that the third-country regime is considered equivalent, and ESMA must establish an appropriate cooperation regime between EU and third-country regulators. Any investment firm wishing to operate under this equivalence regime must apply for registration by ESMA, which should happen within 180 working days (Arts R46, 47).

Where there is no equivalence decision by the EU—or where such decisions have been withdrawn—Member States may authorise third-party investment firms to provide their services to eligible counterparties and professional clients within their territories. Member States may not treat any third-country firms more favourably than firms from the EU, nor may they impose additional requirements on firms authorised under the EU-wide equivalence regime (Art R46).

15.3 Investor Protection

15.3.1 Types of Investors

MiFID recognises three different types of investors: eligible counterparties, professional clients, and retail clients. The most sophisticated group—and therefore the group that is offered the least protection—is the first one. It is defined as follows (Art D30):

> *Eligible counterparties are investment firms, credit institutions, insurance companies, UCITS and their management companies, pension funds and their management companies, other financial institutions authorised or regulated under Union law or under the national law of a Member State, national governments and their corresponding offices including public bodies that deal with public debt at national level, central banks and supranational organisations.*

Eligible counterparties can always opt out of being considered as such, either across the board, or on a transaction-by-transaction basis (Art D30).

Professional clients are defined as follows (Art D4, Annex D2):

- entities which are required to be authorised or regulated to operate in the financial markets (eg banks, investment firms, insurance companies, etc.)
- large companies (balance sheet > €20m; revenues > €40m; equity > €2m)
- public bodies at the national or regional level who are involved in market activities because of their responsibilities (including central banks)
- other institutional investors whose main activity is to invest in financial instruments.

Note that eligible counterparties are typically also professional clients under this definition. Retail clients, finally, are those clients who are not professional clients (Art D4). Professional clients can be asked to be treated as retail clients and vice versa. The latter, however, is only possible under specific circumstances. In any case those reclassifications have to be agreed in advance in writing (Art D30).

Most of the rules under Articles 24, 25, 27, 28 do not apply to eligible counterparties (D30). The only rules that apply to them are: under Article D24 the requirement to inform on the basis and cost of services provided (Art D24.4, 5), under Article D25 that adequate periodic reports must be provided (Art D25.6), and under Article D28 the rules with respect to limit orders (Art D28.2). Article D27—most favourable execution—does not apply at all. The rules on intermediary investment firms (Art D26) and tied agents (Art D29) apply unchanged.

15.3.2 General Investor Protection Rules

There are a number of investor protection rules, some of which recast what has been said earlier regarding the manufacture of financial instruments (Art D24). An important additional requirement that was not mentioned before is that financial instruments can be offered or recommended only when it is in the best interest of the client (Art D24.2) and marketing communications must always be clearly identifiable as such (Art D24.3).

15.3.3 Customer Information Requirements

Before investment advice is provided, firms must inform their customers whether or not the advice is provided on an independent basis, whether it is based on a broad or a narrow scan of the market, and whether or not there will be a periodic suitability assessment in the future. They must also include an appropriate description of the risks taken, and detailed and comprehensible information on all associated costs and charges (Art D24.4, 5). To the extent that firms provide independent advice they must ensure that the universe of options considered is sufficiently wide, including with respect to the providers of the financial products (Art D24.7).

To the extent that a packaged product or service is also offered as a combination of its constituent parts, a client must be made aware of this fact, and must be provided with a breakdown of costs—and risks, where different from the package—for each of the constituent parts (Art D24.11).

15.3.4 Retention of Fees or Commissions

Investment firms cannot retain fees or accept monetary benefits from providers (Art D24.7). Similarly, where a firm manages a portfolio on behalf of a client it cannot receive monetary benefits from any third party in this respect (Art D24.8). Those provisions are very important: traditionally both advisory and discretionary portfolio management services relied to a large extent on third-party payments—eg from brokers, and from the firms manufacturing the investment products—to finance their services. Under MiFID this is no longer allowed, and those services must be financed via direct fees paid by the client.

15.3.5 Alignment of Advisors' Interest

Investment firms must be able to demonstrate that the investment advisors they employ are sufficiently competent (Art D25.1). Before providing investment advice—or before managing a portfolio on behalf of a client—the advisor must assess the clients' level of knowledge and experience as well as their appetite and objective capacity for taking risks (Art D25.2). The requirement to assess the client's individual circumstances also applies in a number of other cases. Under those circumstances clients must be warned before they enter into a transaction that is not in line with their profile

(Art D25.3). This requirement can be waived by the Member States if the services provided only consist of execution, reception, or transmission of client orders in relation to a number of specific low-complexity instruments such as shares, bonds, and UCITS (Art D25.4).

Also, an investment firm's remuneration policies must not be structured in such a way as to create a conflict with the duty to act in the best interest of their clients. When a client is a retail client, then remuneration policies and related measures such as sales targets must not be structured in such a way that it could encourage staff to recommend a particular financial instrument when the firm could offer a different one which could better meet that client's needs (Art D24.10). Note that if interpreted strictly this can become an impediment to providing anything but a fixed remuneration without specific sales targets to sales staff.

15.3.6 Most Favourable Execution

Investment firms have an obligation to execute a client order on terms most favourable to the client, unless the client's instructions specify a venue. The *most favourable terms* requirement is to be understood with regard to the entire consideration paid, including fees and commissions, not only based on the headline execution price (Art D27.1). Investment firms cannot usually receive any benefits for routing client orders to a particular venue (Art D27.2). They must be transparent about—and regularly report on—the venues they access, and they must have an order execution policy in place. This policy must be available to their clients, who also can ask that a firm demonstrated compliance with this policy with respect to a specific transaction they made (Art D27.3–8). Appropriate procedures must ensure that client orders obtain prompt, fair, and expeditious execution when compared to other clients, ie clients cannot be unfairly privileged (Art D28).

15.3.7 Out-of-Court Settlement Procedures

There must be an efficient method for settling customer complaints out of court, and the respective organisations shall coordinate with each other for settlement of cross-border disputes (Art D76). In certain cases, disputes between regulators in different jurisdictions are subject to binding mediation by ESMA (Art D82).

15.3.8 Record Keeping Requirements

The exact terms under which the services an investment firm has agreed to provide to a client are provided must be recorded, and the firm must provide the client with regular reports. Before any transaction—or, in some cases where this is not practical and where the client has consented to this, immediately after the transaction—the client must be provided with a suitability statement with respect to this specific transaction (Art D25.6).

15.3.9 Responsibilities of Intermediary Investment Firms

An investment firm that has no direct contact with the client but receives its instructions via another firm does not have to independently try to obtain that information but can assume that the information provided by the firm that has the client contact is correct. Similarly, suitability analysis is the sole responsibility of the firm that has the contact with the client (Art D26).

15.3.10 Use of Tied Agents

When firms employ tied agents, those agents must be registered, and the firm remains fully responsible vis-à-vis the client for their agent's actions. Tied agents must be registered in a public register, and must satisfy certain conditions with respect to competence and repute in order to be registered. It is the investment firm's duty to ensure that the other activities of their agents have no negative impact with respect to their duties under this directive (Art D29).

Tied agents in this respect are defined as follows (Art D4):

> *'tied agent' means a natural or legal person who, under the full and unconditional responsibility of only one investment firm on whose behalf it acts, promotes investment and/or ancillary services to clients or prospective clients, receives and transmits instructions or orders from the client in respect of investment services or financial instruments, places financial instruments or provides advice to clients or prospective clients in respect of those financial instruments or services.*

In the Fintech space this definition could become important in particular for platform businesses relying on non-employed providers who in some cases might have to be considered tied agents, with all the consequences that this implies.

15.4 Trading Venues

15.4.1 Types of Trading Venues

This regulation defines four classes of trading venues: regulated exchanges, multilateral trading facilities (MTFs), organised trading facilities (OTFs) and systematic internalisers (Art D4). The last one is the odd one out, in that it refers to a firm that trades on its own account with clients with the intention of earning the bid/offer spread rather than matching clients who want to trade and earning a fee, ie it is a dealer rather than a broker in our earlier nomenclature.

Regulated exchanges, MTFs, and OTFs are similar in nature, except that exchanges are usually bigger and more strictly regulated than MTFs and OTFs. Also, OTFs are restricted to trading *bonds, structured finance products, emission allowances, and derivatives,* ie in particular they cannot list shares (Art D4).

15.4.2 Regulated Markets, MTFs, and OTFs

For regulated markets, the organisational requirements are similar to those of investment firms, albeit slightly different due to the nature of their business. Notably, they must establish robust technical operations, including contingency arrangements, and more generally have robust risk management arrangements in place. They must also have *transparent and non-discretionary rules and procedures that provide for fair and orderly trading and establish objective criteria for the efficient execution of orders,* and they must show that they have sufficient financial resources (Art D47).

For MTFs and OTFs the procedures general to all investment firms apply, plus some specific rules similar to—but slightly easier than—those applicable to regulated markets (Arts D18–20).

15.4.3 Operational Requirements for Regulated Markets

Trading systems must be designed and tested to be resilient to deal with *peak order and message volumes,* and must ensure *orderly trading under conditions of severe market stress* (Art D48). Regulated markets must have agreements with a number of market makers who commit in writing to usually post *firm quotes at competitive prices* in exchange for rebates received. Compliance with this commitment must be monitored. There must be a system in place that rejects clearly erroneous orders, and there must be circuit breakers that halt trading in situations where market distress has been objectively established (Art D48).

Operators must ensure that only authorised firms can gain access to electronic trading APIs, and that algorithmic trading does not disrupt the markets. In the trade data capture it must be possible to distinguish algorithmic trading, and it must be possible for a regulator to monitor trading if need be. Operators are allowed to impose a fee structure that takes into account the load that algorithmic traders generate, eg by charging for order cancellations

(Art D48). There must also be an instrument-level tick size regime that is adapted to the structure of the respective market (Art D49).

All markets under the jurisdiction of a regulator must synchronise the clocks they use for recording, to a precision to be determined by the regulators (Art D50).

15.4.4 Admission of Instruments to Regulated Markets, MTFs, and OTFs

The rules governing the admission of instruments to a regulated market must be clear and transparent. Operators of regulated markets must monitor that issuers comply with their listing requirements as well as with the applicable disclosure requirements anchored in the applicable law (Art D51). Similarly, operators of MTFs and OTFs must ensure that members, participants, and users comply with their rules, in particular with respect to orders sent and order cancellations, in order to ensure that behaviour that contravenes the Market Abuse Regulation is caught (Art D31). Significant infringement must be reported to the regulators immediately, who—provided they agree with that assessment—must communicate this to ESMA and other concerned regulators (Art D31, 54).

The operator of a regulated market, an MTF, or an OTF can remove or suspend instruments that no longer comply with their rules, unless this could lead to significant damage to investors' interests, or the functioning of the market. Unless the reason for the removal is specific to that venue, regulators must ensure that the instruments are also removed from all other venues within their jurisdiction. If an instrument is removed, all associated derivatives must be removed as well (Arts D32, 52).

15.4.5 Issuer Consent Requirements

Where a transferable security is admitted to trading on one market, it can be admitted to trading on any other market, with or without the consent of the issuer (Art D51). Under certain circumstances, markets can be designated as SME growth markets. SME issuers must consent before their security can be admitted to trading in another market (Art 33; compare Art D51.5).

15.4.6 Non-discriminatory Membership Requirements in Regulated Markets

The rules governing access to, or membership of, a regulated market must be transparent and non-discriminatory (Art D53). Regulated markets shall not be prevented from using CCPs or settlement systems located in other

Member States (Art D55). Regulators draw up lists of regulated markets in their jurisdiction, which ESMA aggregates and publishes for the entire Single Market (Art D56).

15.4.7 Derivatives Trading and Clearing Obligations

Under EMIR, a significant set of derivative transactions is subject to mandatory clearing (EMIR Art 5). Out of those, ESMA designates a subset of derivatives subject to mandatory exchange trading and publishes it on its website (Art R32–34). This means that if both counterparties are financial counterparties—or non-financial counterparties that have exceeded the clearing threshold under EMIR Art 10—then it is mandatory that they trade on a regulated market, an MTF, an OTF, or an authorised venue in an equivalent third country (Art R28).

All derivatives traded on a regulated market must be cleared by a CCP. The clearing must happen *as quickly as technologically practical using automated systems* (Art R29, 30).

Special rules apply to portfolio compression, ie the process of going through trades of two or more counterparties and closing out all transactions that cancel when aggregated for all participating counterparties (Art R31).

15.4.8 Non-discriminatory Access to CCPs

CCPs—other than those with close links to a particular exchange—are not allowed to discriminate between identical instruments traded on different exchanges; end users must be able choose freely where they want to clear (Art R35). Similarly, exchanges—other than those with a close link to a particular CCP—must provide CCPs with trade feeds on a non-discriminatory basis so as to allow CCPs to clear that exchange's products (Art R36). Finally, providers of benchmark indices (eg, stock market indices like the FTSE 100) must provide both exchanges and CCPs with access to those benchmarks on a non-discriminatory basis.

All of this together allows customers to choose the venue independently from the CCP, which is important, as having to split a portfolio across multiple CCPs is usually expensive in terms of additional collateral requirement, especially if the portfolio contains partially hedged positions that would be separated.

15.4.9 Access by Third-country Trading Venues and CCPs

A trading venue established in a third country can only access a CCP established in the EU if the Commission has made an equivalence decision with respect to the country where that venue is authorised according to Article R28.4 (Art R38).

A CCP established in a third country may request access to a trading venue in the EU only if (a) it is authorised in a third country whose equivalence has been previously established by the Commision according to EMIR Art 25.6, and (b) the CPP itself then has been recognised by ESMA under EMIR Article 25. A CCP may request access to benchmark providers according to Article R37, but only if the Commission has established that its country of authorisation has reciprocal access rules in place for EU CCPs wanting to access the third country's benchmark providers (Art R38).

15.5 Data Reporting

15.5.1 Reporting Requirements

There are a number of pre- and post-trade transparency requirements for equity-like instruments on all venues, ie regulated markets, MTFs, and OTFs (Arts R4–7), and a similar but different set for non-equity instruments like bonds (Art R811). Pre- and post-trade data must be available separately, on reasonable commercial terms (Arts R12, 13).

There are similar but less stringent rules affecting systemic internalisers as well as investment firms trading OTC, ie not on an exchange (Arts R14–22). Systemic internalisers must make firm quotes available on a reasonable commercial and non-discriminatory basis, but they can deny this for genuine commercial reasons (Art R23).

For shares—but not other financial instruments like bonds or derivatives—that are traded on a regulated market or an MTF, investment firms must execute trade in those shares on regulated markets, MTFs, or with systemic internalisers. An exception to this are non-systematic, ad hoc, irregular, and infrequent trades, or trades that are carried out between eligible and/or professional counterparties that do not contribute to the price discovery process (Art R23).

There are specific reporting requirements for all investment firms who execute financial transactions to report them completely and accurately to their regulator as soon as possible, but no later than the close of the following business day (Art R26). Before an instrument can start trading, identifying reference data must be communicated to the regulator. This data, for example, allows the regulators to match instruments that are traded at more than one venue (Art R27).

15.5.2 Data Retention on Customer Order and KYC Data

Investment firms must retain the relevant data relating to all orders and all transactions in financial instruments which they have carried out, whether on thier own account or on behalf of a client. To the extent that those orders are customer-related, the corresponding information required under anti money laundering legislation must also be retained. They also must retain relevant data relating to all orders in financial instruments which are advertised through their systems, and this data must be linked to execution records where relevant. The minimum retention period is five years (Art R25).

15.5.3 Data Reporting Services

There are three types of data reporting services described under this regulation (Art D4):

- *approved publication arrangements* or *APAs*, who publish trade reports on behalf of investment firms pursuant to Articles R20, 21
- *approved reporting mechanisms* or *ARMs*, who report details of transactions to regulators or ESMA on behalf of investment firms
- *consolidated tape providers* or *CTPs*, who collect trade reports for financial instruments listed in Articles R6, 7, 10, 12, 13, 20, 21 from regulated markets, MTFs, OTFs, and APAs and consolidate them into a continuous electronic live data stream, providing price and volume data per financial instrument.

Those services are subject to authorisation and supervision in their home Member State (Art D59). The authorisation specifies the exact scope of the activities. It is valid throughout the Single Market (Art D60). Authorisation is decided within six months, and can be withdrawn. There are certain requirements as to the management of those providers, and operational requirements specific to the class of services they provide (Arts D61–66).

Packaged Retail
and Insurance-based
Investment Products
Regulation

Packaged Retail and Insurance-based Investment Products Regulation—The regulation governing the provision of the so-called Key Information Documents that must be provided to retail investors

Summary

The PRIIPR deals with the Key Information Documents that manufacturers, sellers, and advisors have to provide to retail clients who want to invest in Packaged Retail Investment or Insurance Products (PRIIPs). It establishes its form and content, and when and how it is to be provided. It also specifies administrative fines whose maximum levels must be at least €5m or 3% of annual turnover for companies, and €700k for individuals.

Relevance for Fintech Companies

This is a short regulation that is relevant for most Fintech companies that are engaged in the provision of retail investment products, whether it be as a seller, an advisor, or a manufacturer. The potential fines are steep—up to at least €5m for companies and €700k for individuals—so non-compliance poses a significant risk for resource-constrained start-ups.

References

- Regulation EU 1286/2014 (PRIIPR)
- Directive 2014/65/EU (MiFID2)
- Directive 2011/61/EU (AIFMD)
- Directive 2009/138/EC (Solvency 2)
- Directive 2009/65/EC (UCITS 4)
- Directive 2003/71/EC (Prospectus D)
- Directive 2002/92/EC (Insurance Mediation D)
- Directive 2002/65/EC (DMFSD)

The Packaged Retail and Insurance-based Investment Products Regulation is 1286/2014. It has a number of touch points with other regulations in the investment space, notably MiFID 2014/65/EU, AIFMD 2011/61 EU, Solvency 2

2009/138/EC, UCITS 2009/65/EC, the Prospectus Directive 2003/71/EC, the Insurance Mediation Directive 2002/92/EC, and the Distance Marketing Directive for Financial Services 2002/65/EC.

16.1 Definition and Scope

The purpose of this directive is to establish the requirement of companies that manufacture, sell, or provide advice on Packaged Retail and Insurance-based Investment Products (PRIIPs) to provide a Key Information Document (KID) to retail investors, where retail is defined either using the definition from MiFID or from the Insurance Mediation Directive. It also describes in great detail the contents and appearance of the KID (Arts 1, 2).

A PRIIP is roughly defined as an investment product—insurance-based or not—whose performance is driven by market fluctuations (Art 4). There are a number of important exceptions, including non-life insurance products, life insurance products payable only on death or in respect of incapacity due to injury, sickness, or infirmity, and pension products (Art 2). Also exempt are a number of very low-risk investments issued or guaranteed by the state or by banks, including deposits. However, this specifically excludes subordinated, equity-linked or derivative-linked securities, and structured deposits, which do fall under this directive (Art 2; Prospectus Directive Art 1.2).

Before a PRIIP is made available to retail investors, a KID in accordance with this regulation must be drawn up and published on the manufacturer's website. Some Member States might require the regulator to be notified of all PRIIPs marketed in their jurisdiction (Art 5).

16.2 Form and Content

The KID must be accurate, fair, clear, and not misleading, and it must be consistent with the contractual documents, the offer documents, the terms and conditions, and the marketing documents. The latter in particular must contain a reference to the KID, including a link to where it can be found on the internet (Arts 6, 9). The KID must be a stand-alone document, clearly separated from and without cross-references to any marketing material. It must be short—at most three single-sided A4 sheets in a readably-sized font—and concise. It must be laid out in a manner that it is easy to read, and if colour is used it must print or photocopy well in black and white. It must focus on the information relevant for retail investors and must use language that is clear, succinct and comprehensible (Art 6).

Unless local regulators agree something different, the KID must be provided in one of the official languages of the Member States where it is distributed.

Whenever a marketing document exists in a language, a KID must exist in the same language (Art 7).

The title of the KID must be *'Key Information Document'* and a specific explanatory statement must be included, as well as the name of the PRIIP, the names and the contact details of the manufacturer and the regulator, and the date. Also, the following section headings must appear, and there are some specific requirements regarding what information must appear under those headings (Art 8):

- *What is this product?*
- *What are the risks and what could I get in return?*
- *What happens if [the name of the PRIIP manufacturer] is unable to pay out? What are the costs?*
- *How long should I hold it and can I take money out early?*
- *How can I complain?*
- *Other relevant information.*

Content of the KID must be reviewed and if necessary revised on a regular basis, with regulatory standards being defined by the Joint Committee of the ESAs (Art 10).

Under EU law, a manufacturer only incurs civil liability if the KID is misleading, inaccurate, or inconsistent with other key documents; however, Member States might extend this. Investors who demonstrate loss under those circumstances can claim damages (Art 11). For an insurance contract, the obligation is only towards the policy holder, not towards the beneficiary if different (Art 12).

16.3 Provision

The KID must be provided to the retail investor—or the person making investment decisions on behalf of the retail investor as the case may be—by either the seller or the advisor in good time before the contract is legally binding. An exception to this is where a retail investor is contacting a seller on its own initiative by a means of distant communication where provision of this document is not possible—typically, if the contact is via phone, but not usually via the Internet—and the investor has been adequately informed and has consented (Art 13). A KID that has already been provided in the context of the previous transaction only has to be provided again if it has changed since then (Art 13). The KID must be provided free of charge, on paper, or—if certain conditions are met—on another durable medium or on the Internet. If retail investors have provided an email address, providing the KID via the Internet is usually acceptable (Art 14).

16.4 Monitoring, Invervention, Complaints, and Fines

For insurance-based investment products, both EIOPA and the local regulators—both in the Member State of the seller and the investor—must monitor the market and have certain intervention powers, including suspension and prohibition of marketing of a product and public warnings (Arts 16–18, 24). The maximum penalty for companies in the Member State law must be at least €5m or 3% of annual turnover for legal entities, or €700k for individuals, or twice the amount of gains made/losses avoided for both (Arts 24, 25). Sanctions are subject to appeal (Art 26) and in many cases public reporting (Arts 27–29).

There must be effective extrajudicial complaints procedures for retail investors, including in cases where the product has been sold on a cross-border basis (Arts 19–21).

16.5 Technical Provisions

Articles 30–33 deal with technical provisions.

Payments Services Directive

Payments Services Directive—The directive regulating institutions providing payments services in the EU

Summary

PSD 2 is the 2015 revision of the EU Payments Services Directive, taking into account the recent development in the payments space, especially with relation to Fintech companies. Together with the Electronic Money Directive it defines the requirement for all players in the electronic payments market, both incumbents and new entrants.

It defines new roles, in particular that of the *PISPs* who initiate payments on behalf of customers, and that of the *AISPs* who can aggregate account information on behalf of customers, both without actually running any payment accounts. This regulation defines minimum standards in terms of conduct and security to which those players must adhere. It also puts a requirement on incumbent players to open up their systems, and give those new players non-discriminatory access to their APIs, thereby encouraging innovation in the payments space.

Relevance for Fintech Companies

A lot of Fintech players are active in the payments space, and for them this directive is very important. A key point here is the establishment of AISPs and PISPs to whom banks must grant API access to customers' payment accounts, provided the customers agree that, and provided the companies fulfil certain conditions, in particular with respect to security.

This is a good example of a two-edged sword that Fintech companies must be aware of in the regulations space: on the one hand, banks must provide APIs, but (as far as the regulation is concerned—ultimately, transitional exceptions may apply) screenscraping is no longer allowed. A situation where some banks do not have APIs in place in time is not unimaginable, and whilst they might be fined about this, this does not help Fintech companies whose business model might fall apart if they have no API access and can no longer use screenscraping. An early regulatory dialogue is important here to ensure that the business can run properly through the API transition.

This regulation also goes into very minute details about who in a payment chain is responsible for what, and who takes responsibility vis-à-vis the customer and other participants in the chain if things go wrong. Again, this is something that every company in this space must be aware of in detail, to (a) ensure compliance (and avoid fines), and (b) avoid being unexpectedly responsible for indemnifying others in the event of a breach.

Last but not least, some non-bank companies in the payment space might suddenly find themselves on the other side of the fence, and they might be under an obligation to provide open APIs for other Fintech companies—again something that is important to consider when looking at a Fintech company's product and service strategy.

References

- Directive EU 2015/2366 (PSD2)
- EBA RTS 2017/02 (strong auth)
- Directive 2009/110/EC (e-money)
- Directive 2002/65/EC (DMFSD)
- Directive 2007/64/EC (PSD1)

The Payment Services Directive is 2015/2366. It replaces the previous PSD 2007/64, and it amends the e-money Directive 2009/110 and the directive covering distance marketing for financial services 2002/65. EBA RTS 2017/02 covers the requirement for strong customer authentication.

17.1 Definition and Scope

This directive defines the players in the payment space, and establishes the rights and obligations of users and providers of payment services, as well as a number of conditions around transparency around the services provided and the associated costs (Art 1). It applies to payments within the EU, and under some conditions for cross-border payments where one leg is in the EU (Art 2). There are a number of exclusions to the scope of this directive (Art 3), notably transactions

- using a traditional paper-based system (cash, cheques, traveller's cheques, cash-to-cash foreign exchange, cash withdrawals)
- where the payment function is incidental to the service provided (eg agents purchasing goods on behalf of a principal)
- in a limited-network environment (eg store cards), or related to some purchases of digital items (eg ring tones paid via phone bill).

17.2 Players in the Payment System

The directive defines a number of important roles. Most important is the *payment service provider* (*PSP*), which is a generic term for a player offering a wide range of services in the payments space. A PSP might be *account servicing*, in which it not only offers services, but also payment accounts. In many cases a payment service provider will be a bank, otherwise it will be a *payment institution* (*PI*), which is an entity that operates like a bank in the payments space, but that is only authorised under this directive, and not as a bank. New roles defined here are the *payment initiation service provider* (*PISP*) and the *account information service provider* (*AISP*). The former can initiate payments on behalf of a customer from the customer's payment accounts held at a PSP, and the latter can obtain account information from all a customer's PSPs and aggregate them in an appropriate manner (Art 4).

The directive defines a *payment instrument* as follows (Art 4.14):

'payment instrument' means a personalised device(s) and/or set of procedures agreed between the payment service user and the payment service provider and used in order to initiate a payment order.

The important point here is the *set of procedures* part, meaning that a payment instrument does not need to correspond to a card or any other physical device.

17.3 Authorisation and Regulatory Requirements

17.3.1 Authorisation and Passporting

Only authorised payment institutions are allowed to provide payment services (Art 37). Authorisation is not required for services that are not in scope of this directive (Art 3; see first paragraph). Every payment institution must be incorporated in at least one Member State, and must apply for authorisation there (Arts 5, 28). It is subject to ongoing supervision (Arts 29–31), and it must provide its services in the state where it is authorised, also referred to as home Member State (Art 11). Once authorised in any Member State, a payment institution is passported to operate throughout the Single Market (Art 11). Disagreements between local regulators regarding the supervision of an entity are to be resolved with the help of EBA (Art 27). There are no equivalence provisions in this directive that would allow companies incorporated and regulated in third countries to operate in the Single Market. Both Member States and the EBA maintain a public register of authorised payment institutions (Arts 14, 15).

Authorisation can be withdrawn, for example if the business is not being taken up within 12 months of granting it, if the business is discontinued for 6 months, the initial conditions are no longer met, or the institution is a threat to stability (Art 13). Regulators must be informed in advance of intended changes of control (Art 6).

17.3.2 Capital Requirements

There is a minimum initial capital requirement (Art 7), and there is an ongoing requirement that capital (aka own funds) not fall below a certain level (Arts 8, 9). There are a number of different ways in which an institution can calculate this requirement; regulators can then adjust the raw number up or down by up to 20% (Art 9):

- Method A: 10% of fixed annual overheads
- Method B: percentage of monthly payment volume, starting at 4% for the first €5m, and going down to 0.25% marginally for everything beyond €250m
- Method C: indicator approach based on interest income and expense, commissions, fees, and other income.

17.4 Operational Requirements

17.4.1 Safeguarding of Customer Funds

Users' funds must be safeguarded, by ensuring that they are either held in a separate account held at an institution authorised to take deposits and are not commingled with the institution's own funds, or are covered by a suitable insurance policy (Art 10). Payment institutions cannot engage in lending except in very narrow circumstances, and they are not allowed to hold insured deposits (Art 18). There is a record-keeping requirement (Art 21).

17.4.2 Framework Contracts

The directive distinguishes between single payment transactions where there is no ongoing relationship with the customer and the PSP, and relationships that are governed by framework contracts. The differences are not large, but framework contracts differ slightly in the information requirements, mostly with respect to timing, as some information has to be provided when the contract is entered into, and some whenever a transaction takes place. Framework contracts also allow for custumers to disclaim certain rights that they would otherwise have. For example, a framework contract can give the PSP the right to block a payment for security reasons (Art 68.2), or a custumer can disclaim his right for refund under certain circumstances (Art 76.3), or it can allow the PSP to charge certain fees it otherwise could not charge, eg when payments are being refused for objectively justified reasons (Art 79.1). Framework contracts must be cancellable by the user with at most one month's notice, and at moderate cost or no cost at all (Art 55).

17.4.3 Information Requirements

For single payment transactions it is mandatory to provide certain information ahead of the transaction, in an easily accessible manner (Arts 38–58). This information must be provided free of charge (Art 40). The burden of proof that the consumer has received the information required lies with the PSP (Art 41). The information required includes things like charges payable, reference exchange rate where applicable, and maximum execution time, as well as contact details of the head office, the branch, and the regulator (Art 45). There is a detailed breakdown of who has to provide which information to whom in Arts 46–49.

The equivalent articles to Art 45 for framework contracts are Art 52 (pre-contract information) and Art 56 (pre-transaction information). The information required is more or less the same, plus additional items that are relevant for an ongoing relationship. The post-transaction information requirements are in Arts 57, 58. There is a derogation to the information requirement for certain low-value payment framework contracts (transaction size smaller €30 and overall spending limit of €150; Art 42).

17.4.4 Blocking of Funds

In the event of transactions where the exact amount is not known, payment service providers can block funds for later payment only when the payer explicitly consents to the amount blocked, and funds must be released without undue delay. In some cases the customer has a right of refund if such transactions are unexpectedly large (Arts 75, 76). Also, for authorised transaction initiated by a payee, the customer has the right to claim a refund for up to 8 weeks. The service provider must within 10 days either refund the amount, or justify refusal and explain the right of appeal under Arts 99–102 (Art 77).

17.4.5 Execution Times

Electronic payments in Euro or within a non-Euro country must arrive at the payee at the latest one business day after the instructions have been received. Paper-initiated transactions are allowed to take one business day longer (Arts 82, 83). Cash placed on a payment account by a consumer must be available in the account immediately, for non-consumers the latest on the business day after (Art 84). Member States may demand shorter execution times for national payments (Art 85). Funds received by a customer's PSP must usually be available immediately, in some circumstances at the end of the business day (Art 87).

17.4.6 Security

PSPs must establish a framework to manage the operational and security risks, and maintain effective incident management procedures. They must report to their regulator on this topic at least once per year. In the event of an incident, PSPs must notify their regulator without undue delay (Art 96). PSPs must apply strong customer authentication whenever the account is accessed remotely and there is a risk of payment fraud or other abuses. This includes accessing the account online, and initiating a transaction. The authentication must be specific to the amount and payee in question (Art 97). EBA is tasked with preparing specific guidelines in this respect (Art 98), and also in respect to more general security measures (Art 95.3).

17.4.7 Complaints and Dispute Resolution

Regulators must set up a mechanism to allow customers and other interested third parties to complain to them about alleged infringement by the PSPs (Arts 99, 100). There must be an *alternative dispute resolution* procedure in place in every country where the PSP offers payment services, in the official language of that country. PSPs must reply to customer complaints, addressing all issues raised, in writing, at the latest within 15 business days of receipt, or up to 35 business days in exceptional circumstances (Arts 101, 102).

17.5 Third-party Access

An important theme within this regulation is that incumbents—and everyone else holding customer payment accounts for that matter, including Fintech start-ups operating in the payments space—must give non-discriminatory access to other players provided those other players satisfy certain conditions:

> *Art 35. Member States shall ensure that the rules on access of authorised or registered payment service providers [...] to payment systems are objective, non-discriminatory and proportionate and that they do not inhibit access more than is necessary to safeguard against specific risks [...].*

> *Art 36. Member States shall ensure that payment institutions have access to credit institutions' payment accounts services on an objective, non-discriminatory and proportionate basis. Such access shall be sufficiently extensive as to allow payment institutions to provide payment services in an unhindered and efficient manner.*

Access can only be blocked for an objectively justifiable reason, notably related to security, fraud or—in cases where credit is provided—where there is a significantly increased risk of default (Art 68). There are specific rules with respect to account security, and the various procedures and obligations for dealing with those (Arts 68–72).

PSPs cannot refuse to execute a payment for reasons other than those referred to in their framework contract with the customer (Art 79). PSPs are not allowed to deduct fees from the amount transferred, the only exception being a payee's PSP if this has been previously agreed (Art 81).

17.5.1 Payment Initiation Service Providers (PISPs)

Whenever a payment account is accessible online, the institution running it must make it accessible to PISPs (Art 66). PISPs are not allowed to hold payers' funds, and are only allowed to ask for data they actually need to execute the transaction. They are not allowed to modify amount, payee, or any other feature of the transaction (Art 66). The institutions holding the account must not discriminate against differently originated payments for other than objective reasons, and must not require a contractual relationship between them and the PISP (Art 66). PISPs are deemed to provide payment services (Art 3, Annex I) and therefore require authorisation (Art 37).

17.5.2 Account Information Service Providers (AISPs)

Likewise, whenever a payment account is accessible online, the institution running it must make it accessible to AISPs (Art 66). AISPs are only allowed to access information with the explicit consent of the customer, and are not allowed to access, use, or store data for any purpose not directly related to the account information service they provide. Note, however, that direct account access (aka screenscraping—ie the practice of using a customer's credentials to access a customer's account by simulating a web-browser) is no longer acceptable as per EBA guidance (Speech EBA Enria, Feb 2017). AISPs are deemed to provide payment services (Art 3, Annex I) and therefore require authorisation (Art 37).

17.6 Liability and Refunds

17.6.1 Unauthorised Transactions

Except in cases where fraud is suspected—and where this suspicion is reported to the regulator—a payment service provider must refund the payer in the event of an unauthorised transaction immediately, and in any case no later than one business day after notification. Also, the refund must undo all effects of the transaction, eg with respect to the value date and associated interest or overdraft fees (Art 73.1). Where the transaction has been initiated by a PISP it is still the obligation of the account servicing payment provider to refund the transaction, and to seek recourse from the PISP if appropriate. The latter has the burden of proof to show that it is not responsible for the breach (Art 73.2).

Notwithstanding the above, in cases where an unauthorised payment is due to a lost payment instrument, the payer is liable for losses up to a maximum of €50, unless the payer could either not possibly have known about the loss of the instrument, or the responsibility for its loss is in the sphere of influence of the provider (Art 74). Also, notwithstanding the above, if a payer acts fraudulently or negligently in relation to its obligations under Art 69—eg keeping credentials safe, immediate notification upon noticing a loss—the €50 cap does not apply (Art 74.2). On the other hand, the payer is not responsible for any losses—not even the €50—incurred *after* he notified the provider of the loss, or if there is no appropriate means of notifying a provider of the loss (Art 74.3). Finally, where a service provider does not require *strong customer authentication* the payer is never liable except if he acts fraudulently. In this context, strong customer authentication is defined as follows (Art 4.30):

> *Strong customer authentication means an authentication based on the use of two or more elements categorised as knowledge (something only the user knows), possession (something only the user possesses) and inherence (something the user is) that are independent, in that the breach of one does not compromise the reliability of the others, and is designed in such a way as to protect the confidentiality of the authentication data.*

17.6.2 Attribution of Liability

In general, the payer's PSP is liable for non/late/defective execution of a transaction, and in event of non-execution or defective execution must immediately restore the account as if the transaction never happened. The exception is where it can be proved that the payee's PSP received the funds, in which case the payee's PSP needs to rectify the issue accordingly on the payee's account (Art 89). If a such transaction has been initiated by a PISP it is still the responsibility of the payer's account-servicing PSP to indemnify the customer. However, the PISP has the burden of proof that the error did not come from their side, otherwise they'll have to indemnify the PSP (Art 90). More generally, if another PSP in the chain is responsible for an error then they should indemnify the PSP who initially indemnified the customer (Art 91).

It is the customer's responsibility to use the correct unique identifier (eg IBAN) for the intended recipient. However, PSPs shall make a reasonable effort to recover funds mis-sent because of incorrect identifiers (Art 88).

Where payment institutions rely on third parties (branches, agents, outsourcing companies), satisfactory processes must be in place to ensure that they can fulfil their obligations. In any case this does not release the institution or its staff from its obligations, and it remains fully liable vis-à-vis the customer (Arts 19, 20).

Rating Agencies Regulation

Rating Agencies Regulation—The regulation establishing
a supervisory regime for rating agencies across the
Single Market

Summary

Credit rating agencies opine on the creditworthiness of potential borrowers, and their rating reports are important for the functioning of
the market as well as for a number of regulatory purposes. The EU
has therefore decided to apply a common standard to their regulation.

The scope of the present regulation is publicly available or through
subscription-based credit ratings. It excludes private ratings as well as
(typically consumer) credit scores.

Relevance for Fintech Companies

This regulation is not of particular relevance for most Fintech start-
ups, unless they are active in the securities or rating space themselves.

References

- Regulation EC 1060/2009 (RAR)
- Directive 2013/36/EU (CRD4-CID)
- BCBS 189 (Basel 3)

The Rating Agencies Regulation is 1060/2009. One of the key reasons for regulating agencies is the prevalence of ratings in regulations
like CRD 2013/36, implementing the Basel 3 framework BCBS 189.

Note: the regulation refers to CESR, but CESR was replaced by ESMA since this regulation has been published so references here are to ESMA throughout.

18.1 Definition

This directive regulates credit rating agencies (CRAs) across the Single Market. The stated reason is that it contributes to the *smooth functioning of the internal market while achieving a high level of consumer and investor protection* (Art 1). Also—despite the unease of regulators about this—ratings continue to play an important role in the prudential regulatory framework, especially for banks, despite them having greatly contributed to the development of the financial crisis.

The regulation contains a number of annexes that provide detail on what is expected from rating agencies, notably on *Independence and the Avoidance of Conflicts of Interest* (Annex I), which contains parts on *Organisational requirements* (Section A), *Operational requirements* (Section B), *Rating analysts* (Section C), *Presentation of ratings* (Section D), and *Disclosures* (Section E). Annex II details the information required when applying for registration.

18.2 Scope

This directive applies to *public ratings* that are either made available to everyone, or that can be obtained via a subscription agreement. It does not apply to private or company internal ratings, and—importantly—neither does it apply to credit scores as they are being used in the consumer space (Art 2). A CRA whose registration has been accepted is referred to as an *External Credit Assessment Institution* (*ECAI*). To the extent that credit ratings are used by companies (eg banks, insurance companies etc.) for regulatory purposes they must have been issued or endorsed by an ECAI. Endorsement hereby refers to a specific process that ECAIs must follow to ensure that ratings issued by a third-country agency are of equally high standard (Art 4). It is most often used in relation with an EU-incorporated entity endorsing a non-EU-incorporated entity operating under the same umbrella. For example, US ratings are generally produced by a US entity, and are not eligible to be used in a regulatory context without endorsement.

18.3 Registration and Equivalence

CRAs incorporated in a Member State apply for registration with ESMA, in the language of that Member State as well as *in a language customary in the sphere of international finance*, ie probably in English. ESMA then considers the application together with the home regulator, and possibly a college of other regulators where the CRA is planning to become active (Arts 15–18). A registration fee commensurate with the cost incurred can be charged (Art 19). Registration can be withdrawn in the event of misconduct, or if the CRA has not issued new ratings for 6 months (Art 14). See also Annex II for more detailed information.

There is an equivalence process that allows ratings issued CRAs from third countries to be used in the regulatory context described in Article 4. For this, the Commission must have declared the third-country regime equivalent, and the CRA must register with ESMA. Importantly, equivalence cannot be used if the CRA in question is systemically important in any Member State (Art 5).

18.4 General Operational Requirements

CRAs must be independent and avoid conflicts of interest (Art 6). Rating analysts must have an appropriate level of competence, and they can not participate in commercial discussions with employees of the entities they rate. Analysts must be rotated on a regular basis (Art 7). A CRA must disclose publicly the *methodologies, models and key rating assumptions it uses in its credit rating activities*, and shall subject its analysis to historical analysis and back testing. Methodology must be reviewed regularly—at least annually—and if methodology is changed, the likely impact must be disclosed immediately, and all affected ratings must be adjusted within at most six months, being marked as under review in the meantime (Art 8). CRAs cannot refuse to rate a deal that is relying on other agencies' ratings, eg a structured finance deal where they have not rated all underlying securities (Art 8). See also Annex I, Section A–C for more detailed information.

18.5 Structured Finance Ratings

Structured finance ratings must be distinguished from corporate ratings by using a different symbol (Art 10.3) (note: this is considered important because whilst it is widely acknowledged that corporate and structured finance ratings are not equivalent, many by-laws and investment mandates fail to make this distinction, leading to unnecessary ambiguity).

18.6 Unsolicited Ratings

A CRA must clearly disclose their policy on unsolicited ratings, unsolicited ratings must be marked as such, and the level of cooperation from the company must be disclosed (Art 10.4–5) (note: unsolicited ratings tend to be lower if the rated entity is not given the opportunity to provide non-publicly available information, so unsolicited ratings can be used to nudge a company into requesting a paid-for rating instead).

18.7 Disclosure and Transparency

Disclosure on ratings must be made in a timely and non-discriminatory manner (Art 10). A CRA must make data on the historical performance available in a repository established by ESMA, where it will be publicly available (Art 11). It also must prepare an annual transparency report (Art 12). The disclosures under Arts 8–12 must be free of charge (Art 13). More details on disclosures are in Annex I, Sections D–E.

18.8 Role of EBA

EBA is working with the local regulators, third-country regulators, and colleges of regulators in the manner prescribed by this regulation. It also from time to time issues guidance, and establishes a mediation mechanism to settle disputes. The usual data protection rules apply (Arts 21–35).

Undertakings for Collective Investment in Transferable Securities Directive

UCITS Directive—The directives establishing a regulatory regime for a certain class of fund companies in the EU

Summary

UCITS 5 is the latest revision of the directive regulating certain aspects of Undertakings for Collective Investment in Transferable Securities (UCITS), ie a certain class of relatively low-risk open-ended funds. It establishes requirements for the key players in this field, notably for management companies, depositaries, and intermediaries, all of whom have to be authorised. It also sets up a passporting regime that, once a firm is authorised in one Member State, allows it to do business across the entire Single Market.

    The directive defines in detail which investments are and which are not acceptable for UCITS. It also defines the requirements for marketing of UCITS to end-customers that both managers and intermediaries have to fulfil. In particular it defines the key investor information document, which is a document that must be produced for all UCITS and made available to all customers before they invest.

Relevance for Fintech Companies

The core of the regulations is about requirements for asset management companies and depositaries, none of which is a role where the more recent crop of Fintech companies will operate. However, many of them operate in the intermediation space, so the provisions surrounding provision of information and in particular the key investor information document are important.

References

- Directive 2014/91/EU (UCITS 5)
- Directive 2009/65/EC (UCITS 4)
- Directive 2001/107/EC (UCITS 3 Management)
- Directive 2001/108/EC (UCITS 3 Product)
- Directive 85/611/EEC (UCITS 1)
- Directive 2004/39/EC (MiFID 1)

The latest UCITS Directive—number 5—is 2014/91. It amends the UCITS 4 directive 2009/65, which in turn amends the two UCITS 3 directives 2001/107 (Management) and 2001/108 (Product). Those in turn amend UCITS 1 85/611, as there was no UCITS 2.

Note: the latest revision of the UCITS directives, UCITS 5, amends UCITS 4, so both of them need to be considered together. In terms of references, unqualified references like 'Art 1' are references to the UCITS 4 document. References to the UCITS 5 are, for example, of the form 'Art 23[V:6]', which indicates that the referred Article 23 is found in the UCITS 5 document in Article 1, paragraph 6 (all changes are part of Article 1; UCITS 5 only has three articles).

19.1 Key Elements

19.1.1 Scope

The purpose of this directives is to establish and regulate *Undertakings for Collective Investments in Transferable Securities* (*UCITs*), which are open-ended, diversified, and lowly- or unlevered funds that invest into typically liquid assets. '*Open-ended*' indicates that the investors can invest in or redeem units at any time, at close to net asset value. Alternatively, units can be traded on an exchange with a mechanism that ensures that units always trade close to net asset value, as is the case for ETFs. UCITS can have several investment compartments, which for most purposes look like individual UCITS (Art 1).

A number of fund types are specifically excluded from this directive, notably closed-ended funds—ie funds that don't allow redemption and investment during the lifetime of the fund—as well as funds that are either not marketed to the general public, or only marketed outside the Single Market, and funds that do not qualify either on the basis of the assets they invest in or the leverage they apply (Art 3).

19.1.2 Authorisation and Passporting

A key focus of the UCITS Directive is the passporting regime that allows managers domiciled in one Member State to manage funds domiciled every where in the Single Market, and that also allows funds that are domiciled in one Member State to be marketed all across the Single Market. In this respect, whilst Member States have some freedom to establish additional requirements on UCITS funds, those requirements must not be applied in a discriminatory manner (Art 1.6–7).

UCITS' must be authorised in their home Member State, and authorisation is valid across the entire Single Market. An application to authorise a UCITS shall be decided within two months. UCITS' can only be authorised if both their management company and the depositary are authorised in their respective home Member States, and the directors of the depositary are of sufficiently good repute, and sufficiently experienced in relation to the type of UCITS to be managed. Both management company and depositary can only be changed if authorised by the relevant regulator (Art 5).

If UCITS' are intending to merge, a number of rules safeguarding the unit holders apply (Arts 37–48). UCITS can be organised in a master-feeder structure where the feeder UCITS invests in the master, in which case a number of specific rules apply (Arts 58–67).

19.2 Management Companies

Management companies must be authorised in their home Member State—the state where both their head office and registered office are located—and authorisation is valid across the entire Single Market. An application shall be decided after a maximum of six months. Management companies cannot engage in any other activities, with the exception of managing funds that are not covered by this directive, and a few ancillary services that Member States can allow (Art 6; activities in Annex II). Management companies are subject to capital requirements of 0.02% of their assets under management, with a minimum of €125k and a maximum of €10m, up to half of which can be provided by means of a bank guarantee. The staff must be *of sufficiently good repute and are sufficiently experienced* to perform their duties (Art 7).

Member States must subject management companies to prudential and conduct rules following certain guidelines (Arts 12, 14). In particular there must be a remuneration policy in place that satisfies certain detailed requirements, including that part of the compensation might have to be paid in units of the managed funds, and deferral requirements (Art 14 a–b[V:2]).

Management companies can only be authorised if their significant shareholder or members are known to the regulator and considered suitable (Arts 8, 11). The main responsibility for supervision rests with the home regulator, but host regulators have a role where specified in the Directive (Art 10). Delegation to third parties—including outside the Single Market—can be allowed, but must be subject to specific safeguards. However, the management company itself must retain a substantive part of the overall responsibilities, and remains ultimately responsible for all delegated work (Art 13). Management companies must have a complaints procedure for investors in place, and it must be accessible in the language of all the Member States in which they are operating (Art 15).

19.2.1 Passporting of Management Companies

Management companies authorised in one Member State have the right to provide services all across the Single Market, either via branches, or as cross-border services. If they only market UCITS they manage in another Member State there are very few additional requirements. For most other activities they have to notify their home regulator and can only start providing services in the other Member State after about a month (Art 18; notification Arts 17–18). The majority of the supervisory responsibility rests with the home regulator (Arts 19–20). However, host regulators can ask for regular reporting for statistical purposes, and to ensure compliance with host-country specific rules. Requirements for passported companies shall not be more stringent than those for locally resident companies. Infringement discovered by a host regulator will generally be reported to and dealt with by the home regulator (Art 21).

19.2.2 Third-country Management Companies

Branches of management companies from third countries cannot be accorded better terms than those from within the Single Market (Art 8.2). Notwithstanding that, management companies authorised in a Member State have the right to delegate the actual investment management task to persons outside the EU, provided that certain conditions are fulfilled (Art 13). In the case of issues with reciprocal access with third parties, the same escalation and retaliation rules as under MiFID apply (Art 9, MiFID1 Art 15).

19.2.3 Investment Companies

Investment companies are one possible vehicle of how investors can hold their investment, the other one being common funds (Art 2). Investment companies must have their registered office in, and be authorised in, a Member State (Art 27).

Their activities are restricted to holding the assets for the UCITS (Art 28).

If an investment company has no dedicated management company, certain more restrictive rules apply that mirror those that would otherwise apply to the management company (Arts 29–30 and Art 30[V:11]).

19.3 Depositaries

Depositaries must either be established in a Member State or have their registered office in one (Art 23) and they must be regulated (Art 23[V:6]). Managers can't be depositaries and vice versa, and depositaries cannot engage in any activities that would create a conflict of interest (Art 25[V:8]). The Commission is providing more detailed guidance on the requirements that depositaries must fulfil (Art 26b[V:10]).

Managers must appoint a single depositary for each of the funds they manage, and this appointment must be evidenced by a written contract. The depositary is inter alia responsible for ensuring that fund transactions (sale, issue, repurchase, redemption and cancellation of units) and valuation is done in accordance with applicable national law and reconciliation of all payments. To the extent that assets can be held at the depositary, they must be held there. Where this is not possible, the depositary must have a specific procedure in place to assert ownership of the assets. The assets under custody must be safe in the event of bankruptcy of the depositary (Art 22[V:4]).

Depositaries are not allowed to reuse the assets (eg use them in securities lending or repo transaction) unless under instructions by the UCITS management company, for benefit of the unit-holders, and covered by high-quality and liquid collateral (Art 22[V:5]).

There are restrictions as to what tasks depositaries can delegate, and all delegation has to happen for objective business reasons, and in particular not for avoiding regulatory requirements. For sub-delegation, similar rules apply (Art 22a[V:5]). Depositaries are directly liable both to UCITS and unit-holders for damages they cause, and this cannot be limited by agreement. (Art 24[V:7]).

19.4 Investment Policies

UCITS funds and investment companies have to follow certain specific investment rules. In the case of compartmented UCITS, each of the compartments must follow the rules independently (Art 49). UCITS can only invest in the following assets (Art 50):

1. transferable securities and money market instruments traded on a regulated market, or some other specified venues, including third-country stock exchanges
2. recently issued securities that will be trading on a market as under point 1 within at most a year
3. other UCITS', provided that no more than 10% of investors in the target UCITS are other UCITS' (except in the case of feeder-master structures)
4. deposits at banks with a maturity of less than 12 months
5. derivatives that are traded on a market as under point 1, or OTC derivatives under some circumstances
6. some money market instruments that are issued by a public body, a regulated entity, or an entity that has other securities listed on a market as under point 1
7. real estate which is *essential for the direct pursuit of its business* in the case of investment companies.

Management or investment companies must engage in an adequate risk management process, in particular also with respect to derivatives, and there are certain limits as to the use of derivatives for hedging (Art 51).

There are concentration limits. Notably, not more than 5% of the assets can be invested in securities issued by the same body, not more than 20%

in deposits with the same bank, and not more than 10% in investments in any specific other UCITS. Aggregate investment in non-UCITS collective investment schemes is limited to 30%. Derivative counterparty exposure is limited to 10% against banks, and 5% otherwise. Member States have some discretion to change those limits (Arts 52–55).

There are also rules that are meant to avoid a UCITS—or a management company acting via multiple UCITS'—being in a position to *exercise significant influence over the management of an issuing body.* In this context, a UCITS cannot acquire more than 10% of either of the non-voting shares, debt instrument, and money market instruments issued by a single body (Art 56).

Where UCITS' have substantial investments in other UCITS', this has some implications with respect to disclosure of fees (Art 55). The above limits do not have to be adhered to if securities are acquired in relation to subscription rights, or for reasons beyond the control of a UCITS (Art 57).

19.5 Investor Information

19.5.1 Prospectus and Reports

Every fund and investment company must produce a prospectus, an annual report, and a half-yearly report (Art 68). Those must be provided to investors as paper copy on demand and free of charge. They must also be *provided in a durable medium or by means of a website.*

The prospectus must contain as an annex the rules or instruments of incorporation, possibly by referring to a location from where they can be easily obtained (Art 71). The prospectus must allow *investors to be able to make an informed judgement of the investment proposed to them, and, in particular, of the risks attached thereto,* including a *clear and easily understandable explanation of the fund's risk profile.* It also must contain the information specified in Schedule A of Annex I, as amended by UCITS 5 under point 25 (Art 69). It also must include specific information as to the fund's investment policy, especially if higher-risk strategies are followed (Art 70). It must be kept up to date (Art 72).

The annual report must include a balance sheet, an income statement, and a report on the activities of the financial year, as well as the specific information in Schedule B of Annex I. The information required in the half-yearly report is slightly less (Art 69). The annual report must be audited, and the auditor's statement must be reproduced in full (Art 73).

19.5.2 Key Investor Information

The central document that must be produced by UCITS is the key investor information document. It must include (Art 78)

> *appropriate information about the essential characteristics of the UCITS concerned, which is to be provided to investors so that they are reasonably able to understand the nature and the risks of the investment product that is being offered to them and, consequently, to take investment decisions on an informed basis.*

It must contain a specified set of information, including (Art 78.3) investment objectives and policy, costs and associated charges, and risk/reward profile.

A fund marketed in multiple jurisdictions must use the same key investor information document across all jurisdictions, the only allowed difference being due to translation. The document must be written in a concise manner and in non-technical language, and must be comprehensible to the investor without any reference to other documents. It also must clearly specify where and how to obtain additional information. It must follow a common format, the details of which are being defined by the European Commission (Art 78).

The key investor information document must be provided to customers free of charge in good time before they purchase units, regardless of whether they purchase them directly or via an intermediary. It also must be available on the website in an up-to-date version (Arts 80–81).

19.5.3 Other Information

UCITS' must make publicly available the issue, sale, repurchase, or redemption price of its units each time it issues, sells, repurchases, or redeems them, and at least twice a month (Art 76).

Marketing communication must be clearly identifiable as such, and must be fair, clear, and not misleading. In particular it must make no statement that contradicts or diminishes the significance of the information contained in the prospectus and the key investor information, and it must explain in which languages those other documents are available and how to get them (Art 77).

19.6 General Obligations of UCITS'

UCITS funds and investment companies are not generally allowed to borrow, ie they must be unlevered except in the case of foreign currency holdings. However, Member States may allow them to borrow up to

10% of their assets on a temporary basis, plus another 10% for acquiring real estate used for operating their business, up to a grand total of 15% (Art 83).

UCITS' must repurchase or redeem units at the request of any unit-holder, except in cases where it—in accordance with local law—temporarily suspends redemptions, or is ordered by their regulator to do so (Art 84). Issue and redemption prices—and more generally valuations—have to be done in accordance with applicable law, fund rules, or instruments of incorporation (Art 85), as do the distribution or reinvestment of income (Art 86) and the calculation of fees that can be charged by the management company (Art 90). Units can only be issued when the adequate cash consideration has been received (Art 87). Funds and investment companies cannot engage in lending activities—including guaranteeing loans—unless those loans are eligible investments under Arts 50–51 (Art 88), and neither can they engage in uncovered sales (Art 89).

19.7 Cross-border Distribution and Passporting of Funds

UCITS' that seek to distribute their fund in other than their home Member State must submit a certain set of documents—including a translated copy of the key investor document—to their home regulator, who forwards it to the host regulator within 10 days. From the point where the information has been forwarded the UCITS is free to market the units (Art 93). Member States are not allowed to impose any additional requirements on foreign funds *within the field governed by this Directive*. The UCITS must however comply with the usual local requirements outside this field, and the KID must be easily accessible from a distance and by electronic means. Information on those requirements must be *available in a language customary in the sphere of international finance, is provided in a clear and unambiguous manner and is kept up to date* (Art 91).

In all countries where a UCITS is marketed, the key investor information must be available in at least one official local language. The other documents can be provided—at the choice of the UCITS—in one of the official languages, in a language approved by the regulator, or—importantly—in a language customary in the sphere of international finance such as English. The manner in which those documents must be provided is determined by applicable local laws and regulations (Art 94).

19.8 Regulators and Regulatory Powers

The directive establishes a requirement for Member States to appoint a regulator (Art 97), the general powers of the regulator (Art 98), and a requirement for them to cooperate in a specific manner (Arts 101, 109–110). Regulators are bound by professional secrecy rules (Art 102), which can be softened in some specific circumstances, eg in a liquidation event (Art 103). Also, they are allowed to transmit information to the central bank and similar bodies (Art 104, Art 104a[V:18]). Certain persons must report breaches of this regulation if they become aware of them (Art 106). Regulators must generally provide reasons for refusals in writing (Art 107), and the main sanction power lies with the home regulator, even for infringements that happened in another Member State (Art 108).

There must be an out-of-court settlement procedure in place for customer disputes, and it must work on a cross-border basis (Art 100).

19.8.1 Fines

The regulation requires that the maximum amount must be at least the bigger of €5m and twice the benefit derived, and 10% of turnover for legal persons (Art 99[V:16]). The regulation specifies circumstances which must attract penalties, eg running a business without obtaining authorisation (Art 99a[V:17]). Similar to other directives, this one specifies which circumstances should be taken into account when deciding about the size of a penalty (Art 99c[V:17]). The presumption is that penalties should be made public unless specific circumstances warrant keeping it secret (Art 99b[V:17]). In any case, ESMA must be informed (Art 99e[V:17]). Member States should put structures in place that allow whistleblowers to come forward, and ensure that they receive adequate protection (Art 99d[V:17]).

19.9 Other

The European Commission has been given power to make certain technical amendments (Art 111, Art 112a[V:23]). It is supported by the *European Securities Committee* (*ESC*) (Art 112[V:22]).

There are a number of derogations, notably for Danish *pantebreve*, and in relation to bearer certificates (Art 113). Certain investment firms currently regulated under MiFID can choose to be regulated under UCITS instead (Art 114).

Unfair Commercial Practices Directive

Unfair Commercial Practices Directive—The directive dealing with unfair practices when selling products and services to consumers

Summary

When selling to consumers, unfair business practices—in particular misleading and aggressive practice—are forbidden, and this directive provides the framework around this.

Relevance for Fintech Companies

This directive contains high-level principles applicable when marketing products and services—including financial services—to consumers and is therefore highly relevant for every Fintech company operating in the consumer space.

References

• Directive 2005/29/EC (UCPD)

   This directive is 2005/29.

20.1 Definition and Scope

The purpose of this directive is to improve customer protection by restricting unfair commercial practices harming consumers' economic interests (Art 1). It applies to unfair business-to-consumer practices before, during, and after a commercial transaction in relation to a product, ie a good or service (Art 3). For this purpose, 'consumer' is as usually defined as a *natural person acting for purposes which are outside his trade, business, craft, or profession* (Art 2).

The directive prohibits unfair commercial practices, whereby a practice is considered unfair if it is *contrary to the requirements of professional diligence* and it is likely to materially distort the average targeted consumer. In particular, practices which are *misleading* or *aggressive* as defined below are considered unfair (Art 5).

20.2 Misleading Practices

A practice is misleading if it contains false or misrepresented information in a number of specific areas that is likely to deceive the average consumer and to cause him to take a transactional decision that he would not otherwise have taken. Those specific areas include the nature and main characteristics of the product, and its price. Other areas that can be considered unfair are: when the customer is made to believe they need a specific product eg to repair one they already own; when the trader lies about the reasons why he is offering the product (eg suggesting a store closure when this is not the case); or when the trader lies about the consumer's rights in relation to the product. Finally, making products appear as if they were a competitor's products can be an unfair practice, as can be claiming to adhere to a specific code of conduct if this is not the case (Art 6). A trader can also mislead by omitting important information, including by providing it in an unclear, unintelligible, ambiguous, or untimely manner. However, in this context the characteristics of the medium have to be taken into account (Art 7). There is a list of examples for unfair practices in Annex 1.

20.3 Aggressive Practices

A practice is aggressive if by use of harassment, coercion, or undue influence it is likely to significantly impair the average consumer's freedom of choice and to cause him to take a transactional decision that he would not otherwise have taken (Arts 8, 9). There is a list of examples for aggressive practices in Annex 1.

20.4 Enforcement

Member States must provide adequate means of enforcement, inter alia by allowing competitors to take legal action, or to complain to an administrative authority that has the power to impose adequate sanctions and penalties (Art 1113). The burden of proof that a certain claim is factually correct is usually on the trader (Art 12).

Appendix A: Important Definitions from European Legal Texts

Entity	Definition	Source
AIF	see Alternative investment fund	-
AIFM	see Alternative investment fund manager	-
AISP	see Account information service provider	-
APA	see Approved Publication Arrangement	-
APR	see Annual percentage rate	-
Accepted Market Practice	Accepted Market Practice means a specific market practice that is accepted by a competent authority in accordance with Article 13 MAR	MAR Art 3.1(9)
Account Information Service	Account Information Service means an online service to provide consolidated information on one or more payment accounts held by the Payment Service user either with another Payment Service Provider or with more than one Payment Service Provider	PSD2 Art 4(16)
Account Information Service Provider (AISP)	Account Information Service Provider means a Payment Service Provider pursuing business activities as referred to in point (8) of Annex I	PSD2 Art 4(19)
Account Servicing Payment Service Provider	Account Servicing Payment Service Provider means a Payment Service Provider providing and maintaining a payment account for a payer	PSD2 Art 4(17)

Entity	Definition	Source
Algorithmic Trading	Algorithmic Trading means trading in financial instruments where a computer algorithm automatically determines individual parameters of orders such as whether to initiate the order, the timing, price, or quantity of the order or how to manage the order after its submission, with limited or no human intervention, and does not include any system that is only used for the purpose of routing orders to one or more trading venues or for the processing of orders involving no determination of any trading parameters or for the confirmation of orders or the post-trade processing of executed transactions	MiFID2 Art 4.1(39)
Alternative Investment Fund (AIF)	Alternative Investment Funds means Collective Investment Undertakings, including investment compartments thereof, which raise capital from a number of investors, with a view to investing it in accordance with a defined investment policy for the benefit of those investors and who do not require authorisation pursuant to Article 5 of Directive 2009/65/EC (UCITS)	AIFMD Art 4.1(a)
Alternative Investment Fund Manager (AIFM)	Alternative Investment Fund Manager means legal person whose regular business is managing one or more AIFs	AIFMD Art 4.1(b)
Ancillary Services	Ancillary Services means any of the services listed in Section B of Annex I MiFID2	MiFID2 Art 4.1(3)
Annual Percentage Rate (APR)	Annual Percentage Rate of charge means the total cost of the credit to the consumer, expressed as an annual percentage of the total amount of credit, where applicable including the costs referred to in Article 19(2)	CONSCD Art 2(i)
Approved Publication Arrangement (APA)	Approved Publication Arrangement or APA means a person authorised under this Directive to provide the service of publishing trade reports on behalf of Investment Firms pursuant to Articles 20 and 21 of MiFIR	MiFID2 Art 4.1(52)

Entity	Definition	Source
Approved Reporting Mechanism (ARM)	Approved Reporting Mechanism or ARM means a person authorised under this Directive to provide the service of reporting details of transactions to Competent Authorities or to ESMA on behalf of Investment Firms	MiFID2 Art 4.1(54)
Authentication	Authentication means a procedure which allows the payment service provider to verify the identity of a payment service user or the validity of the use of a specific payment instrument, including the use of the user's personalised security credentials	PSD2 Art 4(29)
Benchmark	Benchmark means any rate, index, or figure, made available to the public or published, that is periodically or regularly determined by the application of a formula to, or on the basis of the value of, one or more underlying assets or prices, including estimated prices, actual or estimated interest rates or other values, or surveys, and by reference to which the amount payable under a financial instrument or the value of a financial instrument is determined	MAR Art 3.1(29)
Biometric Data	Biometric Data means Personal Data resulting from specific technical processing relating to the physical, physiological, or behavioural characteristics of a natural person, which allow or confirm the unique identification of that natural person, such as facial images or dactyloscopic data	GDPR Art 4(14)
CCP	CCP means a legal person that interposes itself between the counterparties to the contracts traded on one or more financial markets, becoming the buyer to every seller and the seller to every buyer	EMIR Art 2(1)
CTP	see Consolidated Tape Provider	-
Certificates	Certificates means those securities which are negotiable on the capital market and which in the event of a repayment of investment by the issuer are ranked above shares but below unsecured bond instruments and other similar instruments	MiFIR 2.1(27)

Entity	Definition	Source
Clearing	Clearing means the process of establishing positions, including the calculation of net obligations, and ensuring that financial instruments, cash, or both, are available to secure the exposures arising from those positions	EMIR Art 2(3)
Clearing Member	Clearing Member means an undertaking which participates in a CCP and which is responsible for discharging the financial obligations arising from that participation	EMIR Art 2(14)
Commodity Derivatives	Commodity Derivatives means Derivatives which relate to a commodity or to an underlying either referred to in Section C(10) of Annex I MiFID2; or referred to in points (5), (6), (7) and (10) of Section C of Annex I MiFIR	MiFIR 2.1(30)
Consolidated Tape Provider (CTP)	Consolidated Tape Provider or CTP means a person authorised under this Directive to provide the service of collecting trade reports for financial instruments listed in Articles 6, 7, 10, 12 and 13, 20 and 21 of MiFID from regulated markets, MTFs, OTFs, and APAs and consolidating them into a continuous electronic live data stream providing price and volume data per financial instrument	MiFID2 Art 4.1(53)
Consumer	A natural person who is acting for purposes which are outside his trade, business, or profession	CCRD Art 3(a)
Consumer	Consumer means a natural person who, in payment service contracts covered by this Directive, is acting for purposes other than his or her trade, business, or profession	PSD2 Art 4(20)
Consumer	Consumer means any natural person who, in contracts covered by this Directive, is acting for purposes which are outside his trade, business, or profession	CONSCD Art 2(b)

Entity	Definition	Source
Controller	Controller means the natural or legal person, public authority, agency, or other body which, alone or jointly with others, determines the purposes and means of the processing of Personal Data; where the purposes and means of such processing are determined by Union or Member State law, the controller or the specific criteria for its nomination may be provided for by Union or Member State law	GDPR Art 4(7)
Counterparty Credit Risk	Counterparty Credit Risk means the risk that the counterparty to a transaction defaults before the final settlement of the transaction's cash flows	EMIR Art 2(11)
Credit Agreement	Credit Agreement means an agreement whereby a creditor grants or promises to grant, to a Consumer, a credit falling within the scope of Article 3 in the form of a deferred payment, loan, or other similar financial accommodation	MCD Art 4(3)
Credit Institution	Credit Institution means an undertaking the business of which is to take deposits or other repayable funds from the public and to grant credits for its own account	CRR Art 4.1(1)
Credit Intermediary	Credit Intermediary means a natural or legal person who is not acting as a creditor and who, in the course of his trade, business, or profession, for a fee, which may take a pecuniary form or any other agreed form of financial consideration: (i) presents or offers credit agreements to Consumers; (ii) assists Consumers by undertaking preparatory work in respect of Credit Agreements other than as referred to in (i); or (iii) concludes Credit Agreements with Consumers on behalf of the creditor	CONSCD Art 2(f)

Entity	Definition	Source
Credit Intermediary	Credit Intermediary means a natural or legal person who is not acting as a creditor or notary and not merely introducing, either directly or indirectly, a Consumer to a creditor or credit intermediary, and who, in the course of his trade, business, or profession, for remuneration, which may take a pecuniary form or any other agreed form of financial consideration: (a) presents or offers Credit Agreements to consumers; (b) assists consumers by undertaking preparatory work or other pre-contractual administration in respect of Credit Agreements other than as referred to in point (a); or (c) concludes Credit Agreements with Consumers on behalf of the creditor	MCD Art 4(5)
Credit Transfer	Credit Transfer means a Payment Service for crediting a payee's payment account with a payment transaction or a series of payment transactions from a payer's payment account by the payment service provider which holds the payer's payment account, based on an instruction given by the payer	PSD2 Art 4(24)
Creditor	Creditor means a natural or legal person who grants or promises to grant credit in the course of his trade, business, or profession	CONSCD Art 2(b)
Creditworthiness Assessment	Creditworthiness Assessment means the evaluation of the prospect for the debt obligation resulting from the Credit Agreement to be met	MCD Art 4(17)
Cross-border Payment	Cross-border Payment means an electronically processed payment transaction initiated by a payer or by or through a payee where the payer's payment service provider and the payee's payment service provider are located in different Member States	CBPR Art 2(1)
Data Controller	see Controller	—
Data Processor	see Processor	—

Entity	Definition	Source
Data Reporting Services Provider	Data Reporting Services Provider means an APA, a CTP, or an ARM	MiFID2 Art 4.1(63)
Depositary	Depositary means an institution entrusted with the duties set out in Articles 22 and 32 and subject to the other provisions laid down in Chapter IV and Section 3 of Chapter V UCITS4	UCITS4 Art 2.1(a)
Depositary Receipts	Depositary Receipts means those securities which are negotiable on the capital market and which represent ownership of the securities of a non-domiciled issuer while being able to be admitted to trading on a Regulated Market and traded independently of the securities of the non-domiciled issuer	MiFID2 Art 4.1(45)
Derivatives	Derivatives means either securities giving the right to acquire or sell transferable securities or giving rise to a cash settlement determined by reference to transferable securities, currencies, interest rates or yields, commodities or other indices or measures or those instruments referred to in Annex I, Section C 4–10 of MiFID2	MiFIR 2.1(29)
Digital Content	Digital Content means goods or services which are produced and supplied in digital form, the use or consumption of which is restricted to a technical device and which do not include in any way the use or consumption of physical goods or services	PSD2 Art 4(43)
Direct Debit	Direct Debit means a payment service for debiting a payer's payment account, where a payment transaction is initiated by the payee on the basis of the payer's consent given to the payee, to the payee's payment service provider or to the payer's own payment service provider	CBPR Art 2(14)
Direct Debit Scheme	Direct Debit Scheme means a common set of rules, practices, and standards agreed between payment service providers for the execution of direct debit transactions	CBPR Art 2(15)

Entity	Definition	Source
Direct Electronic Access	Direct Electronic Access means an arrangement where a member or participant or client of a Trading Venue permits a person to use its trading code so the person can electronically transmit orders relating to a financial instrument directly to the trading venue and includes arrangements which involve the use by a person of the infrastructure of the member or participant or client, or any connecting system provided by the member or participant or client, to transmit the orders (direct market access) and arrangements where such an infrastructure is not used by a person (sponsored access)	MiFID2 Art 4.1(41)
Durable Medium	Any instrument which enables to store information in a way accessible for future reference for a period of time adequate for the purposes of the information and which allows the unchanged reproduction of the information stored	CCRD Art 3(m)
ETF	see Exchange-traded Fund	-
Electronic Money	Electronic Money means electronically, including magnetically, stored monetary value as represented by a claim on the issuer which is issued on receipt of funds for the purpose of making payment transactions as defined in point 5 of Article 4 of Directive 2007/64/EC (PSD1), and which is accepted by a natural or legal person other than the Electronic Money Issuer	EMONEYD Art 2(2)
Electronic Money Institution	Electronic Money Institution means a legal person that has been granted authorisation under Title II EMoneyD to issue electronic money	EMONEYD Art 2(1)
Electronic Money Issuer	Electronic Money Issuer means entities referred to in Article 1(1), institutions benefiting from the waiver under Article 1(3) and legal persons benefiting from a waiver under Article 9	EMONEYD Art 2(3)

Entity	Definition	Source
Exchange-traded Fund (ETF)	Exchange-traded Fund means a fund of which at least one unit or share class is traded throughout the day on at least one trading venue and with at least one market maker which takes action to ensure that the price of its units or shares on the trading venue does not vary significantly from its net asset value and, where applicable, from its indicative net asset value	MiFID2 Art 4.1(46)
Feeder AIF	Feeder AIF means an AIF which invests at least 85% of its assets in units or shares of another AIF (the master AIF), invests at least 85% of its assets in more than one master AIF where those master AIFs have identical investment strategies, or has otherwise an exposure of at least 85% of its assets to such a master AIF	AIFMD Art 4.1(m)
Financial Holding Company	Financial Holding Company means a Financial Institution, the subsidiaries of which are exclusively or mainly Institutions or Financial Institutions, at least one of such subsidiaries being an Institution, and which is not a Mixed Financial Holding Company	CRR Art 4.1(20)
Financial Instrument	Financial Instrument means those instruments specified in Section C of Annex I MiFID2	MiFID2 Art 4.1(15)
Funds	Funds means banknotes and coins, scriptural money, or electronic money	PSD2 Art 4(25)
High-frequency Algorithmic Trading Technique	High-frequency Algorithmic Trading Technique means an algorithmic trading technique characterised by: (a) infrastructure intended to minimise network and other types of latencies, including at least one of the following facilities for algorithmic order entry: co-location, proximity hosting or high-speed direct electronic access; (b) system-determination of order initiation, generation, routing or execution without human intervention for individual trades or orders; and (c) high message intra-day rates which constitute orders, quotes, or cancellations	MiFID2 Art 4.1(40)

Entity	Definition	Source
Inside Information	Information of a precise nature, which has not been made public, relating, directly or indirectly, to one or more issuers or to one or more Financial Instruments, and which, if it were made public, would be likely to have a significant effect on the prices of those financial instruments or on the price of related Derivative Financial Instruments	MAR Art 7.1(a)
Institution	Institution means a credit institution or an investment firm	CRR Art 4.1(3)
Insurance Undertaking	Insurance Undertaking means a direct life or non-life Insurance Undertaking which has received authorisation in accordance with Article 14 Solv2D	Solv2D Art 13.1
Interchange Fee	Interchange Fee means a fee paid between the Payment Service Providers of the payer and of the payee for each Direct Debit Transaction	CBPR Art 2(13)
Interoperability Arrangement	Interoperability Arrangement means an arrangement between two or more CCPs that involves a cross-system execution of transactions	EMIR Art 2(12)
Investment Advice	Investment Advice means the provision of personal recommendations to a client, either upon its request or at the initiative of the investment firm, in respect of one or more transactions relating to Financial Instruments	MiFID2 Art 4.1(4)
Investment Firm	Investment Firm means any legal person whose regular occupation or business is the provision of one or more investment services to third parties and/or the performance of one or more investment activities on a professional basis	MiFID2 Art 4.1(1)
Investment Recommendations	Investment Recommendations means information recommending or suggesting an investment strategy, explicitly or implicitly, concerning one or several Financial Instruments or the issuers, including any opinion as to the present or future value or price of such instruments, intended for distribution channels or for the public	MAR Art 3.1(35)

Entity	Definition	Source
Investment Services and Activities	Investment Services and Activities means any of the services and activities listed in Section A of Annex I relating to any of the instruments listed in Section C of Annex I MiFID2	MiFID2 Art 4.1(2)
Issuer (of a Financial Instrument)	Issuer means a legal entity governed by private or public law, which issues or proposes to issue Financial Instruments, the issuer being, in the case of Depository Receipts representing financial instruments, the issuer of the Financial Instrument represented	MAR Art 3.1(21)
Liquid Market	Liquid Market means a market for a Financial Instrument or a class of Financial Instruments, where there are ready and willing buyers and sellers on a continuous basis, assessed in accordance with the following criteria, taking into consideration the specific market structures of the particular Financial Instrument or of the particular class of Financial Instruments: (a) the average frequency and size of transactions over a range of market conditions, having regard to the nature and life cycle of products within the class of Financial Instrument; (b) the number and type of market participants, including the ratio of market participants to traded instruments in a particular product; (c) the average size of spreads, where available	MiFID2 Art 4.1(25)
Local Firm	Local Firm means a firm dealing for its own account on markets in financial futures or options or other derivatives and on cash markets for the sole purpose of hedging positions on derivatives markets, or dealing for the accounts of other members of those markets and being guaranteed by clearing members of the same markets, where responsibility for ensuring the performance of contracts entered into by such a firm is assumed by clearing members of the same markets	CRR Art 4.1(4)
MTF	see Multilateral Trading Facility	—

Entity	Definition	Source
Management Company	see UCITS Management Company or AIFM	—
Market Maker	Market Maker means a person who holds himself out on the financial markets on a continuous basis as being willing to deal on own account by buying and selling financial instruments against that person's proprietary capital at prices defined by that person	MiFID2 Art 4.1(7)
Market Operator	Market Operator means a person or persons who manages and/or operates the business of a regulated market and may be the regulated market itself	MiFID2 Art 4.1(18)
Master AIF	Master AIF means an AIF in which another AIF invests or has an exposure in accordance with point (m)	AIFMD Art 4.1(y)
Microenterprise	Microenterprise means an enterprise which, at the time of conclusion of the payment service contract, employs fewer than 10 persons and whose annual turnover and/or annual balance sheet total does not exceed EUR 2 million	PSD2 Art 4(36), Recommendation 2003/361/EC
Mixed Activity Holding Company	Mixed Activity Holding Company means a parent undertaking, other than a Financial Holding Company or an Institution or a Mixed Financial Holding Company, the subsidiaries of which include at least one Institution	CRR Art 4.1(22)
Mixed Financial Holding Company	Mixed Financial Holding Company means a parent undertaking, other than a regulated entity, which, together with its subsidiaries, at least one of which is a regulated entity, constitutes a Financial Conglomerate	ConglD Art 2(15)
Money Remittance	Money Remittance means a Payment Service where funds are received from a payer, without any payment accounts being created in the name of the payer or the payee, for the sole purpose of transferring a corresponding amount to a payee or to another payment service provider acting on behalf of the payee, and/or where such funds are received on behalf of and made available to the payee	PSD2 Art 4(22)

Entity	Definition	Source
Money Market Instruments	Money Market Instruments means those classes of instruments which are normally dealt in on the money market, such as treasury bills, certificates of deposit, and commercial papers and excluding instruments of payment	MiFID2 Art 4.1(17)
Multilateral System	Multilateral System means any system or facility in which multiple third-party buying and selling trading interests in financial instruments are able to interact in the system	MiFID2 Art 4.1(19)
Multilateral Trading Facility (MTF)	Multilateral Trading Facility or MTF means a multilateral system, operated by an investment firm or a market operator, which brings together multiple third-party buying and selling interests in Financial Instruments—in the system and in accordance with non-discretionary rules—in a way that results in a contract in accordance with Title II of this Directive	MiFID2 Art 4.1(22)
National Payment	National Payment means an electronically processed payment transaction initiated by a payer, or by or through a payee, where the payer's Payment Service Provider and the payee's Payment Service Provider are located in the same Member State	CBPR Art 2(2)
Non-credit Institution	Non-credit Institution means any creditor that is not a Credit Institution	MCD Art 4(10)
OTF	see Organised Trading Facility	-
Organised Trading Facility (OTF)	Organised Trading Facility or OTF means a multilateral system which is not a regulated market or an MTF and in which multiple third-party buying and selling interests in bonds, structured finance products, emission allowances or derivatives are able to interact in the system in a way that results in a contract in accordance with Title II of this Directive	MiFID2 Art 4.1(23)

Entity	Definition	Source
Originator	Originator means an entity which: (a) itself or through related entities, directly or indirectly, was involved in the original agreement which created the obligations or potential obligations of the debtor or potential debtor giving rise to the exposure being securitised; or (b) purchases a third party's exposures for its own account and then securitises them	CRR Art 4.1(13)
Overdraft Facility	Overdraft Facility means an explicit Credit Agreement whereby a creditor makes available to a Consumer funds which exceed the current balance in the Consumer's current account	CONSCD Art 2(d)
PISP	see Payment initiation service provider	-
Payment Initiation Service	Payment Initiation Service means a service to initiate a payment order at the request of the payment service user with respect to a payment account held at another Payment Service Provider	PSD2 Art 4(15)
Payment Initiation Service Provider (PISP)	Payment Initiation Service Provider means a Payment Service Provider pursuing business activities as referred to in point (7) of Annex I	PSD2 Art 4(18)
Payment Institution	Payment Institution means a legal person that has been granted authorisation in accordance with Article 11 to provide and execute payment services throughout the Union	PSD2 Art 4(4)
Payment Instrument	Payment Instrument means a personalised device(s) and/or set of procedures agreed between the payment service user and the payment service provider and used in order to initiate a payment order	PSD2 Art 4(14)
Payment Service	Payment Service means any business activity set out in Annex I	PSD2 Art 4(3)
Payment Service Provider	Payment Service Provider means a body referred to in Article 1(1) or a natural or legal person benefiting from an exemption pursuant to Article 32 or 33	PSD2 Art 4(11)

Entity	Definition	Source
Payment System	Payment System means a funds transfer system with formal and standardised arrangements and common rules for the processing, clearing and/or settlement of payment Transactions	PSD2 Art 4(7)
Payment Transaction	Payment Transaction means an act, initiated by the payer or on his behalf or by the payee, of placing, transferring or withdrawing funds, irrespective of any underlying obligations between the payer and the payee	PSD2 Art 4(5)
Personal Data	Personal Data means any information relating to an identified or identifiable natural person ('data subject'); an identifiable natural person is one who can be identified, directly or indirectly, in particular by reference to an identifier such as a name, an identification number, location data, an online identifier or to one or more factors specific to the physical, physiological, genetic, mental, economic, cultural, or social identity of that natural person	GDPR Art 4(1)
Portfolio Management	Portfolio Management means managing portfolios in accordance with mandates given by clients on a discretionary client-by-client basis where such portfolios include one or more Financial Instruments	MiFID2 Art 4.1(8)
Prime Broker	Prime Broker means a Credit Institution, a Regulated Investment Firm or another entity subject to prudential regulation and ongoing supervision, offering services to Professional Investors primarily to finance or execute transactions in financial instruments as counterparty and which may also provide other services such as clearing and settlement of trades, custodial services, securities lending, customised technology, and operational support facilities	AIFMD Art 4.1(a–f)

Entity	Definition	Source
Processing	Processing means any operation or set of operations which is performed on personal data or on sets of Personal Data, whether or not by automated means, such as collection, recording, organisation, structuring, storage, adaptation or alteration, retrieval, consultation, use, disclosure by transmission, dissemination, or otherwise making available, alignment or combination, restriction, erasure, or destruction	GDPR Art 4(2)
Processor	Processor means a natural or legal person, public authority, agency, or other body which processes Personal Data on behalf of the Controller	GDPR Art 4(8)
Professional Client	Professional Client means a client meeting the criteria laid down in Annex II MIFID2	MiFID2 Art 4.1(10)
Professional Investor	Professional Investor means an investor which is considered to be a professional client or may, on request, be treated as a professional client within the meaning of Annex II of MiFID2	AIFMD Art 4.1(ag)
Profiling	Profiling means any form of automated processing of Personal Data consisting of the use of Personal Data to evaluate certain personal aspects relating to a natural person, in particular to analyse or predict aspects concerning that natural person's performance at work, economic situation, health, personal preferences, interests, reliability, behaviour, location, or movements	GDPR Art 4(4)
Pseudonymisation	Pseudonymisation means the processing of Personal Data in such a manner that the personal data can no longer be attributed to a specific data subject without the use of additional information, provided that such additional information is kept separately and is subject to technical and organisational measures to ensure that the personal data are not attributed to an identified or identifiable natural person	GDPR Art 4(5)

Entity	Definition	Source
Public Sector Entity	Public Sector Entity means a non-commercial administrative body responsible to central governments, regional governments or local authorities, or to authorities that exercise the same responsibilities as regional governments and local authorities, or a non-commercial undertaking that is owned by or set up and sponsored by central governments, regional governments, or local authorities, and that has explicit guarantee arrangements, and may include self-administered bodies governed by law that are under public supervision	CRR Art 4.1(8)
Recognised Exchange	Recognised Exchange means an exchange which meets all of the following conditions: (a) it is a Regulated Market; (b) it has a clearing mechanism whereby contracts listed in Annex II are subject to daily margin requirements which, in the opinion of the competent authorities, provide appropriate protection	CRR Art 4.1(72)
Regulated Market	Regulated Market means a Multilateral System operated and/or managed by a Market Operator, which brings together or facilitates the bringing together of multiple third-party buying and selling interests in financial instruments—in the system and in accordance with its non-discretionary rules—in a way that results in a contract, in respect of the Financial Instruments admitted to trading under its rules and/or systems, and which is authorised and functions regularly and in accordance with Title III of this Directive	MiFID2 Art 4.1(21)
Reinsurance Undertaking	Reinsurance Undertaking means Reinsurance Undertaking as defined in point (4) of Article 13 of Directive 2009/138/EC	-
Remote Payment Transaction	Remote Payment Transaction means a payment transaction initiated via Internet or through a device that can be used for distance communication	PSD2 Art 4(6)

Entity	Definition	Source
Retail Client	Retail Client means a client who is not a Professional Client	MiFID2 Art 4.1(11)
Retail Investor	Retail Investor means an investor who is not a Professional Investor	AIFMD Art 4.1(a–j)
SME Growth Market	SME Growth Market means a MTF that is registered as an SME Growth Market in accordance with Article 33	MiFID2 Art 4.1(12)
SSPE	see Securitisation Special Purpose Entity	-
Securitisation Special Purpose Entity (SSPE)	Securitisation Special Purpose Entity or SSPE means a corporation trust or other entity, other than an Institution, organised for carrying out a securitisation or securitisations, the activities of which are limited to those appropriate to accomplishing that objective, the structure of which is intended to isolate the obligations of the SSPE from those of the originator institution, and in which the holders of the beneficial interests have the right to pledge or exchange those interests without restriction	CRR Art 4.1(66)
Sovereign Debt	Sovereign Debt means a debt instrument issued by a sovereign issuer	MiFID2 Art 4.1(61)
Sponsor	Sponsor means an Institution other than an Originator Institution that establishes and manages an asset-backed commercial paper programme or other securitisation scheme that purchases exposures from third-party entities	CRR Art 4.1(14)
Strong Customer Authentication	Strong Customer Authentication means an authentication based on the use of two or more elements categorised as knowledge (something only the user knows), possession (something only the user possesses), and inherence (something the user is) that are independent, in that the breach of one does not compromise the reliability of the others, and is designed in such a way as to protect the confidentiality of the authentication data	PSD2 Art 4(30)

Entity	Definition	Source
Structured Deposit	Structured Deposit means a Deposit under Article 2.1c of the Deposit Scheme Directive (2014/49/EU), which is fully repayable at maturity on terms under which interest or a premium will be paid or is at risk, according to a formula involving factors such as: (a) an index or combination of indices, excluding variable rate deposits whose return is directly linked to an interest rate index such as Euribor or LIBOR; (b) a financial instrument or combination of financial instruments; (c) a commodity or combination of commodities or other physical or non-physical nonfungible assets; or (d) a foreign exchange rate or combination of foreign exchange rates	MiFID2 Art4.1(43)
Structured Finance Products	Structured Finance Products means those securities created to securitise and transfer credit risk associated with a pool of financial assets entitling the security holder to receive regular payments that depend on the cash flow from the underlying assets	MiFIR 2.1(28)
Systematic Internaliser	Systematic Internaliser means an Investment Firm which, on an organised, frequent systematic and substantial basis, deals on its own account when executing client orders outside a Regulated Market, an MTF, or an OTF without operating a multilateral system	MiFID2 Art 4.1(20)
Tied Agent	Tied Agent means a natural or legal person who, under the full and unconditional responsibility of only one Investment Firm on whose behalf it acts, promotes investment and/or ancillary services to clients or prospective clients, receives and transmits instructions or orders from the client in respect of Investment Services or Financial Instruments, places Financial Instruments, or provides advice to clients or prospective clients in respect of those Financial Instruments or Services	MiFID2 Art 4.1(29)

Entity	Definition	Source
Tied Credit Intermediary	Tied Credit Intermediary means any Credit Intermediary who acts on behalf of and under the full and unconditional responsibility of: (a) only one creditor; (b) only one group; or (c) a number of creditors or groups which does not represent the majority of the market	MCD Art 4(7)
Trade Repository	Trade Repository means a legal person that centrally collects and maintains the records of Derivatives	EMIR Art 2(2)
Trading Venue	Trading Venue means a Regulated Market, an MTF, or an OTF	MiFID2 Art 4.1(24)
Transferable Securities	Transferable Securities means those classes of securities which are negotiable on the capital market, with the exception of instruments of payment, such as: (a) shares in companies and other securities equivalent to shares in companies, partnerships or other entities, and depositary receipts in respect of shares; (b) bonds or other forms of securitised debt, including depositary receipts in respect of such securities; (c) any other securities giving the right to acquire or sell any such transferable securities or giving rise to a cash settlement determined by reference to transferable securities, currencies, interest rates or yields, commodities, or other indices or measures	MiFID2 Art 4.1(44)
UCITS Management Company	UCITS Management Company means a company, the regular business of which is the management of UCITS in the form of common funds or of investment companies (collective portfolio management of UCITS)	UCITS4 Art 2.1(b)
Unfair Terms	Unfair Terms means the contractual terms defined in Article 3	CONSCD Art 2(a)

Appendix B: Abbreviations Used for Legal References

Abbreviation	Name	Reference
AIFMD	Alternative Investment Fund Manager Directive	Directive 2011/61/EU
AMLD 4	Anti Money Laundering Directive	Directive EU 2015/849
BRRD	Bank Recovery and Resolution Directive	Directive 2014/59/EU
CBPR	Cross-Border Payments Regulation	Regulation EC 924/2009
CCOD	Consumer Contracts Directive	Directive 1993/18/EEC
CCRD	Consumer Credit Directive	Directive 2008/48/EC
CID	Credit Institutions Directive (part of CRD4)	Directive 2013/36/EU
CRD4	Capital Requirements Directive	see CRR and CID
CRR	Capital Requirements Regulation (part of CRD4)	Regulation 575/2013
ConglD	Conglomerate Directive	Directive 2002/87/EC
DGSD 2	Deposit Guarantee Scheme Directive	Directive 2014/49/EU
EBAR	Regulation establishing EBA	Regulation EU 1093/2010
ECBPRUR	Regulation establishing ECB's role in prudential supervision	Regulation EU 1024/2013
EIOPAR	Regulation establishing EIOPA	Regulation EU 1094/2010
EMIR	European Market Infrastructure Regulation	Regulation EU 648/2012
EMONEYD 2	Electronic Money Directive	Directive 2009/110/EC
ESMAR	Regulation establishing ESMA	Regulation EU 1095/2010
ESRBR	Regulation establishing ESRB	Regulation EU 1092/2010
GDPD	General Data Protection Directive (superseded by GDPR)	Directive 95/46/EC

Abbreviation	Name	Reference
GDPR	General Data Protection Regulation	Regulation EU 2016/679
IORPD	Institutions for Occupational Retirement Provisions Directive	Directive 2003/41/EC
MAR	Market Abuse Regulation	Regulation 596/2014
MCD	Mortgage Credit Directive	Directive 2014/17/EU
MiFID 1	Markets in Financial Instruments Directive	Directive 2004/39/EC
PRIIPS	Packaged Retail and Insurance-based Investment Products Regulation	Regulation EU 1286/2014
RAR	Ratings Agencies Regulation	Regulation EC 1060/2009
SOLVD 2	Solvency Directive	Directive 2009/138/EC
UCITS 4	Undertakings for Collective Investment in Transferable Securities Directive	Directive 2009/65/EC
UCITS 5	Undertakings for Collective Investment in Transferable Securities Directive	Directive 2014/91/EU

Index